Online Education

ONLINE EDUCATION

Perspectives on a New Environment

Edited by
Linda M. Harasim

———————————

Foreword by
Murray Turoff

PRAEGER

New York
Westport, Connecticut
London

Library of Congress Cataloging-in-Publication Data

Online education : perspectives on a new environment / edited by Linda
    M. Harasim.
        p.   cm.
    Includes bibliographical references.
    ISBN 0-275-93448-9
        1. Computer-assisted instruction.   2. Education – Data processing.
    3. Computer networks.   4. Educational technology.   I. Harasim,
    Linda M. (Linda Marie), 1949-
    LB1028.5.049   1990
    371.3'34 – dc20   89-38987

Library of Congress Catalog Card Number: 89-38987
ISBN: 0-275-93448-9

First published in 1990

Praeger Publishers, One Madison Avenue, New York, NY 10010
An imprint of Greenwood Publishing Group, Inc.

Printed in the United States of America

∞

The paper used in this book complies with the
Permanent Paper Standard issued by the National
Information Standards Organization (Z39.48-1984).

10 9 8 7 6 5 4 3 2 1

For

Tanikka and Tasya

Contents

Foreword

Murray Turoff

Having observed and participated in the evolution of computer-mediated communications (CMC) since the late 1960s, I am firmly convinced that educational delivery is the key application for this technology as a public form of communication. It will some day have the same criticality for citizen utilization as the telephone has today.

The introduction of CMC into the field of education promises to bring about important changes in the educational process. The underlying reasons for this are the following:

- Students and instructors do not have to meet at the same time because the computer stores their communications. Online education is available at any hour of the day or night, seven days a week.
- Students can communicate with one another to promote collaborative learning. This is increasingly understood to be as important a part of the learning process as student-to-teacher communications.
- Students anywhere in the world can be part of a single class. Teachers can be anywhere in the world and still team-teach a class.
- The computer provides specialized communication structures that can actually improve on what can be done in face-to-face classes. For example, if the instructor asks a discussion question, the computer can prevent a student from seeing the other answers until his/her own answer has been supplied.
- The technology is inherently cheaper than telephone or video conferencing for providing communications. For example, students anywhere in the state of New

Jersey can call an educational network utilizing the
Virtual Classroom™ facilities at a charge of only $2.00
per hour. This is considerably less than hourly rates
for telephone calls beyond ten miles.

These factors take on increased significance in the context of
changes in the demographics of education. An increasing proportion of university and college students are working adults who
have families, and are returning for additional education. One
result is that the biggest growth in student populations occurs on
campuses close to concentrations of work places or homes. By the
end of the century the majority of students in universities and colleges will not be fresh out of high school. These students find that
even if they are close to a campus, attending face-to-face classes on
a regular basis can be difficult because of business and family commitments. Further, such students are much more selective and
mature in their understanding and judgments of what they need
in the way of education. They are far more likely to have personal
computers, and to be willing to go electronically wherever they can
find the program of study that they feel they need. They are far
more likely to view their fellow students as peers who have experience and knowledge from which they can benefit and with
whom they want to engage actively in collaborative learning activities.

As a result, many of the traditional characterizations of student bodies and of typical students for remote education will be
completely overturned. In terms of colleges and universities, the
most startling implication is that there will no longer be any
geographic monopolies in higher education. It can no longer be assumed that the good student will go to the closest or most
geographically convenient institution.

Comparisons of educational delivery via CMC and via face-
to-face classrooms show another startling result: On the average,
students can learn just as well, as measured by midterms, finals,
and grades. However, the more mature and better students learn
more, while students without good study habits and with basic
reading and writing difficulties learn less.

This result comes out of controlled experimental studies of
regular classes conducted by Professor Starr Roxanne Hiltz (see
Chapter 7). Working students and those with families become extremely enthusiastic about the convenience of this form of communication. The more the courses have to deal with pragmatics of
a subject area, as opposed to just learning skills, the greater are
the benefits of increased collaborative student participation. It is
possible to have guest lecturers who participate under pen names;

they and the organization with which they are affiliated may never be identified. In a management course, a practicing manager can talk in great detail about how real mistakes in decisionmaking occur. In a sociology course, an ex-convict can present his experiences on life in prison. Through online education, the real world can be brought into the classroom.

It is also clear that this technology provides some important psychological benefits to students. There is more of a sense of equal participation. Students who are not learning in their mother tongue spend considerably more time rereading material and in the end participate equally in terms of written contributions. Women and minority students often feel their comments and ideas are taken more seriously than in traditional face-to-face classrooms. Finally, there is often a sense of greater closeness to the instructor and of an increased ability to get advice and counseling. Many teachers expect that more students will now discuss such topics as life-long ambitions and goals.

From an economic standpoint, the costs of establishing a brand-new educational program for a few thousand students are far less than the cost of a building to house the same number of students. The introduction of optical disks and more powerful personal computers has made possible the creation of "simulated laboratories" where a student can experiment with the laws of physics on the moon, dissect a virtual frog or human, design and operate a factory floor, or create a primitive society and watch it evolve over generations. Optical disks that contain all of Shakespeare's plays in a searchable manner will cost about the same as a single book.

If colleges and universities do not perceive the long-term changes that are coming and do not move to incorporate this form of educational delivery into their programs, companies that have moved into continuing and vocational education will. The results will be further erosion of the student population on which colleges and universities draw.

The use of CMC for educational delivery at the college and university level is linked to a growing demand for adult education from the more educated segments of the population, and a corresponding shortage of instructors. The shortage of instructors in many technical and even business fields is now also becoming a major factor.

The most serious bottleneck to the introduction of this technology in colleges and universities is not the technology itself or its costs, nor the adaptability of students; it is the retraining and adaptability of faculty. The teaching methods and approaches to communication with students are different from those suited to the face-to-face environment: The instructor is more a facilitator of group communications, organizer of group learning activities, and resident consulting expert. Ten to 20 percent of faculty adapt to this without training because it is already a part of their style of education. Another 10 to 20 percent will never adapt and should not be forced to try. The remainder need help and a period of acclimation. The best method is for new faculty to apprentice with experienced faculty in existing CMC courses; another approach is to use CMC to augment existing face-to-face classrooms.

Another significant problem is that the work load for faculty is linearly dependent upon the number of students: leaving grading aside, the amount of communication generated is a direct function of the number of students. As a result, compensation practices and load limits for faculty need to be reexamined. Moreover, the initial effort of developing material in electronic form is similar to the complete development of a new course or of a small book. On the other hand, the cumulative memory of the computer is a distinct advantage for maintenance and updating of courses. If students are assigned to teach a particular subtopic to the rest of the class, the better lesson material can be incorporated into future offerings of the course. Student reviews of recent professional articles can be incorporated into a growing database for use by future classes. Students simulating company performance in a sequence of management courses can operate the company on a continuing basis instead of starting afresh every semester.

There have been a host of efforts to provide online education via CMC. There is also a growing but scattered body of literature on the subject. Most of it is naive: "Gee whiz, we were able to do it, and this is our impression of what happened!" It is quite easy to do a bad job of educational delivery via CMC. The approaches that teachers take in the face-to-face classroom are not appropriate. Understanding whether improvements have occurred in the educational process is by no means a simple judgmental process. It is time to develop a general understanding of what is known about this area. This book has gathered together a core body of work that goes beyond mere reports of experiences, and deals directly with what we now know with respect to theory, design, and methodology of online education. Therefore, this book is an important foundation for anyone interested in understanding this approach to educational delivery. It also serves as an important introduction for those who want to generate further understandings of online education. To date we have only scratched the surface of what is possible.

NOTE

Virtual Classroom™ is trademarked by the New Jersey Institute of Technology.

Preface

This book introduces the new environment of online education by presenting theoretical, design, and methodological perspectives that can help us to better understand, use, and benefit from computer-mediated communication (CMC). Online education already exists as a field of practice; there is an urgent need, now, to build a research discipline and knowledge base to guide research, practical, and technical developments in this new field. This book addresses that need.

Online Education is itself the product of an online educational collaboration. The need to build a scholarly community and discipline for studying, developing, and promoting online education was acknowledged in 1986-1987 in the "Online Educational Research Workshop," which brought "together," on a computer conferencing system, twenty educators from Canada, the United States, and the United Kingdom. Over a period of almost three months, participants explored and developed ten perspectives on online education. These ten topics have been refined into the chapters that make up this book.

Each of the principal authors—Andrew Feenberg, Linda Harasim, Roxanne Hiltz, Jim Levin, Paul Levinson, Robin Mason and Tony Kaye, Elaine McCreary, Denis Newman, and Richard Wolfe—moderated a computer conference on the theme of her/his chapter. Discussants active in the online conferences—Terry Anderson, Gary Boyd, Liz Burge, Lynn Davie, France Henri, Rob Higgins, Craig Montgomery, Ron Ragsdale, and Tina Vozick—also made a significant contribution to the development of this book. As moderator of the online workshop and editor of this collection, I am pleased to acknowledge the valuable input of each of the workshop participants, whose intellectual and social contributions form the substance of this text. Once the workshop ended, I continued to work closely with the contributors to this collection; it has been a pleasure to work with such a dedicated and innovative group.

I would like to thank as well those who created the conditions that enabled me to make this book a reality. First, with regard to the Online Workshop, I thank the Canadian Social Sciences and Humanities Research Council's Strategic Grant for financial support. I am also grateful to the Ontario Institute for Studies in Education (OISE) where I was employed during the period that the online workshop and this book were produced: OISE encouraged my efforts in implementing and moderating the online workshop by providing financial assistance and the use of OISE's computer conferencing system. Craig Montgomerie, as co-moderator, and Rob Higgins, as research assistant, provided valuable assistance in the design and implementation of the online workshop. Work on the manuscript for the book benefited greatly from Kate Hamilton, who read the draft and made invaluable comments to improve the style of the text, and Frances Tolnai, who provided text-processing and formatting expertise.

I would also like to acknowledge with affection and gratitude the important roles of Lucio Teles, my husband; Mary Harasim, my mother; and my two daughters, Tanikka and Tasya, who have been an endless source of energy and inspiration. The vision of a better educational future makes such undertakings seem worthwhile and important. I therefore dedicate this book to my daughters and to learners and teachers everywhere. May advances in educational communication enhance intellectual and social collaboration on a global basis; and may this book contribute to that vision.

Introduction to Online Education

Linda Harasim

OVERVIEW OF ONLINE EDUCATION

Online education introduces unprecedented options for teaching, learning, and knowledge building. Today, access to a microcomputer, modem, telephone line, and communication program offers learners and teachers the possibility of interactions that transcend the boundaries of time and space. New social and intellectual connectivities are proliferating as educational institutions adopt computer-mediated communication (CMC) for educational interactions. Courses—including degree and diploma programs—are offered totally online. Online collegial exchange and joint writing are becoming commonplace, particularly within universities but increasingly at all levels of education. We find growing numbers of school-based networks that link learners (locally, regionally, and internationally) to discuss, share, and examine specific subjects, such as environmental concerns, science, and local and global issues, or to enhance written communication skills in first- or second-language proficiency activities. Computer networking for and by teachers offers opportunities for in-service education and peer information sharing and support. CMC is being adopted as well by organizations in the corporate, government, and nonprofit sectors for educational applications such as training and professional development.

Practical applications have developed rapidly and, until very recently, have outpaced research. Some applications of online education were developed with neither theory-based design at the outset nor assessment of the experience at the conclusion. There have been successes, and there have been problems and failures.

We know little about the factors involved in these experiences. But we are beginning to learn more. And we need to systematize and share what we have learned. There is a critical need for research to inform and guide future developments in the field and to make the promise—as welcome as it might be—a viable and useful reality.

Online Education: Perspectives on a New Environment initiates a research base and discipline for educational CMC, presenting theoretical frameworks, design paradigms, and research methodologies for analyzing and shaping this new field of educational activity. It provides, in one volume, a range of perspectives and approaches for understanding educational applications of electronic mail (e-mail) and computer conferencing networks. The final chapter provides a comprehensive bibliography for further reading in this field to assist researchers, developers, and educators working in or interested in learning more about educational CMC.

The three sections of this book—each of which contains contributions from leading theoreticians and practitioners—tackle the questions posed by educational CMC from different perspectives: theory, design, and methodology. But despite the diversity of approach, common themes link the chapters. The first such theme is that online education is a new environment, with new attributes, and requires new approaches to understand, design, and implement it. A second theme is the essentially group or socially interactive nature of the online educational environment as the conceptual basis for research and design. A third theme explores the augmented environment that the computer provides for educational activity. Finally, each author in some way addresses the fundamental practical issue: What are effective uses of these new CMC media? Can we just transfer our existing set of conventional instructional practices, or do we need to develop a new set of practices better suited to the new tools?

Theoretical Perspectives

"Theoretical Perspectives" initiates the discussion of CMC as a new educational environment, emphasizing the social or group nature of CMC, especially computer conferencing, and the importance of understanding the attributes of the new medium. Although a concern for theoretical perspective underlies all the chapters of the book, the three chapters of this first section offer explicit theoretical frameworks for online education.

Paul Levinson's "Computer Conferencing in the Context of the Evolution of Media" draws on media history and philosophy. Situating educational CMC within the historical development of other media, Levinson analyzes the current characteristics and consequences of computer conferencing in light of the impact, on education and on society, of four prior developments in human communication: spoken language, alphabetic writing, the printing press, and electronic audiovisual media. The thesis proposed is that we can better understand the current performance of CMC, and plan for its future use and development, if we consider what prior media have done in similar educational situations. Important innovations in communication made possible by CMC include the liberation of text from the printed page—making the text infinitely revisable, readable by an infinite number of people at the same time, transmissible at the speed of light to anywhere in the world—and various capacities for interactivity not possible in either in-person or printed communication.

In Chapter 2, Robin Mason and Tony Kaye, distance educators at the Open University, United Kingdom, examine computer conferencing as a new paradigm within their field. "Toward a New Paradigm for Distance Education" looks at the revolutionary effect of computer conferencing on traditional distinctions between distance education and place-based education. How do educational computer communications change the instructional and administrative roles traditional in distance education—the roles of faculty, adjunct tutors, administrative and support staff? What opportunities are presented by this medium for collective thinking and peer exchange? This chapter grows out of an online discussion among educators who have used mass and small-group computer conferencing to deliver online education. The differing viewpoints of the discussants generated what the authors call "new paradigms" for future educational programs. The chapter concludes by outlining one such new paradigm: decentralized institutions where students choose courses at the regional or global level, delivered by varying combinations and levels of electronic and other media, and including access to resources and support people drawn from a much broader base than the teaching profession.

The final chapter of this section, "Online Education: An Environment for Collaboration and Intellectual Amplification," also views online education as a new environment, examining the novel attributes of computer conferencing for education. Using collaborative learning as the conceptual base for understanding, designing, and developing online educational activity, Linda Harasim examines how many-to-many, time- and place-independent, text-based and computer-mediated interactions create a new educational environment. Online education, in this theoretical perspective, has similarities to, but also significant differences from, the other two major educational domains: the face-to-face and distance modes. This environment is much more than a technical device for exchanging information; it can support and amplify intellectual activity by facilitating the sharing of knowledge and understanding among individuals who are not in the same location nor working at the same time, by enhancing active discovery learning and by contributing to metacognitive skills. Parallel but converging sociotechnologies, such as hypertext and hypermedia, suggest ways of drawing upon and organizing the richness of the conferencing environment to enhance connectivity and amplify intellectual activity.

Design Perspectives

"Design Perspectives" treats online education in terms of system design and—perhaps more important—in terms of social and cognitive activities. The mere introduction of CMC does not in itself improve learning: design (or method) is crucial. The chapters in this section bring social science approaches to the study of online education; the authors' concern is to develop conceptual and organizational tools that enhance learning and the adoption, use, and impact of online education.

Chapter 4, "Social Factors in Computer-Mediated Communication," by Andrew Feenberg and Beryl Bellman, argues that as CMC begins to offer study and work environments for groups of users rather than simple tools for individual work, it will be increasingly important to take social considerations into account in designing programs.

The design of electronic social environments requires attention to what the authors call the "social factors" determining user acceptance and satisfaction where the "users" are not individuals but social groups. This chapter offers two approaches to the study of social factors. First, practicing consultants in social networking design are repositories of a great deal of relevant practical knowledge. Second, various social theories can be employed to develop testable hypotheses about the needs of different types of user groups. To bring these two forms of knowledge about social factors to bear on program design, the chapter presents a model for relating group needs to communication requirements and program features. This model is intended to serve as a basis for tailoring systems in socially specific configurations.

Denis Newman's "Cognitive and Technical Issues in the Design of Educational Computer Networking" examines the design of online educational environments from the perspective of issues in computer networking. Newman undertakes three related tasks: (1) the development of three design principles that arise out of the desire to maintain a common "conversation" or conference in the diverse contexts arising from the growing use of powerful microcomputers; (2) the analysis of the components of current network systems in terms of the connections among various levels of the systems; and (3) the analysis of cognitive issues in terms of the degrees of coordination that can be achieved both in local settings and over longer distances. Newman argues that understanding the system in terms of both face-to-face and computer-mediated conversations is especially important in designing systems for education, where the nature of the educational activity may require coordination around immediate concrete objects.

In "Three Behavioral Models for Computer-Mediated Communication," Elaine K. McCreary analyzes the social roles that emerge from CMC. Three roles are given special attention: the individual participant, who is defined as a "CMC collaborator"; the "conference moderator"; and a role that will be introduced in her chapter, the "diffusion manager." McCreary presents three possible models previously derived from direct observation of human behavior, and examines their heuristic potential as tools to guide our indirect observation of humans as they present themselves, via electronic print, in online communities. Each section begins by discussing the nature or demands of one of these new social roles, cites a model relevant to the online role, and examines how the model can be applied to CMC to elucidate what is observed, to train people for the role, or perhaps to be transformed into a new model, more representative of CMC phenomena.

Methodological Perspectives

The research methodologies presented in "Methodological Perspectives" are not mutually exclusive but complementary, each exploring different approaches to and issues within the study of online education. Each analytical approach is illustrated by application to online educational activities.

In "Evaluating the Virtual Classroom," Roxanne Hiltz discusses evaluation methodologies and their applications to online education. This chapter builds upon a major study whose goal was to demonstrate that it is possible to use computer conferencing systems to improve access to and the effectiveness of postsecondary educational delivery. The most important "product" of the project was knowledge about the influence of variations in student characteristics and implementation techniques and settings. The chapter presents the data collection methods developed, discusses problems that arose, and assesses the relative fruitfulness of the different methodologies for evaluating the Virtual Classroom. It also includes some of the major findings derived from the research.

Four research methodologies are presented by Jim Levin, Haesun Kim, and Margaret Riel in "Analyzing Instructional Interactions on Electronic Message Networks." These methodologies were developed for analyzing educational interactions conducted via electronic (e-mail) networks: (1) participant analysis, (2) intermessage reference analysis, (3) message flow analysis, and (4) message act analysis. Each methodology is applied to a variety of different educational interactions, and the implications of the results are discussed. The corpus for this study is the set of e-mail messages sent over one year (approximately 750 messages) on the InterCultural Learning Network.

In the final chapter of this section, Richard Wolfe presents "Hypertextual Perspectives on Educational Computer Conferencing." Computer conferencing can be conceptualized as a form of "hypertext," defined as a nonlinear networking of textual information. Wolfe applies hypertext systems to educational computer conferencing transcripts to illustrate the possibilities of the hypertext perspective, and concludes by exploring issues that the hypertext perspective raises for computer conferencing analysis and design. Existing computer conferencing programs provide only weak hypertext tools for organizing and viewing a conference, and so one finds that conference users invent their own hypertext adjuncts. Taking hypertext as an interface design model would provide a better grasp of the overall content and structure of a conference in progress, better navigation tools, and a more efficient process of contribution and interpretation.

In examining the three aspects of the new field of online education—theory, design, and methodology—this book brings together some of the most recent and most exciting research on this topic. It is the first book dedicated to theory building for online education. It is the authors' hope that the perspectives presented here will contribute to systematizing knowledge about online education, and hence advancing the field; and that the juxtaposition of such diverse approaches will introduce us to new ways of viewing and studying online education, and inspire future activities and developments in this environment.

PART I
Theoretical Perspectives

Chapter 1
Computer Conferencing in the Context of the Evolution of Media

Paul Levinson

MEDIA EVOLUTION

An ecological approach to technology suggests that in order to understand a device or a technique, we need to do more than place it under
the microscope of dissective examination and research. We also need to look at the new technology through the telescope, that is, to relate it to nearby and distant technologies, to place it in a context of cultural (and even biological) history, and to derive from this a set of bearings and metaphors with which to make sense of our new creation.[1] Applying the telescope to computer conferencing entails placing computer conferencing in the ongoing history of the evolution of media—looking at the major stages of media development, assessing their merits and debits, and seeing how and where computer conferencing stacks up in this lineage.

The evolution of media begins with speech, which in giving us the capacity to communicate about things not physically present—ranging from lions over the next hill to lions that were over the hill to lions that might be over the hill tomorrow, and, most portentously, to the utterly nonphysical concept (such as, say, a concept) that has little to do with lions at all—likely helped make us human. But being human—knowing about things not physically present—also entails wanting more, and in the case of speech this meant wanting more than the communication within earshot and memory that speech prescribes. Thus the fluidity and abstraction of speech created evolutionary pressure for communication beyond fluid biological boundaries.

Writing answered this need; it is "the voice of an absent person," as Freud put it (*Civilization and Its Discontents*).[2] The written word indeed freed human thought from the confines of space and time. But it sacrificed the interactivity of in-person speech; you cannot receive a reply from a written page, Socrates complained in the *Phaedrus*.[3] And so the modus operandi of media evolution was set: always a price to pay, a loss in prior communicative ability, with each step forward.[4] The steps make sense because new media rarely obliterate their predecessors—writing did not replace the power of speech—and thus we have the benefit of both.

Still, pressure continued for a writing system that sacrificed less of speech than the scarce carving on a wall or handwritten manuscript. The printing press arose: just as one voice can be heard by a multitude of ears, so one page can be read by multitudes of eyes, Stradanus wrote.[5] The press re-created the sustenance of audience that handwritten communication had so drastically reduced. Here is a second principle of media evolution: new media often retrieve elements of biological (natural) communication eclipsed by primitive media (which extended communication only by sacrificing some of its natural benefits).

But the printed page, no less than the handwritten, was mute to the questioner. Electronics restored interactivity with a rush in the nineteenth century. But the telegram was too clipped and formal, and the telephone not formal enough, to support the intellectual exchange that one imagined from, let us say, the interactive book. Radio and TV make sounds and pictures available throughout the world virtually simultaneously, but still leave us merely audiences, with no hope of participation.

Into this vortex comes computer conferencing—instant but permanent, global but interactive, highly malleable throughout. How does it contribute to this history of pros and cons in communication?

In "Human Replay: A Theory of the Evolution of Media" (1979),[6] I explain the historical and continuing development of communications technologies as a three-stage process:

(A) Our species begins with a communications environment in which all features of the naturally perceived world are present, but in which communication can take place only within the biological boundaries of eyesight, earshot, and memory.

(B) We thus are motivated to develop means —technologies—for communication beyond these biological boundaries. Our initial technologies do so, but at the price of sacrificing much of the natural "pretechnological" communications environment. Thus, writing permits communication across great distances and time; yet the written word has neither the intrinsic emotional shading of speech nor the form and color of images.[7]

(C) We thus are motivated to develop additional technologies that both extend communication across biological boundaries and retrieve elements of process and form of "pretechnological" (Stage A) communication that were lost in Stage B primitive technologies. I call this third stage—and thus the evolution of media in general—"anthropotropic" or evolving towards human function. Thus, contrary to many critics of technology who see our world becoming increasingly artificial,[8] I see our world becoming increasingly natural—albeit on a (life enhancing) extended basis—courtesy of technology.

THE CHALLENGE OF TEXT

Text—the written word—has played a pivotal role in this process. As the quintessential Stage B medium (extending beyond biological boundaries at the expense of the full representation of the real world), it has itself been the object of a series of developments whose effect has been to make the written word more human. At the same time, it has given impetus since the late nineteenth century to the development of a series of photochemical-electric and audio media that abandon text altogether in pursuit of human perceptual ends. Computer conferencing (or computer-mediated communication, CMC) at present figures most prominently in the first area: the humanization of text and its transmission.

Communication of text via electronic means usually begins with the creation of text electronically or via word processing. (Electronically scanned text, facsimile mail, and the like are exceptions—as, indeed, is the telegraph, the first electronic medium.) Word processing, with its capacity for infinite manipulation of text prior to transmission, provides enormous benefits to the initial creation of text, for the writer is now freed of the need to negotiate and compromise that inevitably occurs the instant text is fixed in some permanent way. The possibility of easy revision carries the possibility of new error introduced in the revision process; nonetheless, the capacity to revise seems likely to produce the closer fit between ideas/emotions and their expression in writing that is the goal of all writers.[9]

Once the product of word processing is set on a physical page—the letter or article or book is printed—the capacity to

revise ends. Thus the conventional products of word
processing—letters, papers, books—may be superior (owing to
their circumstances of creation) to products of ink and typewriting;
but once they become products, they are no different in transmissibility than products of the traditional media.

This is where CMC shows part of its mettle: text electronically transmitted, and stored in electronic form, is (a) in principle
infinitely revisable, (b) capable of transmission at the speed of
light, (c) capable of being read by an infinite number of people at
the same time, (d) indeed subject to all the properties of electronics
as opposed to the physical object of paper.

MEDIA INTERACTIVITY

CMC also makes a profound contribution to the evolution of
interactivity in media. In the "pretechnological" (Stage A) environment, all communication offers the possibility of interaction, or exchange between sender and receiver. (In some cases, Myles Stan-
dish may use John Alden or a human surrogate to send a message
to Priscilla Mullins. But at the point of communication—between
John and Priscilla—interaction is always possible.) Personal writing on paper continues this—in an asynchronous sense—but the
printing press dispensed with interaction. The loss of interactivity
was the price paid for the huge gain in audience across space and
time. At the dawn of the electric age, the telegraph and telephone
set the foundation for person-to-person interactivity on a global
level. The telephone continues to fulfill this expectation, but the
headlining media of the twentieth century—motion pictures, radio,
and TV—have instead exalted the one-way mass audience first
brought into being by the press. And, indeed, attempts to improve
upon the book as the sole vehicle of formal education have by and
large been confined to similarly unidirectional audiovisual
media.[10]

CMC—the combination of word processing and
telecommunications via personal computers, telephone lines, and
central computer conferencing systems—in effect puts a telegraph
in everyone's home and place of business. This might logically
have been the next step after the telegraph's introduction—but the
evolution of media is far from precisely logical, and the development of the telephone after the telegraph has a logic of its own.
Further, the enormous ease of telephone use (requiring, as distinct
from word processing, virtually no learning) spurred the develop-

ment of the massive networks of telephone lines that form a natural resource for computer conferencing today.

THE SOCIAL MATRIX

The impact of any technological system is a function not only of the technology itself but also of the web of social expectations and consequences that inseparably accompany and indeed make possible the operation of the technology. For example, education via computer conferencing is often erroneously compared to traditional "correspondence school" learning;[11] the comparison is erroneous not only because information can be exchanged at much faster rates in computer conferencing (a technical difference with social consequences) but also because the electronic classroom on a computer conferencing system encourages group exchanges (between faculty and many students, among groups of students, etc.) that are simply not possible in correspondence school education. Nor is education via computer conferencing in any way similar to "computer assisted instruction," the use of computer programs for individual learning or drill.[12] The student who computer conferences is communicating *through* computers to other people, rather than *to* an already determined computer program. These examples show that research into education via computer conferencing must be sensitive to the ways that seemingly subtle differences in the technology of education can engender radical change in the social educational environment. The importance of social factors suggests that "computer conferencing" may be a better name for the process than is "computer-mediated communication": the term "conferencing" accentuates the inherent "groupness" of this educational medium.
The inextricable social matrix of computer conferencing also suggests that the designers of online educational systems must be not only technical but also social engineers. (The development of the Electronic Information Exchange System by technical designer Murray Turoff and sociologist Roxanne Hiltz over the years provides a personal embodiment of this joint technical-social need in computer conferencing system design.) But, as Karl Popper and others have pointed out,[13] the naturally selective quality of human design and its consequences—which are often unintended—resist careful planning. Media design and planning conducted in an evolutionary context, then, needs to be a flexible, feedback process in which the social consequences of technical design spur changes

or attempted improvements in the design, which in turn will engender slightly different social consequences, and so on.

Let us consider, as an example, a real issue in computer conferencing that has been addressed in a variety of ways by different systems designers: the question of to what extent a text already sent or entered on the system should be malleable or amendable, and by whom.[14] The question arises because, from a technical standpoint, electronically stored text is infinitely malleable. The decision about how much amendability/malleability to allow is a social one. This creates a need for new technical features on the system; for example, the social decision to limit who can modify text leads to a technical feature on the system that prevents anyone other than, say, the instructor from modifying an already entered text.

An evolutionary approach to this problem (and, indeed, all technological problems) begins by consulting the testimony of previous media and their performance in the area under investigation. In the case of letter writing, phone calls (with or without answering machines), and in-person classroom conversation, no possibility exists for amending a communication other than issuing a new one. The same applies to book publishing and, indeed, most media: once disseminated, the original message cannot be altered—it is in the hands, so to speak, of the receivers.

Good reason exists for this, especially in scholarly activities. Were an author able to change his/her original text at will, then dialogue and discussion of the text would be severely jeopardized, for no one would know whether the text under discussion was the original or one of the amended versions. (Indeed, this problem arises in revised editions of books. Karl Popper attempts to deal with this danger by indicating all new edition material in a way that makes clear that the material is new. In the case of footnotes, he retains footnotes from earlier editions, and presents footnotes to new editions as new footnotes—1 in original edition, *1 in second edition, **1 in third edition, etc.)

The weight of previous media practice thus favors placing sharp limits on the technical ability to modify an already entered text. Yet who of us who has written a letter—or published an article or book—hasn't yearned to correct an annoying typo or an inelegant statement? The capacity of computer conferencing for easy modification of such errors seems wasted if we forbid modifications by the sender of a text. (Note that if a receiver of a computer conference text records that text on his/her personal computer disk, or prints the text on paper, then of course the author loses the ability to modify the recipient's text. In many cases of computer conferencing, however, the primary reading and responding to text

take place entirely online or when connected to the central computer system, and in these instances the author's ability to modify
previously entered text becomes a very serious issue.)

Where are we in the technical → social → technical → etc.,
model described above? A technical capacity (modifiability) controlled by human fiat (no modifications allowed by authors) engenders a situation that asks for yet further technical capacities:
to wit, a system that allows for modifications, but in a way that
does not obliterate the original texts and thus does not confound
the dialogue. The Electronic Information Exchange System (EIES)
has already taken a step in this direction: modifications are allowed, but the modified comment is clearly labeled, and all participants in the conference (or electronic classroom) are notified
that such a modification has occurred. I would go one step further
to suggest a technical design that (a) allows modifications to occur,
(b) notifies all participants of the modification (as in EIES), but (c)
keeps the original text retrievable by all participants, so everyone
can be clear about exactly what was modified in the discussion. In
this way, the manipulability of computer text can allow participants to have their cake and eat it.

TOMORROW'S MEDIA

Discussion of the evolution of anything, including computer
conferencing and media, entails a consideration not only of the
past and the present, but also of the future. Thus far, we have
attempted to understand the impact of computer conferencing, and
to suggest a context for research into computer conferencing and
education, by situating computer conferencing in the evolution of
media in the past.

Two frames of reference for computer conferencing seem pertinent to assessment of the future. One, the more narrow frame,
concerns the liberation of text from fixed paper—the "fungibility"
of text (to use Harvey Wheeler's term[15]), its capacity in electronic
form for infinite and easy revisability, interactivity delayed and
immediate, duplicability, transmissibility, storage, and attendant
cognitive enhancement that we have looked at in this chapter, and
that makes text a much finer, more supple, and more propagative
tool of the intellect. From the point of view of written text, computer conferencing constitutes the first progress in the evolution of
media since the mass application of the printing press in fifteenth-
century Western Europe. Accordingly, we can expect a second

golden age of print in the next century—a renaissance of letters as print is utilized to potentials impossible on the page. If, as David Riesman said, print was the "gunpowder of the human mind"[16]—an explosive stimulant of ideas and their impact that, as Innis, McLuhan, I, and others have detailed,[17] gave rise to the Protestant Reformation, hegemony of national states, the Scientific Revolution, development of public education, and capitalism (in short, the mutually escalating currents of inquiry and self-expression that constitute the modern world)—we may be in for an unleashing of mental energies on an atomic-fusion level as a result of electronic creation and dissemination of text.

But the ascension of electronic text need not inhibit the continued development of nonliterate media of sight and sound, nor should any educator recommend such an inhibition. As Rob Higgins, participant in our online (and in person) discussions argued, the human intellect and sensorium are entitled to the fullest array of media we can muster. This is indeed the thesis of my Human Replay: that we strive to create media that both extend the range of our communication and recapture elements of the natural communication environment lost in this extension. As indicated above, the initial creation of audiovisual media in this and the last century was a quite natural response to prior media environments in which colorless, quiet print was the only game in town. Computer conferencing may be seen as an evolutionary development that rectifies the slow, fixed, noninteractive quality of print—but text electronically communicated is no improvement over print's inability to convey literally the scope and subtlety of what old-time philosophers quite rightly called the sensuous world.

For the world of the nonabstract senses—which continues to be an important human realm—media that convey sight and sound in a literal way will be essential educational tools. I would not trust an art critic, nor want to be operated upon by a brain surgeon, who had been educated solely via online text environments. Brain surgeons of the future requiring online education would be best served not by hypertext but by "hypermedia," an interactive, modifiable system that "pulls in" not only all conceivable text associations but also holographic moving and still images and sounds that supplemented and where appropriate, completely replace the nonliving letters of text.

On the other hand, the realm of the abstract—of physical objects not present, of entities that were not ever physical at all—is the hallmark of human existence, a realm that apparently separates us from all other living organisms on this planet. For this realm, liberated text will likely be as profound as the invention of the alphabet and the printing press before it.

NOTES

1.   The microscope-telescope analogy was first offered by literary critic I.A. Richards.   See Harry Levin, "I. A. Richards (1893-1979)," *The New York Review of Books*, December 6, 1979, p. 42:   "When he [Richards] took what he termed 'the Copernican step,' substituting the telescope for the microscope, he was perforce an explorer not a guide."   The same can be said for the pioneering media analyses of Marshall McLuhan; see Paul Levinson, "McLuhan and Rationality," *Journal of Communication* 31 (3) (Summer 1981): 179-88, and "McLuhan's Contribution in an Evolutionary Context," *Educational Technology* 22 (1) (January 1982): 39-46, for discussion of McLuhan's "telescopic" approach to media theory.

See also Paul Levinson's "Marshall McLuhan and Computer Conferencing," *IEEE Transactions of Professional Communication*, March 1986, pp. 9-11, for discussion of the form of McLuhan's writing as computer conferencing in a preelectronic (print) environment.

2.   Sigmund Freud, *Civilization and Its Discontents*, trans. J. Riviere. New York: Cape and Smith, 1930, p. 38.

3.   *Phaedrus*, 275-276.

4.   See Paul Levinson's "Human Replay: A Theory of the Evolution of Media," Ph.D. diss., New York University, 1979, for a detailed development of my theory of tradeoffs in media evolution. Examples include the telegraph (which allowed instant transmission at the expense of fidelity to the real world: the dots and dashes of the telegraph are abstractions of written letters, which are themselves abstractions of spoken sounds, which are in turn already abstractions of the real-world events they describe; the telegraph is thus three levels of abstraction removed from reality), the telephone (which permitted human vocal communication but lost the permanence of telegraph transmissions), and photography (which at first captured the real world at the expense of the color already achieved in painted portraiture).   Note that each of these deficits was eventually rectified by later media (telephone and videophone allow instant transmission with high fidelity to sensory reality; telephone answering machines permit permanence if desired in telephone conversations; color photography became commercially available by the 1930s).

5.   Caption to a Stradanus engraving of a print shop; reprinted in Joseph Agassi, *The Continuing Revolution*, New York: McGraw-Hill, 1968, p. 26.

6.   Ph.D. diss., New York University.

7.   See Marshall McLuhan, *The Gutenberg Galaxy*. New York: Mentor, 1962, for more on the sensory inadequacies of the written word. See also the discussion of writing in Paul Levinson, *Mind at Large: Knowing in the Technological Age*. Greenwich, CT: JAI Press, 1988, pp. 119-37.

8.   Jacques Ellul, *The Technological Society*, trans. J. Wilkinson. New York: Vintage, 1964 [1954], is a prime example. See Levinson, *Mind at Large*, pp. 224-25 ff for discussions and critiques of Ellul, Karl Jaspers, Lewis Mumford, and other critics of technology. I describe Ellul's critique of artificial technology as the "Ellulian error"—the mistake of judging current technology, which is in its infancy or adolescence, as the final technological state. See also Levinson, "Human Replay"; and his "The Human Option: Media Evolution and Rationality as Checks on Media Determinism," in *Studies in Mass Communication and Technology*, ed. S. Thomas. Norwood, NJ: Ablex, 1984, pp. 231-37 for more on the Ellulian error and other problems with Ellul's critique of technology.

9.   See Levinson, *Mind at Large*, "Electronic Facilitations of Print," for further discussion of this point.

10.   This argument is developed further in Paul Levinson, "Social Consequences of Computer Conferencing," plenary address, Second International Conference on Computer Conferencing, University of Guelph, June 1987 (published acoustically on audiotape by The Powersharing Series Riverside, CT; no. 161, ed. Charles K. Mann).

11.   For example, Murray Turoff's remarks at the Conference on Computer Conferencing, Newark, New Jersey Institute of Technology, February 23, 1985. (Turoff is designer and director of the Electronic Information Exchange System, a computer conferencing system in operation since 1985.) McLuhan termed this tendency to judge new media in terms of past structures "rear-view mirrorism": "When faced with a totally new situation, we tend to attach ourselves to the objects, to the flavor of the most recent past. We look at the present through a rear-view mirror. We march backwards into the future." Marshall McLuhan and Quentin Fiore, *The Medium is the Massage*. New York: Bantam, 1967, pp. 74-75. Examples of rear-view mirrorism include the "horseless carriage" (early name for the automobile) and the "wireless" (early name for radio). In fact, automobiles were much more than horseless carriages and radios much more than wireless telegraphs. See Paul Levinson, "Cosmos Helps Those Who Help Themselves: Historical Patterns of Technological Fulfillment, and Their Applicability to Human Development of Space," paper presented at

MIT Conference on Space Agenda: Context and Opportunity, Cambridge, MA, April 1986; published in *Research in Philosophy and Technology*, Vol. 9, ed. F. Ferre. Greenwich, CT: JAI Press, 1989, pp. 91-100.

12.   See *Electronic Learning*, March 1989, entire volume, for recent developments in computer-assisted instruction.

13.   See Karl Popper, *The Poverty of Historicism*. London: Routledge and Kegan Paul, 1944-1945/1957, for his now classic critique of social planning, and his *Objective Knowledge*, Oxford: Oxford University Press, 1972/1979 for his evolutionary epistemology.   See Paul Levinson, "What Technology Can Teach Philosophy," in *In Pursuit of Truth: Essays on the Philosophy of Karl Popper*, ed. P. Levinson.   Atlantic Highlands, NJ: Humanities Press, 1982, pp. 157-76 for a discussion of Popper, Donald T. Campbell, and other evolutionary epistemologists.   See also Levinson, *Mind at Large*.

14.   See "The Book in History" and "Electronic Facilitations of Print," in Levinson, *Mind at Large*, for further comparison of print and electronic text.   See also Paul Levinson, "Intelligent Writing: The Electronic Liberation of Text," presented at the 1989 AAAS Annual Meeting, San Francisco, January 16, 1989, and published in *Technology in Society* 11 (3), Fall 89 (in press).

15.   See Wheeler, *The Virtual Society*, currently available from the author on computer disk, and Paul Levinson's review of this disk-book in *The Journal of Social and Biological Structures* (forthcoming).

16.   Cited in Neil Postman, *Teaching as a Conserving Activity*. New York: Delacort, 1979, p. 65.

17.   See note 13 above.

REFERENCES

Agassi, J. (1968). *The continuing revolution*. New York: McGraw-Hill.

Ellul, J. (1964 [1954]). *The technological society*, trans. J. Wilkinson. New York: Vintage.

Freud, S. (1930). *Civilization and its discontents*, trans. J. Riviere. New York: Cape and Smith.

Levin, H. (1979). I. A. Richards (1893-1979). *The New York Review of Books* (December 6): 42.

Levinson, P. (1979). Human replay: A theory of the evolution of media. Ph.D. diss., New York University.

——— (1981). McLuhan and Rationality. *Journal of Communication, 31* (3): 179-88.

——— (1982). McLuhan's contribution in an evolutionary context. *Educational Technology, 22* (1): 39-46.

——— (1982). "What technology can teach philosophy." In P. Levinson (ed.), *In pursuit of truth: Essays on the philosophy of Karl Popper*. Atlantic Highlands, NJ: Humanities Press, pp. 157-76.

——— (1984). "The human option: Media evolution and rationality as checks on media determinism." In *Studies in mass communication and technology*, ed. S. Thomas. Norwood, NJ: Ablex, pp. 231-37.

——— (1986). Marshall McLuhan and computer conferencing. *IEEE Transactions of Professional Communication* (March): 9-11.

——— (1987). "Social consequences of computer conferencing." Plenary address, Second International Conference on Computer Conferencing, University of Guelph, June 1987. (Published acoustically on audiotape by The Powersharing Series, Riverside, CT, no. 161, ed. Charles K. Mann.)

——— (1988). *Mind at large: Knowing in the technological age*. Greenwich, CT: JAI Press.

——— (1989a). Cosmos helps those who help themselves: Historical patterns of technological fulfillment, and their applicability to human development of space. In F. Ferre (ed.), *Research in Philosophy and Technology*, Vol. 9, Greenwich, CT: JAI Press, pp. 91-100.

——— (1989b). "Intelligent writing: The electronic liberation of text." *Technology in Society, 11* (3), Fall (in press).

——— (in press). "Review of Harvey Wheeler's *The virtual society*." *The Journal of Social and Biological Structures*.

McLuhan, M. (1962). *The Gutenberg galaxy*. New York: Mentor.

McLuhan, M., & Q. Fiore. (1967). *The medium is the massage*. New York: Bantam.

Popper, K. (1944-1945/1957). *The poverty of historicism*. London: Routledge and Kegan Paul.

——— (1972/1979). *Objective knowledge*. Oxford: Oxford University Press,

Plato, *Phaedrus*, 275-276.

Postman, N. (1979). *Teaching as a conserving activity*. New York: Delacort.

Wheeler, H. (1988). *The virtual society*. Santa Barbara, CA: University of Southern California/Martha Boaz Endowment.

Chapter 2
Toward a New Paradigm for Distance Education

Robin Mason and Tony Kaye

INTRODUCTION

The field of distance education includes many different organizational structures and, just like face-to-face teaching, includes programs based on various models of teaching and learning
(see, for example, Holmberg 1981;
Keegan 1986; Hodgson et al. 1987). At one extreme, there are dedicated institutions dealing with mass audiences that produce multimedia courses centrally, and support their presentation to students through regional centers and part-time tutors (see Kaye and
Rumble 1981; Rumble and Harry 1982). Some colleges and universities operate a "mixed-mode" model, with extension studies
departments where an individual lecturer can give a version of
his/her face-to-face course to off-campus students. Many of these
distance programs deal with relatively small numbers of students,
although some (for example, the University of Wisconsin) are very
extensive. There are also numerous postgraduate, specialist
programs that rely on the greater experience and independence of
mature students to control their own learning and research within
the framework of small-group and individual study at a distance.

In recent years, computer-mediated communication (CMC)
has started to be used by a small number of institutions in each of
the above distance education settings. An example of the integration of CMC into an existing multimedia distance education system is described by Kaye (1987); the use of CMC in a mixed-mode
institution has been reported by Haile and Richards (1984); and
the use of CMC for postgraduate seminar courses has been

described by Davie (1987) and by Harasim (1987). This chapter is the outcome of a discussion among various educators involved in such experiments. The result of the discussion is presented here as an attempt to define a new paradigm for distance education. This is based on the assumption that if the potential of CMC and networking is to be exploited to the full, existing implementations of distance learning will need to be reconceptualized, just as some would claim that the introduction of telematics into the school will bring about radical changes in the classroom teaching paradigm (Gooler 1986). In fact, the distinctions currently drawn between distance and classroom-based education may become less clear as applications of the new computer-based communication technologies become more widespread.

IMPLICATIONS OF CMC FOR DISTANCE EDUCATION

For the purposes of this chapter we use the description of distance education presented by Keegan (1980) and subsequently developed by Henri and Kaye (1985) and by Rumble (1986). This description contains six major elements, all of which are required to define a distance education program. For each element we will examine the implications of the introduction of CMC and present our view of the role that it could play in distance education.

The Separation of Teacher and Learner

The separation in time and place of teachers and learners does not imply that distance education is synonymous with all teaching and learning carried out over a distance. Distance education should not be the mere delivery, "at a distance," of classroom-based instruction. A verbatim transcript of a lecture circulated by post to students spread over the country does not constitute distance education. Information should be designed for a particular medium to best exploit its unique advantage. Although distance learners have more control over when and where studying takes place, they need correspondingly more support in terms of resources they can access in order to carry out the learning process. CMC, as one of these resources, can provide vastly enhanced opportunities for dialogue, debate, and conversational learning. Furthermore, it provides a real sense of community and affiliation through its networking potential (Boyd 1985), which in turn gives access to other students' experience and opinion. Contributions to a computer conferencing environment come without the visual and status-determining cues of face-to-face exchanges. This tends to produce a relatively democratic atmosphere where individual contributions are valued on their own merit. The content of the message becomes the primary focus, which can lead to an ideal situation for developing the tools of critical thinking.

The Influence of an Educational Organization

The educational institution exists to design and provide learning materials, to enroll and guide students, and to select and review faculty. Small-scale organizations usually have a direct link between the design of the course, the delivery of it, and the guidance of the students—in other words, one academic "teaching" his/her course. Large-scale organizations usually have many "interfaces" with students: course teams to develop courses, part-time tutors to interact with students, and regional centers to support students. The danger with the "massification" of distance education is the prepackaging of knowledge; education becomes a product that largely determines what the learning process will be. It could be argued that CMC is the ideal vehicle for breaking up the educational "package" and facilitating the processes of internal reflection and reorganization through dialogue, argument, and debate. The part-time tutor can hold continuing tutorials for the duration of the course with a small group of students, encouraging and modeling a deeper engagement with the issues of the course. CMC allows course material, which is presented over a number of years, to be continuously updated and brought to life by current references to daily events. It provides a much faster turnaround time than postal correspondence for communication between student and tutor. An essentially literary medium, it places a premium on the skills of analysis and written expression in the language of the discipline. These are the very objectives of most postsecondary learning programs. Though the benefits of conferencing are more obvious in large-scale distance educational institutions, many of them apply to short-distance learning programs as well. In fact, conferencing offers very exciting possibilities to the academic who manages his/her own course. The potential for interaction and dialogue is one aspect of developing independence in the distance learner; the freedom to negotiate learning objectives and evaluation procedures is another (Garrison and Baynton 1987). In order to maintain quality and standards, large educational organizations need to control the curriculum and the examination process. The academic responsible for only a small number of distance students can, through conferencing, offer them the opportunity to diagnose their own learning needs and formulate their own goals. Thus students have the freedom to choose not only where and when to study, as all distance students can, but also what and how to learn.

The Use of Technical Media, Usually Print, to Unite Teacher and Learner

The different forms of distance education can be identified by the technical media they choose as the basis for their learning materials. By far the majority of programs are print-based, but a few are audio based, fewer still video-based; recently, some are CMC-based. Some, of course, are multimedia; in the average British Open University course, for instance, approximately 80 percent of the student's study time is spent working with text (print) materials, around 10 percent with audiovisual media (cassettes, broadcasts), and about 10 percent on interaction with other students and tutors (face-to-face seminars, summer schools, telephone, correspondence). The role that CMC has taken so far in distance education has varied with the subject matter and the academic level of the students. In seminar-based courses run for small groups of relatively knowledgeable adults[1] who have a lot of highly relevant personal knowledge and experience to contribute, and in many ways are able to provide much of the course content themselves, the time spent in CMC activities is considerable, especially when CMC is used not only for conferencing and e-mail, but also for accessing publications and database information. On the other hand, in an Open University multimedia undergraduate course using CoSy, or in the CMC-supported external degree program at New York Institute of Technology (where students can opt to use CMC for tutor support rather than correspondence tuition), the proportion of students' time spent in CMC activities may be as low as 5 - 10 percent.

It is self-evident that for effective learning to occur, the student must consciously interact with, and operate on, the learning material and resources at his/her disposal. There are, of course, many ways to interact—dialogue with other people, whether written or spoken, is but one. While reading, for instance, one can underline and actively extract ideas that impinge on one's own thoughts, or work out answers to problems and self-test questions embedded in the text. While listening to a lecture or watching a video, one can take notes and draw diagrams to represent the overall message. CMC technology and microcomputers with word-processing software permit other sorts of interaction: the downloading of text messages and documents that can then be edited, modified, and uploaded again for others to read, comment on, and process. These possibilities change the ways in which text material is perceived and apprehended — the authority of a finished, polished product (e.g., a book) is replaced by something dynamic and modifiable, much more under the learner's control. Perhaps the most important contribution of the new technologies to distance education will be that of the communicating text processor, an "intelligent" work station linked to a CMC system.

The Provision of Two-Way Communication

Two-way communication between student and tutor in distance education usually takes the form of written comments on assignments, occasional phone calls or letters, different forms of audio and video conference, and varying amounts of face-to-face tuition in a group situation (see Abrioux 1985). The extent to which students can initiate the communication process varies from one program to another, but this is an important influence on their sense of control over their learning environment (Garrison and Baynton 1987). Electronic mail has an obvious advantage over postal correspondence between an individual student and tutor, in terms of shorter turnaround time and flexibility in manipulating text. Computer conferencing vastly increases the opportunities for turns at expressing one's ideas and for receiving more feedback on them from a wider variety of people, and in a format that is easily retrievable (unlike audio conferencing). Growing out of this high level of interaction and the permanence of the discussion record is the possibility of a group creation, where people make leaps in understanding that are unlikely to happen when working in isolation. Thus, by enhancing the potential for interactivity, CMC allows students to personalize and control their learning activities and environment far more easily than with traditional methods.

The fact that CMC possesses certain advantages over other interactive media, however, does not necessarily mean that it should be
considered as a complete substitute for other forms of interaction.
Lack of choice in teaching media is an impoverishment of the
learning environment, and it is surely better to make available a
range of options for interactivity than to assume that one technology can cope with people's varying communication needs, moods,
and situations. Furthermore, although electronic mail and conferencing may well replace a certain proportion of the telephone
communications that typically take place between tutors and students, CMC cannot effectively substitute for certain specific
properties of voice communication, especially the intimacy and the
spontaneity of response. Likewise, at least in the immediate future, it is difficult to imagine how CMC can replace the carefully
positioned hand written comments, sketches, and other graphic
codes that a tutor might write on the draft of a piece of work submitted by a student.

The Possibility of Occasional Meetings

Most distance education programs include face-to-face meetings as an essential element of the learning system. Such meetings
are used for tutorial discussion, seminars, practical work,
troubleshooting, and counseling, as well as to provide opportunities for socializing for students who feel particularly isolated.
CMC should probably not be seen as a substitute for such face-to-
face events, but rather as a means of continuing to serve a number
of the above functions conveniently and effectively in between occasional meetings. A group of learners who have already met each
other in person, in the presence of a tutor/animateur, are more
likely to be able to communicate effectively online because the personal meeting has provided a number of contextualizing cues that
would otherwise be absent from discussions held exclusively
within the framework of a computer conference.[2] The advantages
of conferencing in the context of group tutorial work lies in the
time it provides for reflection and reading, as well as the
retrievability of other participants' messages. Its educational
potential lies in the entirely new possibilities it opens up for collaborative work and joint projects between students—projects that
might be launched at a face-to-face meeting, pursued in the
framework of a conference, and then finalized at a further face-to-
face meeting.

The Participation in an Industrialized Form of Education

This last element of the description refers to the application to distance education of paradigms drawn from the industrial sector in the design and mass production of learning materials and in the planning and organization of logistical activities. The concepts of division of labor, production line methods, market research, product testing, and emphasis on cost effectiveness apply in some dedicated institutions set up in Thailand, Indonesia, China, India, the United Kingdom, and a number of other countries. These institutions are dealing with student numbers in the 100,000-800,000 range. In this context, distance education is about widening educational opportunities for large numbers of adults. Experience from such distance educational institutions around the world indicates that large-scale projects are necessary to produce courses of consistently high quality, to maintain continuity and institutional stability, to achieve economies of scale, and to gain access to the public broadcasting networks, to publishing expertise, to good computing facilities, and—most importantly—to a wide range of adult students and top-quality tutors.[3]

The question of how to use CMC effectively in the context of such large-scale programs is a difficult one: it raises more issues than does the integration of other interactive opportunities, such as face-to-face meetings or telephone audio conferencing, on high-population distance education courses. In these cases, the individual tutor or animateur is more or less entirely responsible for his/her own group of 20 or so students, and each such group is relatively isolated from the others. However, with CMC, any one student or tutor in a large population course can contact any other student, tutor, or central faculty member; this potential for lateral communication and networking brings an entirely new dimension into the traditional "devoluted" distance education model (Mason 1988b). CMC has already shown itself to be a valuable educational tool in small-scale distance education programs. The completely online courses offered by Connected Education under the leadership of Paul Levinson, as well as the graduate courses run largely online by the Ontario Institute of Studies in Education are just two examples of successful applications on a small scale. Can this medium humanize and individualize education on the large-scale model? How can conferencing, which is essentially a labor-intensive medium, have any application in the mass education marketplace? This seemed such a major issue, from our perspective as educational technologists working in a mass distance education institution, that we posed it as a specific question in the online discussion of this chapter. An edited extract from this discussion is contained in the Appendix, which the interested reader should consult at this point.

We can summarize part of this discussion by saying that the satisfactory articulation of the small-group interactivity of CMC with large course populations will depend on the role and expertise of the tutors, who are both mediating the course materials and moderating the small-group tutorial conferences. Their role can be augmented within the framework of an existing large-scale institution by the creation of a network of resource people from the wider community who can take part in the institution's program as adjunct staff, advisers, and guest speakers. This would allow many more people to tutor part-time than is possible in current place-based institutions or in small-scale distance eduction programs. However, as the online discussion demonstrates, there was some doubt expressed about whether CMC is an appropriate medium for use in distance education courses with large student numbers.[4] CMC can also provide alternative channels of communication and "extend organization boundaries" (Rice 1987) in such a way as to enrich the institutional, and often hierarchical, communication and decisionmaking paths typical of any large organization. Most valuable from a humanistic view of education, it can provide a social framework for the development of a growing community of people; the more students, faculty, tutors, and alumni there are—in other words, the larger the "critical mass" of users of the system—the greater the potential for fruitful contacts, exchanges, and stimulating chance encounters.

NEW PARADIGMS FOR DISTANCE EDUCATION

There is no doubt that CMC is a unique medium for teaching and learning, with valuable educational features and a distinct learning atmosphere different from face-to-face tuition and from other forms of teleconferencing. CMC needs, therefore, to be developed both as a medium in its own right and as an important resource to be integrated into the distance education repertoire. However, the introduction of CMC into a distance education system inevitably affects the ways other media are used, because it opens up the potential for doing new things, or doing old things in new ways. It will affect the structure of courses, the roles of central faculty versus part-time tutors, and ultimately the administration and maintenance of courses (e.g., through online registration and help facilities, database access, etc.).

The applications of CMC in distance education have already begun to change the nature and structure of present institutions in subtle ways, and as networking experiments continue, the six features of distance education that we presented in the opening section of this chapter will eventually need rethinking. To summarize, three major implications of using CMC on distance education courses have emerged from our analysis:

- The breaking down of conceptual distinctions between distance education and place-based education,[5] primarily because of the opportunities that CMC provides distance learners for discussion, collaborative work, and the development of autonomy in learning, and also because of the potential for building a sense of community among the participants in large-scale distance education institutions
- The changing of traditional roles of faculty, adjunct tutors, administrative and support staff
- The provision of an opportunity, which never existed before, to create a network of scholars, "space" for collective thinking, and access to peers for socializing and serendipitous exchange.

When looking to the future with only the seeds in hand, it is important to resist thinking that all innovations must somehow reflect the institutional provision that currently exists. In fact, there are those who proclaim that organizations as we know them are obsolete in the information society; human networks thrive, and it is these which are basic to organizing people (Mueller 1986).

Given the evident properties of CMC and networking to provide continuous access to interactive educational and information resources, is it now possible to envision the development of decentralized programs that bring together the advantages of power, prestige, and reputation of large-scale systems with the benefits of human scale, student-centeredness, and small group interaction? We see this as the central research question facing the next generation of distance education establishments. We would like to identify a few of the issues that require consideration, development, and research, in order to facilitate the growth towards this new paradigm.

The need for adequate and appropriate library access both for students and for academics

The presence of large-scale bibliographic databases accessible online indicates that this need can be met. However, the cost of these services and the lack of support in using them have to be overcome.

The need for a curricular review process

Although the departmental structure of universities provides for this at present, the new paradigms envisioned could respond more fully to the basic premises. The belief that in any field there is a core knowledge that must be taught and that deficiencies in any field are caused by a lack of instruction in the core, which can be corrected by curricular review decisions, must be overthrown in the face of the massive growth in the common body of knowledge. The views of Wondoloski (1987) on this issue are very apt:

> Computer assisted communication offers us an alternative to the models based on traditional views of knowledge. In a guided process-oriented environment....students create their own model or system for employing their skills to sift, sort, and distill information. The professor, rather than doing the work for the student, provides the student with process systems skills which empower the student to perform these functions. CAC provides the opportunity for people to inform, question, and touch one another. A community develops which adds emotional color and drama to the rational content.

The need to ensure faculty competence

The quality and selection of faculty for the new educational paradigm make some of the the most far-reaching changes in the place-based scene. First, there is the possibility of a new type of faculty, drawn from anywhere in the world, and from a much wider range of skills than the teaching profession. The adjunct tutor, exploited by some institutions to "mediate" a course designed by others, can with CMC bring much more of his/her own experience and flair to a basic printed curriculum—or, equally, offer a course in an area of expertise while maintaining a job in industry, management, or a profession, or even act as a guest lecturer or team teacher. The tutor may, for better or worse, use the materials of the multimedia system as so many tools placed at his/her disposal to aid the teaching task. This new facility in distance education could lead to the bold and identifiable perspectives of great teaching individuals and equally to the empowerment of the mediocre and the misguided. New measures will be required to monitor the conferences of the "distributed" faculty.

The provision of support and counseling for students

In many ways this is the easiest of the four elements to implement with a student community that is joined by networking. However, networking must not, even with new paradigms, be seen as a substitute for face-to-face contact. One can imagine students in cosmopolitan settings anywhere in the world connecting to their ethereal community with no culture shock, but it is less easy to picture the rural-based, disadvantaged student slipping into the global village with the same ease. Here is where the decentralized, group-based aspects of the new possibilities come into play.

Thus our new paradigms consist of a number of educational choices: small group discussions and large lecture courses, lab and simulation learning through sophisticated computer-assisted learning, and cooperative projects with other students, some at the local level, some at the global level, developed and delivered by a community of scholars and specialists in every field. Some courses would be delivered entirely online, some with a mixture of media, and some based mainly in regional centers with a smaller online element. The choice would depend on the learning style and experience of the student, economic and domestic arrangements, and the nature of the course material.

CONCLUSION: THE LEARNER'S PERSPECTIVE

Let us conclude with the most important element in the whole picture: the student. The principles of andragogy (Knowles 1970) tell us that adult learners perceive themselves as self-directing human beings and define themselves in terms of their own personal achievements and experiences.

In practice, the fundamental social code of teacher and taught, of classroom and students, has in the past often carried the message of passive, dependent learner (Mason 1988a). The fact that this new paradigm offers considerable choice and autonomy to the learner is irrelevant if the learner is not able to make informed choices about his/her learning requirements and to work independently of authority figures. Computer-mediated communication can be used now as a tool in maturing students' learning styles and developing independent learning strategies. Within the context of an online course, students can be asked to reflect on what they already know and to share their experience or expertise in certain areas of the course with everyone in the group, by making a presentation or fielding questions. Computer conferencing also makes available for distance learners the valuable technique of cooperative projects, where a small group of students work together on a joint paper, presentation, or assignment. These two teaching strategies, combined with the relatively status-free environment and general increase in turn-taking and opportunity for feedback, can, we hypothesize, make computer conferencing an unrivaled medium for developing truly independent learners.

However, although we believe that this growth toward autonomy and self directedness in learning can be radically enhanced by CMC, we would like nevertheless to make a number of caveats concerning the "implementation engineering" of CMC in distance education programs.

First, and obviously, access to online technology from the home—and it is at home that most distance learners study—is not yet widespread (France, with the extensive Teletel network, is an exception). So, at the present time, use of CMC is restricted, for cultural, economic, and technological reasons, to a small public. However, in designing a distance education course that uses CMC effectively, one has to assume that all students will have easy access to the necessary technology, and will know how to use it as a medium for educational communication. This requires a certain amount of experience and practice—naive users of CMC systems are often at a loss as to how to use the medium effectively, and end up making verbose, aimless, or irrelevant contributions, which, in turn, can discourage others from participating. Hopefully, the large-scale applications of CMC within multimedia distance courses that are currently being launched by a number of institutions (e.g., at the British Open University) will contribute significantly to a more widespread familiarization with the technology.

Second, future development of CMC for the distance learner should be considered in conjunction with the development of microcomputer-based work station technology and associated software—particularly packages that integrate word processing, hypertext, idea organizers, and graphics with communications software. The ultimate aim should be the development of communicating text and graphics tools that the student can use and control to organize his/her own learning environment—in other words, a "thoughtbox," linked via CMC, to a "scholar's network" (see Alexander 1986).

Third, despite the medium's inherent support of a learner-centered environment, there is still a possibility that old patterns of teaching and learning will predominate. Tutors who were meant to be facilitators and resource people, available to be consulted when needed, might end up, with the complicity of their students, reproducing the social role of the classroom teacher as authority figure. This goes against the potential of CMC for promoting the educational use of "many to many" communication[6] because it puts the teacher at center stage. If, in addition, CMC is seen as a compulsory and key part of a course, with students feeling an obligation to read everything in their conferences and to contribute well-composed messages of their own, there is a risk that the conference situation will become as constraining for some students as regular attendance at face-to-face classroom sessions. We believe it is important that CMC be seen as one of a range of interactive media that can be put at the disposal of the distance learner within the framework of a multimedia course. It is not necessarily a substitute for face-to-face meetings, telephone conversations, audio conferencing, or other forms of communication. Each has its own specificity, just as do the other media of print, broadcasts, cassettes, CAL software, and so on, that are deployed to varying degrees in distance education courses. At any given moment, the learner should be able to decide which medium to use, for which purpose. This implies that a certain amount of overlap and redundancy between media should be built into any distance education program, to cater not only to differences in learning styles and situations between different students, but also to variations in the mood, level of motivation, and situation of any one individual. There are occasions when the student will want to communicate face to face, over the telephone, or via a computer conference; and there will be occasions when no communication at all is desired, and the student wants to watch a video, study a correspondence text, do some CAL exercises, or compose an essay. The challenge to us as educators is to integrate CMC into the wide range of resources available to the distance learner in such a way that the learner's control of his/her environment is enhanced, and that the distance education systems themselves become more flexible, open, responsive, and decentralized in light of the new potential that CMC offers them.

Acknowledgments

This chapter began as draft notes submitted to an online discussion about CMC in distance education. Major contributors to this discussion over a period of three months were Dr. Lynn Davie, Dr. Paul Levinson, Dr. Linda Harasim, and Terry Anderson; an edited extract of the discussion is contained in the Appendix to this chapter. Face-to-face discussions about the subject continued in Toronto over several days, and a final draft of the chapter was submitted for comment online. France Henri made important contributions at this stage. We acknowledge the successive refinements of our original perspective by each of these contributors. Nevertheless, the views and value judgments made throughout the chapter are ours alone, and have been strongly influenced by our experience of working in a mass distance education institution.

NOTES

1. For example, the CEOs taking the Western Behavioral Sciences Institute's (WBSI) management courses, the graduate students studying education at the Ontario Institute for Studies in Education (OISE), and the students of the Connected Education program.
2. Presumably this is one of the reasons why the WBSI management courses open with a week of face-to-face seminars and meetings before starting the online component of a course.
3. The Open University in Britain, for example, ensures the involvement of leading academic consultants, tutors, contributors, and examiners from universities all over the United Kingdom, as well as from many other countries, because of its reputation for quality that was made possible only through the scale of its operation. For a new course on information technology, television programs were made in France (Teletel) and India (education satellites), and access was granted to IBM's most advanced computer-aided manufacturing technology and to Reuters Information Systems. This would be impossible if the Open University were not a large-scale national institution.
4. See notes 23 (Terry Anderson), 34 (Paul Levinson) and 35 (Linda Harasim) of the transcript in the Appendix.
5. This precise and evocative term was first coined by Paul Levinson in 1984, comment 64, 6/29/84 12:39 AM, "Electronics and the Soul."

6. See note 35, by Linda Harasim, of the transcript in the Appendix.

REFERENCES

Abrioux, D. (1985). Les formules d'encadrement. In F. Henri, & A.R. Kaye, (Eds.), *Le savoir domicile: Pédagogie et problématique de la formation distance.* Québec: Les Presses de l'Université du Québec, pp. 179-203.

Alexander, G. (1986). The thought box and the scholar's network: Integrated tools for distributed learning. Milton Keynes, Open University, Faculty of Technology. (mimeo.)

Boyd, G. (1985). Providing for life-long affiliation with distance education institutions and the feasibility of doing so with personal communications. *Canadian Journal of Educational Communication, 14* (1): 8-9.

Davie, L. E. (1987). Learning through networks: A graduate course using computer conferencing. *Canadian Journal of University Continuing Education, 13* (2): 11-26.

Garrison, D. R. & Baynton, M. (1987). Beyond independence in distance education: The concept of control. *The American Journal of Distance Education, 1* (3): 3-15.

Gooler, D. (1986). *The education utility.* Englewood Cliffs, NJ: Educational Technology Publications.

Haile, P. & Richards, A. (1984). *Supporting the distance learner with computer tele-conferencing.* Islip, NY: New York Institute of Technology. (mimeo.)

Harasim, L. (1987). Teaching and learning online: Issues in computer-mediated graduate courses. *Canadian Journal of Educational Communication, 16* (2): 117-35.

Henri, F., & Kaye, A. R. (Eds.). (1985). *Le savoir domicile: Pédagogie et problématique de la formation distance.* Québec, Les Presses de l'Université du Québec.

Hodgson, V. E., Mann, S. J. & Snell, R. (1987). *Beyond distance teaching—Towards open learning.* Milton Keynes, England: The Society for Research into Higher Education and The Open University Press.

Holmberg, B. (1981). Status and trends of distance education. London: Kegan Page.

Kaye, A. R. (1987). Integrating computer conferencing into distance education: A discussion paper. In *Proceedings of the*

Second Symposium on Computer Conferencing and Allied Technologies. Guelph, Ontario: University of Guelph, pp. 23-32.

Kaye, A. R. & Rumble, G. (Eds.). (1981). *Distance education for higher and adult education*. London: Croom Helm.

Keegan, D. J. (1980). On defining distance education. *Distance Education, 1* (1): 13-36.

Keegan, D. J. (1986). *The foundations of distance education*. London: Croom Helm.

Knowles, M. (1970). *The modern practice of adult education*. New York: Association Press.

Lamy, T. (1985). La télématique: Un outil convivial? In F. Henri, and A. R. Kaye, (Eds.), *Le savoir domicile: Pédagogie et problématique de la formation distance*. Québec: Les Presses de l'Université du Québec, pp. 303-28.

Mason, R. (1988a). Computer conferencing: A contribution to self-directed learning. *British Journal of Educational Technology, 19* (1): 28-41.

———— (1988b). Computer conferencing and the university community. *Open Learning, 3* (2): 37-40.

Mueller, R. (1986). *Corporate networking: Building channels of communication*. New York: Free Press.

Rice, R. E. (1987). Computer-mediated communication and organizational innovation. *Journal of Communication, 37* (4): 65-87.

Rumble, G. (1986). *The planning and management of distance education*. London: Croom Helm.

Rumble, G., & Harry, K. (Eds.). (1982). *The distance teaching universities*. London: Croom Helm.

Wondoloski, E. (1987). An educator, a PC, and a modem: A multidimensional approach to knowledge. Paper presented at the Fifth Annual Conference of Nontraditional and Interdisciplinary Programs, George Mason University, Virginia Beach, May 4-6.

APPENDIX

Edited Extract of the Online Discussion from the Distance Education Branch of the Workshop Conference on PARTI, Covering the Issue of the Use of CMC in Mass Distance Education Programs

---

22 (of 70) TONY KAYE Nov. 30, 1987 at 11.29 est (2407 characters)

...

How would you plan to use CC if you were told that, in 6 months' time, you had to modify your existing course...to cater for a student population of 1,000, all starting at the same time?

...

---

23 (of 70) TERRY ANDERSON Nov. 30, 1987, at 13:10 est (1,069 characters)
Let me duck out of providing answers to Tony's questions by questioning one of the assumptions relating to the "industrial" model of DE. Although much traditional DE has been designed for large audiences and utilizes the economics of scale associated with specialized course teams and other strategies, there are other models of DE.
Many of the teachers in this conference (like myself) have used CC for small groups and have taught/learned in models to some degree more related to the classroom (with some obvious improvements) than to "industrial model" distance education design and delivery. I guess trying to create the "virtual classroom."
    Perhaps this decentralized, teacher intensive model will in fact become the predominant model when communications costs and teacher /student ratios improve. Perhaps not.
    However, I also think that we need to address Tony's questions relating to large student numbers, especially if CC is ever going to be a relevant delivery/ learning mode for Third World nations....

---

24 (of 70) LYNN DAVIE Nov. 30, 1987, at 16.22 est
(93,104 characters) Re: note 22...Adaptation of my course
for 1,000 students.
Assumptions:

A. Availability of 10 tutors, each to handle 5 tutorial
sections of 20 students each.

B. Main course content will be published in regular
distance education mode. Course handbook with 6
modules. Each module will contain notes re texts;
cassette tapes; and a list of discussion questions.
CMC design:

I will base the CMC design on PARTICIPATE, which
I know best, and will take advantage of its branching
features. I suspect that the transfer to COSY or EIES
would not be difficult, although the design would be
altered to maximize the features of those systems.

In PARTICIPATE there would be one main
conference, which I will call "Agenda." This conference
would be under the control of the main teacher and
would contain scheduling information, notes regarding
assignments, and other administrative matters.

The first branch would be called "Counselor" and
would have two subbranches: "Academic" and "System".
"Counselor" would be a place where any student (or
tutor) could ask questions and receive help. I envision
the questions to be of the nature of the student's
relationship to the institution under "Academic" and the
usual software and hardware questions under "System."

The next branch would be "Coffee," for social
interaction. Again, students, the instructor, or tutors
would be welcome here.

The next branch would be the "main" conference. This
conference would be set to be read only and would
contain "lectures" by the instructor, "visits" from experts,
and other material common to the whole course. There
might be branches off this to contain optional reading
material, specialized bibliographies, etc. The instructor
would elaborate on course materials or comments
regarding recurring problems found in the tutorial
groups.

Then I would create a branch for each module in the
course materials. In each module branch there would
first be a common conference for the module (staffed by a
tutor) that is read-only. This conference would be similar
to the "main" conference above. It would deal with

common problems found in the tutorial groups for the module.

Within each module would be 50 "tutorial" conferences. Each would contain a tutor and 20 students. These conferences would be the place for discussion of course materials. Students would comment on questions found in the course materials, ask questions, submit assignments, and generally replicate the small discussion sections associated with small groups. One could envision role playing, case analysis, or joint writing projects in these tutorial groups. To encourage student participation, you might require that each student leave at least one note in response to a common question. Each module would in turn be the main focus for the course for a two-week period, after which the conference could be made read-only (to be used for later reference). These tutorial conferences could be edited to make them more useful for reference. Students would be joined only to their own tutorial conference.

---

27 (of 70) TONY KAYE Dec. 4, 1987, at 12:28 est (1,613 characters) Comments on notes 24 and 25

Your two responses were very interesting, Lynn, and I am dying to see how others will react to the questions I asked in note 22. In many ways, it is interesting to see how your proposals match what we are trying to implement here in terms of integrating CoSy with the traditional OU media and methods.

However, there are a few questions I'd like to ask: (1) On the adaptation of your own course for 1,000 students, you would have ten tutors each running five tutorial conferences. What sort of load do you think this would represent in, say, hours per week for each tutor? How do you think they would cope with running, in parallel, five conferences for the same topics with five different groups of students? Would the individual tutors be able to communicate with each other and with you on the system? Would you want to monitor what they were doing within their conferences?

---

28 (of 70) PAUL LEVINSON Dec. 4, 1987, at 19:21 est (1,783 characters)

I'm going to surprise you, Tony, by admitting that I see education via CC as no more amenable than

education in-person to education of all-at-once masses.
In other words, although I see many more topics as
teachable with quality via CC than do you, I do not
include among the values of CC that it can teach a
thousand or more people all at once.

In terms of teacher-student ratios, then, the optimum
online class may well be around the same twenty-ish size
as the in-person class.

This suggests, in turn, that our goals for education via
CC must be the training of large numbers of teachers
(not necessarily from traditional teacher pools, but from
practitioners in industry, etc) so that we can reach the
numbers of people we want to.

But this is ok, because my guess is that in a total
flexitime environment, we'll find many more people
capable of being fine teachers than we do in the world's
current place-based situation.

...

Notwithstanding all of the above, I would, one month
sometime in my life, like to teach a class with as many
people in the world as were willing to register.

My best accomplishment to date in this area was
doing an "E-lecture" on the Source several years ago (on
Space: Humanizing the Universe, my next book). We had
some 400 participants who generated 750 comments in
one month (I wrote about 100 of these).

There was, of course, no way I could grade these people,
and I agree completely with Lynn that large numbers of
people require tutors and small discussion places in
addition to the central lecture. (I had one huge read-only
lecture plus about 15 interactive branches. We did this
on Parti—Version 3—on the Source). Anyway, I'd like to
try my hand at an infinite audience someday.... (But
that's just personal).

---

29 (of 70) LYNN DAVIE Dec. 6, 1987, at 10:17 est (2,176
characters)
Comments on notes 27 and 28

I am also looking forward to seeing how the others
will respond to your problems.

You ask what sort of load the plan would represent for
each tutor. Of course, the amount of instructor
interaction in each conference will depend a lot on the
instructor. For my course, I have had an average of about

20 notes per week for the past 2 years (for a group of about 15 students plus me). My estimate for the time needed to monitor and respond was about a half hour per day. Thus, if there was not an overload of running the 5 different groups, simple addition yields about 3 hours (rounded up) of machine time. Of course, a tutor would have to spend time researching his/her answers, etc., so that is probably a full-time job.

In terms of coping with five simultaneous groups, I think some thinking through is in order. I would think it would be very difficult if you just signed on and banged away at your responses. However, if I were training the tutors, this is what I would suggest.

First, do not respond immediately. Sign on and download the day's notes onto a disk. On the disk, you should have a separate file for each tutorial group. Using some kind of word-processing software that allows for split-screen editing (Microsoft Word, for example), put the conference in one window and construct your responses in another. Read enough of the conference each time to locate yourself and remember the threads of that conference's discussion. Carefully prepare and edit your responses. Then log back in and send your notes. This is the procedure I am using with this conference to keep all the branches straight.

I would set up a separate conference for the tutors and myself to communicate about problems and suggest strategies. Tutors could copy problematic (or interesting) notes into this separate conference. Finally, I would be able to read all tutor conferences. I might not in fact read them all, but I would want to browse.

---

33 (of 70) ROBIN MASON Dec. 10, 1987, at 12:42 est (2,557 characters)

I would like to have a go at summarizing what has developed in this conference so far....It seems to me that the issue of conferencing as a tool in mass education at a distance is critical to every aspect of the discussion. The use of conferencing for education of small groups at a distance is a successful model that, presumably, none of us here doubts.

...

One person, no matter how charismatic, cannot run a

conference for 1,000 students single-handed for very long and still exploit the real value of the medium. The educational value of the medium, as I see it, is the opportunity for greatly increased turns at expressing one's ideas and for receiving more feedback on them from a wider variety of people. Growing out of this high level of interaction is the possibility of a group creation, where people make leaps in understanding that are unlikely to happen when working in isolation. In order for these values to be exploited, 25 students to 1 tutor is about the right allocation for online education, just as in f2f. In order to produce high-quality, standardized course material, the major content is most efficiently produced centrally. The tutor then acts as facilitator, interpreter, even critic.

My conclusions from studying Lynn's model, which is as near as dammit to the OU's use of conferencing, are that maximum efforts need to go into the training of tutors to teach online. For this we need to gather evidence from a variety of moderating styles and analyze the successful attributes of each. We also need to amass a collection of different applications of online teaching to build up expertise in teaching techniques. Some work in these areas has been done, but possibly not as systematically as is now required. Can we now focus on this issue: how to train people—not just traditional teachers, but industrialists, executives, etc., to effectively tutor online courses.

I need to add an addendum to this as I prepared it before the last two messages. It involves the "control" of the course content centrally, which is the essence of the OU teaching model. Obviously this has major implications for the role of the tutor/moderator. Maybe we should plan for both scenarios—the tutor being responsible for the content, as well as the model where the tutor is go-between for centrally produced content.

---

34 (of 70) PAUL LEVINSON Dec. 10, 1987, at 15:54 est (1,613 characters)

Further to what I said before in response to Tony's request for more on the issue of 1,000s taught by CMC ...:

I'm honestly not sure that I see any value in even considering CMC as a medium in which students are construed of as coming in blocks of 1,000s. Here are two indisputable values of CMC in education:

1. One teacher can reach 25 students who are located literally in many parts of the earth.
2. Teacher and students can access their course anytime, 24 hours a day.

Both of these and many other advantages of CMC are obvious and have been often remarked upon; they are nonetheless still extraordinary in comparison with traditional place-based education.
In terms of numbers of students that CMC can handle, why try to make CMC attain an ideal of handling huge numbers at one time? The only advantage I could see, even if CMC could educate such large numbers at once, is if we (the world of educators) were suffering from a punishing paucity of teachers, and we needed to make the most of the tiny number that we had. But in fact, I don't see this as the case at all—indeed, I see a net increase in excellent teachers as a consequence of CMC (e.g., freeing professionals to teach—whereas in the in-person setting they wouldn't have the time).

The bottom line for me: I think the notion of one person teaching a thousand students is not especially germane to CMC and not especially productive. The one to many model is a rear-view mirrorism related to books and television—and one that the very interactivity of CMC should outmode.

---

35 (of 70) Modified by LINDA HARASIM Dec. 11, 1987, at 11:57 est (2,333 characters)

I have been thinking about the concrete problem that Tony and Robin recently set out in this conference: to design a course with 1 instructor to reach 1,000 students (with the use of tutors and a possibility of other media). Perhaps because my experience has always been with small groups and with graduate courses, I have found it difficult to conceptualize something that seemed educationally useful or effective for such a massive student:instructor ratio.

I found Paul's comment (#34) insightful, and it made me wonder if the original question (about how to design an activity for such a ratio) should not be questioned. I find it difficult to understand or accept the underlying assumptions for such a mass student-instructor arrangement. CMC offers the opportunity to do different things educationally, in terms of both f2f and distance ed. New learning opportunities are available, such as to increase interactivity and in some ways to "personalize" and control one's learning activities and environment (including more options for selecting one's instructors and learning peers—these could be from almost anywhere). However, massifying educational interaction does not seem the best way to approach CMC. Even the ratio of 1:25 (suggested by Robin and Lynn) seems to me possibly too high. As I commented in the "testimonials" conference, my course of 28 students over 12 weeks generated 2,600 conference notes and probably close to that again in personal notes. While my online presence was quite minimal (I use a group learning approach), still my online time averaged something like 8-10 hours/week...not counting the reading and preparation that I did offline. That is 8 hours interacting with one course instead of the typical 2.5 to 3 hours (at OISE). That is a heavy load for one course. And even with that I was not satisfied that I provided as much organization and synthesis of the discussions as I would have liked.

So, perhaps one question to consider is what are the advantages and features that CMC offers and how to design new learning environments to make best use of these....interactivity and active participation (many to many) are among these, and it seems to me that the one to many model has implicit, very different educational goals and approaches from the many to many model.

Chapter 3

Online Education: An Environment for Collaboration and Intellectual Amplification

Linda M. Harasim

INTRODUCTION

New communication technologies introduce powerful environments to enhance social and intellectual connectivities. Online education, based on the use of computer communication systems for educational delivery and interaction, is growing rapidly as a field of practice; there is a need for theoretical perspectives to frame our understanding, design and use of online systems for education and to contribute to new developments in the field.

A fundamental question for educators and learners is how educational applications of new online environments may improve learning. Do CMC systems such as computer conferencing introduce a unique set of capabilities that enable us to enhance our social and intellectual capacities? To address such questions and to guide how we study and employ these media for knowledge building, we require a theoretical perspective. Collaborative learning theory, which highlights social and intellectual interaction, offers a valuable starting point.

This chapter examines online education from the perspective of how it facilitates educational collaborations, especially where the activity takes place primarily online, in a computer conferencing system. The chapter begins by locating online education within its historical and educational counterparts, a discussion which leads to identifying five key attributes of the online environment. Using these attributes as a framework we can set out qualities of social and intellectual interaction possible within the online medium that are similar, different, or even impossible using other media or face-to-face. The framework helps us to explore the capabilities of online systems for facilitating educational collaboration and enhancing human thinking; it can also help us to identify limits with current conferencing technology. Developments in related computer-supported cooperative work systems such as hypertext and hypermedia, integrated with computer communication systems, suggest directions to expand the potential of online education for amplifying active and purposeful learning. The final part of the chapter examines theoretical and practical convergences among these new groupware to guide research and development in the field.

BACKGROUND

The search to amplify intellectual processes has been an inspiring force in the development of computer technology. Early visionaries devoted their attention to this issue, highlighting the role of the computer as a tool to augment rather than automate human intellect and interaction. Online education emerged from systems that focused on enhancing intellectual processes through collaboration among knowledge workers.

Vannevar Bush, in the 1940s, presented his vision of the *memex*, "a device in which an individual stores all his books, records, and communications, and which is mechanized so that it may be consulted with exceeding speed and flexibility. It is an enlarged intimate supplement to his memory" (Bush 1945, p. 108). Bush's vision was distinguished by his conception of an associative structure, in electronic form, that closely modeled the structure of human memory. Bush conceived of a system which would operate like the mind, by association, in accordance with some intricate web of trails. While a computer might not equal the speed and flexibility with which the mind follows an associative trail, it should be possible to beat the mind with the speed and clarity of items resurrected from storage (Bush 1945, p. 108). This vision has inspired a growing pursuit of tools to amplify human intelligence, especially at the collaborative/group level.

Douglas Engelbart, like Bush two decades earlier, was concerned with ·augmenting the intellectual capacity of users. He prototyped his NLS (On-Line System), later marketed as *Augment*, at the Augmented Human Intellect Research Center at Stanford Research Institute. One of the most notable design features of Augment is the emphasis on providing tools to support collaborative knowledge work. Second, the Augment project "placed the greatest emphasis on collaboration among people doing their work in an asynchronous, geographically distributed manner" (Engelbart and Lehtman 1988, p. 245). (Augment enabled co-located and simultaneous interaction as well, but time- and place-independent collaboration and communication were highlighted.) Third, Augment enabled idea structuring as well as idea sharing. While linkages among ideas and authors are supported by Augment, the system employs a hierarchical structure.

In the early 1960s Theodore Nelson coined the term *hypertext* to denote online writing and reading that are non-sequential and heavily cross-referenced and annotated; *hypermedia* uses similar associative linkages to include such components as graphics, spreadsheets, video, sound, and animation, whereby an author can create links to diagrams, texts, photographs, video disks, audio recording and the like (Nelson 1974; Yankelovich, Meyrowitz, and van Dam 1985). In Project Xanadu, Nelson designed an experimental self-networking system that permits users to view hypertext libraries, create and manipulate text and graphics, send and receive messages, and structure information intuitively. A user creates linkages between ideas and explores these linkages, using a variety of features that facilitate developing and tracking interconnections (Nelson 1987).

These were the first systems to articulate the potential of computers to create cognitive and social connectivity: webs of connected information and communication among knowledge workers.

The direct ancestry of online education lies in *computer conferencing*. Computer conferencing, a communication system for dispersed human groups, was invented and implemented by Murray Turoff in 1970 (Hiltz and Turoff 1978, p. 43). Turoff designed conferencing to be a "collective intelligence" environment, which would use the computer to structure human communication for information exchange and effective problem solving. Computer conferencing has been adopted commercially, first within government, then by the corporate and scientific sectors, and more recently within the educational community.

KEY ATTRIBUTES OF ONLINE EDUCATION

Educational computer conferencing is a new phenomenon, appearing in the early 1980s. Its use grew significantly in that decade, but theory building was attempted only in the later part of the 1980s.

During the early years of practice, online education was understandably approached from one of two traditional perspectives: as an extension of distance education or as a variant of classroom activity. However, neither perspective is entirely adequate or accurate: to study or design online education most effectively, educators need to take into account the attributes that the environment offers for educational interaction (Harasim 1989b).

Online education is a unique expression of both existing and new attributes. It shares certain attributes with the distance mode and with the face-to-face mode; however, in combination, these attributes form a new environment for learning. Like distance education, online education is time- and place-independent, and the educational interaction is mediated. However, distance education is premised upon a one-to-many or sometimes a one-to-one model of communication. Characterized by Burge (1988) as a "transmittal model," distance education typically relies on mass delivery of pedagogic materials (by mail, radio, or TV), self-study, and, often, access to a tutor (by phone or mail). The interactivity of face-to-face learning modes is not present. Even when the telephone or electronic mail is used, learner-instructor interaction remains weak, while collaboration among learning peers has not been considered even by the literature. Sewart, for example, proposes that "the basis for a theory of distance education is to be found within general educational theory, but not within the theoretical structures of oral, group-based education. This is because distance education is not based on interpersonal communication and is characterised by a privatisation of institutionalised learning" (Sewart 1981, p. 16). Traditional distance education models emphasize the independence of the learner (Moore 1986) and the privatization of learning (Keegan 1986). The emphasis in distance education theory and practice is on individual, rather than group, activity.

Online education, on the other hand, is distinguished by the social nature of the learning environment that it offers. Like face-to-face education, online education supports interactive group communication. Historically, the social, affective, and cognitive benefits of peer interaction and collaboration have been available only in face-to-face learning. The introduction of online education opens unprecedented opportunities for educational interactivity. The mediation of the computer further distinguishes the nature of the activity online, introducing entirely new elements to the learning process.

The potential of online education can be explored through five attributes that, taken together, both delineate its differences from existing modes of education and also characterize online education as a unique mode: (1) many-to-many communication; (2) place independence; (3) time independence (that is, time-flexible, not atemporal); (4) text-based; and (5) computer-mediated interaction.

Many-to-Many Communication

Computer conferencing is essentially a many-to-many communication tool that structures information exchange and group interactions. This attribute deserves serious consideration for theory building, research, and design of online educational activities because—with careful attention to design—computer conferencing supports and facilitates active learning collaborations.

Collaborative or group learning in the face-to-face classroom refers to instructional methods whereby students are encouraged or required to work together on academic tasks. While there are important differences among various theoretical and practical understandings of collaborative learning (Damon and Phelps 1989), all distinguish collaborative learning from the traditional "direct transfer" model in which the instructor is assumed to be the sole source of knowledge and skills. Unlike the teacher-centered models that view the learner primarily as a passive recipient of knowledge from an expert, collaborative or group learning is premised upon a learner-centered model that treats the learner as an active participant. Bouton and Garth (1983) construe learning to be an interactive group process: the learner actively constructs knowledge by formulating ideas into words, and these ideas/concepts are built upon through reactions and responses of others to the formulation.

Educational research identifies peer interaction among students as a critical variable in learning and cognitive development at all educational levels (Johnson, Maruyama, Johnson, Nelson, and Skon 1981; Sharan and Sharan 1976; Slavin 1983; Bouton and Garth 1983; Brookfield 1986). Webb (1982) investigated how participating in group work helps group members learn. Her review of the literature identifies two general approaches to this issue: (1) mediating variables that may create an emotional or intellectual climate conducive to learning; and/or (2) mechanisms directly affecting cognitive processes.

Relevant socioemotional variables include motivation, anxiety (reduced when working with peers instead of with the instructor), and satisfaction. Collegial collaboration can be highly effective in reducing uncertainty as learners find their way through the complex directions of novel tasks (Cohen 1984, pp. 183-84). Peer interaction also assists learners in understanding new concepts and provides learners with an opportunity to commit the new vocabulary to working memory. Collaboration, in the form of peer work groups, increases engagement in the learning process (Cohen 1984, p. 184).

Cooperative groups may also facilitate greater cognitive development than the same individuals achieve when working alone (Stodolsky 1984, p. 122). The conversation (verbalizing), multiple perspectives (cognitive restructuring), and argument (conceptual conflict resolution) that arise in cooperative groups may be the responsible factors (Sharan 1980; Slavin 1980; Webb 1982).

Verbalizing to a peer is related to concept attainment (Durlin and Schick 1976). More than the act of verbalizing, the purpose of the verbalizing was identified as significant. Bargh and Schul (1980) found that learners verbalizing to assist or teach a peer scored better than those verbalizing to demonstrate their own learning: the act of preparing to teach produces a more highly organized cognitive structure. Actively reorganizing the material allows "the teacher to see the issue from new perspectives, enabling him/her to see previously unthought-of new relationships between the discrete elements. It may be this building of new relationships that facilitates a better grasp of the material" (Bargh and Schul 1980, p. 595).

Educational researchers are also examining the ways in which group feedback assist group members in cognitive restructuring, by requiring them to reshape their ideas and learn new information that they might not discover on their own (Slavin 1977). Myers and Lamm (1976) argue that passive receipt of information is not enough for opinion change; the acts of processing, weighing, and reformulating arguments presented by other group members are necessary for internalizing attitude change.

Controversy within the group may lead members to question their own concepts and seek new information and perspectives. Johnson and Johnson (1979) thus propose that conceptual conflict resolution—resolving disagreements in a group—has cognitive benefits: "Students who experience conceptual conflict resulting from controversy are better able to generalize the principles they learn to a wider variety of situations than are students who do not experience such conceptual conflict" (p. 67). The literature on peer collaboration indicates that as ideas are presented, there is a need to actively build linkages and associations and to organize the ideas. Interaction among peers seems important to internalizing attitude change. Information is processed, weighed, reorganized, and structured in this process, both by each individual and also by the group.

The online environment is an effective medium for collaborative learning (see, for example, Chapter 7 of this volume). Computer conferencing software, which automatically files notes into topical discussions and updates users on any new comments in a topic, is currently one of the most appropriate online environments for learning collaborations. Conferencing was designed to support "collective intelligence" and meeting of minds through the topical structure of the system. This structure provides the shared space essential to group interaction: all members of an online group can read the same messages about a particular topic in the same order. The files are a commonly shared object: each member of the group has access, and can read comments and make responses. The shared file holds the individual members of the group together and enables a "conversation" to take place. It also generates a dynamic record or transcript of the interaction.

The theoretical framework of collaborative learning suggests that conferences can provide a fertile forum for interaction. Answering requests for clarification or assimilating responses that disagree with earlier statements from the participants can refine one's own ideas. The interaction necessarily involves formulating arguments or reorganizing material to introduce new (previously unrecognized) relationships, thereby advancing the knowledge of the participants. Rice points out that in a computer conference with geographically dispersed group members, the nonverbal aspects of human communication are generally absent, and so "the emphasis in interaction shifts to the exchange of information. Flows of information into groups, out of groups, and within groups become important attributes of systems and group structure" (Rice 1982, p. 927). Computer conferencing encourages, even demands, active information seeking and discovery: "Users of computer-mediated communication systems often are freer to search for those information exchanges that provide satisfactory resources in return than they would be in typical organizations or communication contexts" (Rice 1982, p. 927).

Place-Independent Group Communication

The second attribute of online education is that it enables place-independent learning and collaboration. With telecommunications linkages, group activities and collaborations need no longer be restricted to participants who are geographically proximate. Computer conferencing offers a kind of "panoptic power" (Zuboff 1988): it becomes possible to access and collaborate with experts and peers anywhere, regardless of location. This feature expands access to learning and intellectual resources. Learners unable to access traditional place-based education (due, for example, to geographical isolation, physical disability, or job or family responsibilities) can nevertheless use computer conferencing to reach learning peers, expertise, and archival information sources. One of the more exciting aspects of this attribute of online education is the access it affords to entirely new communities who, by virtue of personal circumstances, have thus far been excluded from educational opportunities.

Computer-mediated communication also promises the augmentation of personal/professional networks into a global community. Expanded access empowers the learner and enriches her/his resource base: learners, free of geographical constraints, can access a range of input richer and more diverse than available locally. Academics, researchers, educators, and learners can collaborate with colleagues on the basis of shared interests and expertise rather than being constrained in the first instance by the requirement of shared location.

Time-Independent Communication

Time-independent group communication is a third attribute of online education. Most computer conferencing systems are based upon asynchronous (that is, not real-time) communication. Face-to-face and telephone interaction are both real-time communication; conferencing messages, by contrast, are stored in the central computer database awaiting access by the addressee(s). Users can thus participate at a time and at a pace convenient to them and appropriate to the application. This attribute impacts upon group dynamics and the learning process.

The "24-hour classroom" is always open; this facilitates self-pacing and self-directed learning. Asynchronicity expands user control over the time of the interaction, and increases the time available to read or reread a message and formulate a comment. One need neither wait through a slow speaker's delivery nor ask a hasty speaker to repeat. Similarly, the user may write a response immediately or take time to reflect, perhaps accessing a reference or other information resource in the interim. User reports indicate this feature contributes to learning effectiveness (Harasim 1986; Hiltz 1986).

Learning exchanges and interactions can occur over a period of time. A class discussion no longer need be limited to two to three hours per week for the entire group; a "meeting" can extend for as long as required to cover the material and allow each member to participate. Increased opportunities for member input may enhance the quality of decisionmaking (Rice 1984). A workshop or collegial exchange can span several days, weeks, months, or even years, as necessary. This can improve in-depth investigation and development of a topic.

Asynchronous group learning can also reduce competition for air-time among participants (unlike face-to-face or audio conferencing modes). Because the system can accept and display input from all participants, there is no concern that time restrictions or turn taking will limit expression or opportunities to speak. No one need fear going unheard, and each user can participate to the degree that he or she wishes. Participants who require additional time to present their ideas (speakers who are timid, not fluent in the language, or have speech difficulties) are not interrupted by more assertive individuals. Each user can access the system at the time/day of her/his choice, and as frequently and for as long as required. Research also suggests that computer conferencing may suppress the emergence of a group leader. "Thus, more reserved group members may finally gain access to discussions and decision-making, while any individual may have a harder time gaining the group's attention" (Rice 1980, pp. 234-35).

Interpersonal contact among members of the group is extended, since interaction is not limited to a finite period, as in face-to-face or telephone contact. Despite the fact that communication is asynchronous, in an active group responses can be experienced as "near-immediate". On the other hand, asynchronicity is not atemporality. While there is more flexibility over the time of an interaction online, timeliness in discussing the current topic remains important.

Asynchronous collaboration also has drawbacks. Communication anxiety (the feeling of speaking into a vacuum) can occur when a participant receives no immediate response to ideas and comments (Feenberg 1987). Another difficulty is the "rolling present": how does a user know whether a topic is still current or has been overtaken by another theme? Participants may feel they have lost their opportunity to contribute to a particular discussion thread if they log on to the discussion "late" and the focus/momentum has shifted. Being properly located in the asynchronous "timeline" is apparently quite important. Par-

ticipants express annoyance at colleagues who refer to themes that
are perceived by the discussion group as no longer current. Such
thematic threading concerns are an acknowledged problem with
computer conferencing systems (Hiltz and Turoff 1985).

Finally, consensus decisionmaking can be awkward and
time-consuming online. Long delays result if group members do
not log on regularly to present their position or to agree to a
proposal. This is particularly frustrating when deadlines are involved. Moreover, the quality of the decision may be reduced by
delays created through asynchronous group discussion, debate, or
conflict resolution. Members may go along with an initial sugges-
tion, even if they don't agree with it, in order to expedite the
process. Group dynamics can suffer because in many ways this
medium does not offer tools to support such processes as forming
groups and identifying and coordinating group tasks.

Some conferencing systems are based on real-time communication. Real-time communication may be necessary for conducting certain aspects of distributed group work (such as tasks of
short duration which require the simultaneous attention of several
group members) and for coordinating task responsibilities. It may
also be an important asset to such processes as problem solving
and decisionmaking. Real-time is also essential for handling crisis
situations when participants are unable to meet face-to-face (Sarin
and Greif 1988). Educational applications of real-time computer
conferencing systems are being developed within or among face-to-
face classes, primarily as adjuncts to other class activities (Batson
1988).

Text-Based Communication

The fourth characteristic distinguishing online education is
text-based communication. Communication and interaction
among participants in online education is mediated by the
keyboard and video display terminal screen and conducted solely
through text—that is, by sending and receiving messages typed
into the system. Communication in the online medium is thus, at
present, limited to a narrow bandwidth of information: the presentation of text. This feature has both positive and negative implications for educational interactions.

There are cognitive benefits to text-based interaction.
Writing comments is perceived by learners as contributing to more
reflective interaction than talking in a face-to-face class or

telephone conference. Online education provides the opportunity either to respond immediately or first to reflect—that is, compose (and edit) one's response. Reading and writing online can also be conceptualized as unique ways of thinking about and exploring a topic en route to building knowledge. There is a large body of knowledge and sophisticated theorizing about reading and writing that might be relevant to investigating the user's experience of CMC. For example, Vygotsky (1962), although not referring to on-line environments, offers insight into how writing can contribute to knowing. He contends that the process of articulating thoughts into written speech involves deliberate analytical action. "The change from maximally compact inner speech to maximally detailed written speech requires what might be called deliberate semantics—deliberate structuring of the web of meaning" (pp. 99-100). McGinley and Tierney (1989) build on the notion that writing involves purposeful constructing of meaning, and cite an insightful passage from J. Gage (1986):

> Writing is thinking made tangible, thinking that can be examined because it is on the page and not in the head invisibly floating around. Writing is thinking that can be stopped and tinkered with. It is a way of holding thought still enough to examine its structure, its flaws. The road to clearer understanding of one's thoughts is travelled on paper. It is through an attempt to find words for our-selves in which to express related ideas that we often dis-cover what we think. (Cited in McGinley and Tierney 1989, p. 24)

The need to verbalize all aspects of interaction within the text-based environment can enhance such metacognitive skills as self-reflection and revision in learning. Metacognitive skill re-quires the opportunity to make explicit to oneself the aspects of an activity that are usually tacit—for example, expressing the thinking processes by which a decision or conclusion is reached, or the strategy for accomplishing some task. The text-based environ-ment is such a narrow bandwidth of information that, to compen-sate, clear and explicit articulation is essential for effective group interaction.

Other aspects of the text-based environment can affect the learning process. Participants in online courses report increased attentiveness to the content of a written message over one that is verbally presented. Text-based communication, they argue, has no social or physical cues to distract from the cognitive content of a message: the focus is on the content rather than on the presenter (Harasim 1987a). Additionally, the text-based medium offers a so-

cial "equalizing" effect.   Text-based communication lacks
mechanisms for displaying or enforcing social differentiation by
such factors as social status cues or physical cues such as race,
gender, or physical handicap, which in other communication contexts interfere with group interaction (Siegel et al. 1986). Online
learners   report   that   text-based   interactions   diminish   the
stereotyping associated with high external social status or physical
appearance, thereby removing a significant barrier to equal participation (Harasim 1986).

Though these barriers are lost, so is much richness. Physical
cues such as facial expressions, voice intonations, and gestures are
eliminated, and their elimination is perceived by users, particularly in the early stages of online educational activities, as a
loss. The text-based medium is perceived to constrain the expression (and reception) of such nuances as jokes and irony. The concern for presentation is displaced: participants worry about the
"appearance" of their text. For some, the appearance of the text
becomes one's "signature", and making typos or other errors is perceived as a detraction from one's image.

Another issue can be loosely termed the "vulnerability" of
textual communication. This takes several forms. Participants
may feel inhibited within online discussions because their words
will be preserved in the database. Comments in the conference
transcripts can be recalled at other locations or at other times by
conference participants unknown to the user. At issue is who owns
the conference or the particular comment, and who controls how
the comments will be used in future. Will the "authors" have control over the future use of a transcript? How does archiving the
transcripts affect online discourse and how participants interact
online? Will self-censorship result? Closely related is the issue of
copyright or intellectual property rights in the electronic environment, a concern that may be particularly important for professionals (researchers, scientists, academics) for whom advancement
is linked to formal acknowledgment of new ideas.

Text-based communication may contribute to information
overload. Active online discussion results in heavy amounts of
reading for each user; this problem grows with the size of the
group. In online coursework, the problem is compounded because
students must follow both the online discussions and the course
reading list.

Related to overload is the problem of the user interface
which, at present, is awkward and inadequate for navigating
through discussion threads within a conference. Conferencing systems have only limited tools for linking comments (branching,
references, headers), and there are no mechanisms for linking and

relating ideas, for viewing these linkages, for creating and manipulating structures, or for navigating through these webs on current systems. Tools such as concept maps or hierarchies whereby users (individuals and/or groups) can link, organize, and structure comments as part of their own information management system are not available to online learners or instructors. Nor are there structures or prompts to support decisionmaking activities online (Stefik et al. 1988, p. 361).

Finally, because there are no international standards for microcomputer graphics, computer conferencing systems are not yet able to transmit sound nor display such graphical data as mathematical symbols, graphs, spreadsheets, video images, or illustrations. This difficulty in transmitting graphics across different microcomputers currently limits the type of educational activities that can be mounted online.

Computer-Mediated Learning

The mediation of the computer is the most significant attribute: many of the previous attributes hinge on it. This most powerful attribute is the newest for education and the one about which we have least knowledge.

Computers, as media, introduce a unique set of capabilities that can augment learning. Some of the attributes discussed above, such as text-based and time- and place-independent communication, are available through other media—through books, for example. Communication that is computer-mediated is distinct from these other forms of communication. It is interactive: it encourages active involvement, whereas books and radio transmission are oriented toward passive receipt of information. But, above all, computers offer control capabilities—the ability to present, receive, process, and manage information (Kozma 1987; Rice 1984). Online educational interactions, being revisable, archivable, and retrievable, augment the user's control over the substance and process of the interactions.

Collaboration in computer conferencing takes place in a common space. Each conference functions as a shared space, just as a blackboard or newsprint focusses and records the discussion in face-to-face interaction. Unlike the face-to-face event, even with a record keeper, however, the CC system maintains a written transcript of the entire proceedings; additionally, the transcript is stored in the system database: it will not be erased at the end of each session. This record, or community memory, can be sub-sequently searched for discrete items that can then be retrieved.

Users thus have more control over the nature of their inter-actions than they have in face-to-face environments: they may read all items, read items selectively, or merely scan. They may save particular items to disk or print them to be used in later or more intensive review. Transcripts of group interactions can be recalled for retrospective analysis by using the search mechanisms. This last feature deserves particular attention from educational designers and practitioners. For online course activity, learner strategies such as weaving (synthesizing key themes in a conference) and critical reviews of the proceedings encourage mul-tiple passes through the transcripts to enhance analytical think-ing.

New developments in computing, such as hypermedia and structured environments, offer increasingly powerful tools to ac-tivate and amplify the learner's cognitive processes of obtaining, manipulating, organizing, and structuring information (Scardamalia et al. 1989; Kozma 1987, 1989). In these cases the computer is used not only to provide the learner with access to large amounts of information, but is programmed to aid the learner in structuring, interconnecting, and integrating new ideas with previous ones as well as restructuring information as each learner's knowledge base grows. How CMC might benefit from the new directions in software development in order to amplify online education is discussed in the next section.

AMPLIFYING HUMAN INTELLECT ONLINE

Thus far the chapter has considered how the five key at-tributes framing the CC environment influence educational inter-actions. This final section focuses on how online environments could be used to augment intellectual activities, examining current system supports and needed enhancements. Educators active in this field are recognizing that the tools offered by CMC not only increase the learner's access to information—and do so powerfully and successfully—but can also facilitate knowledge building ac-tivities. This is where the interest in CMC and online education lies—and where the challenge lies. We are developing and using new tools: How do they work? In what ways might the new media—particularly computer-based tools—empower our intellec-tual processes, to make us better thinkers, learners, and problem solvers? What new developments might be needed to enhance educational collaboration online?

CMC brings us, as educators and as learners, closer to realizing the goals first envisioned by Bush and Engelbart, that of expanding our intellectual powers beyond what the unaided human could demonstrate. The emphasis on social as well as intellectual connectivity underlies computer conferencing. How well it facilitates active group learning and knowledge building activities is now considered.

Active Learning

Long term understanding requires both active engagement as well as active construction of meaning, which the online environment should support and encourage. Emerging research into online educational collaborations indicates that high levels of active user participation and interaction are possible. We find, for example, in data collected from graduate courses delivered entirely online, that students sent an average of 5 to 10 conference notes per person per week, over a 12-week course (Harasim 1989a). (This figure does not include personal [e-mail] notes, which are not tracked.) The data indicate as well that all learners participated in the messaging and that the volume of input was distributed fairly equitably among the participants (Harasim 1987b). Equitable participation in computer conferencing groups has been identified in research on organizational communication as well (Rice 1984; Siegel et al. 1986), although Thompson (1989) suggests that communication in online small groups may follow similar distribution patterns to that of face-to-face small group discussions. The distribution of communication within online groups, just as with their face-to-face counterparts, is related to the nature and design of the activity; nevertheless, the five attributes of CC augment the possibilities for active participation beyond what can occur face-to-face. Asynchronicity, for example, increases opportunities for active input: the online classroom, open 24 hours per day and seven days a week, allows participation by each class member. Asynchronous and place-independent participation enable each person to access the learning situation at a time and location most convenient to that user or most opportune for that task, thereby facilitating increased activity. By reducing competition for air-time among students, moreover, asynchronous interaction may even enhance collegiality. Opportunities for many-to-many communication within a computer conference can further contribute to amplifying the activity level. Collaboration enhances connectivity and socioemotional engagement to the learning process, as well as creating an intellectual climate that encourages participation. A fourth factor, the text-based nature of the medium, also encourages active learning: to participate online demands active verbalization from each member of the group. Finally, the user control capabilities provided by the computer can enhance and augment the ways in which a participant may interact with the learning activities and resources, affecting the nature and quantity of learner activity.

In addition to supporting active participation, the attributes of online education can contribute to facilitating active construction of meaning. Active text-based interaction generates a database or web of ideas and responses. The exposure to responses—both positive and negative—stimulates cognitive restructuring, in response to new information, and to disagreements or challenges encountered in the group discussions. Since text-based communication is archivable and searchable, cognitive learning strategies such as making multiple passes or directed searches through the rich corpus of ideas are rewarding (Scardamalia et al. 1989). Active sharing and seeking of information and playing with ideas is central to online collaboration. The shared text-based space seems particularly conducive to stimulating brainstorming activities and group synergy, sparking ideas or identifying new associations. The group interaction encourages the generation of a diverse array of ideas and data and the exploration of varied perspectives on these. Users can then manipulate the information: store it, retrieve it, print it, edit it , or share it. The rich corpus of stored, manipulable information is excellently suited for knowledge building activities, but as the next section suggests, additional system supports are required to enable users to take full advantage of the information resources generated online.

Knowledge Building

New online educational environments may be seen as forming part of what has been called "the shift from seeing technology as a cognitive delivery system to seeing it as a means to support collaborative conversations about a topic and the ensuing construction of understanding" (Brown 1989). Brown presents a view of knowledge building as a sense-making pursuit, and argues the need for learning technology to support the individual and social processes associated with such a pursuit.

> Good learning situations...are successful not because they enable a learner to ingest preformed knowledge in some optimal way, but, rather, because they provide initially undetermined, threadbare concepts to which, through conversation, negotiation, and authentic activity, a learner adds texture. Learning is much more an evolutionary, sense-making, experiential process of development than of simple acquisition. We must therefore, attempt to use the intelligence in the learning environments to reflect and support the learner's or user's active creation or co-production, *in situ*, of idiosyncratic, highly "textured" models and concepts, whose texture is developed between the learner/user and the situating activity in which the technology is embedded. (Brown 1989)

What is the learner creating or producing online? And how can the online environment support the conversations and shared explorations that form part of the user's active creation or co-production of knowledge? From my observation, in order to facilitate sense-making and knowledge building within online group discussion activities, the system needs to support three educational processes: idea generating (and gathering), idea linking, and idea structuring. Current computer conferencing systems support idea generating, but additional enhancements are required for idea linking and idea structuring within online group activities. There are specific cognitive tasks associated with these processes that need to be considered in order to address how computer systems might facilitate the procedures involved. The three processes outlined here derive from my work with university and adult learners, and have not been tested with preadult learners.

Idea generating occurs when the learner articulates her/his thoughts on a particular subject. In an online class, ideas are generated in response to readings or comments on a particular topic as the learner begins to assimilate the information and verbalize an understanding of the relevant concepts. This process includes idea gathering, as the learner identifies and obtains (additional) relevant information and perspectives on the topic. Idea-generating activities include brainstorming, information sharing, identifying and discussing alternatives, debating, querying, and elaborating upon ideas presented. Computer conferencing enables the collection and exchange of this input. In an educational conference, each participant has the opportunity to verbalize a position, obtain feedback on that position, elaborate or modify their own ideas and view and interact with the ideas of their colleagues. The CC system has proven valuable for generating a rich, complex, and often informal web of ideas and information. Online courses may generate thousands of notes over a relatively short period of time. These notes are interlinked; they relate to the topic of the conference and build on previous notes (Winkelmans 1988; Harasim and Chandler-Crichlow 1989).

Divergent thinking activities such as exploration, brainstorming, analogy, and idea sharing are facilitated in computer conferences. The exploration of several different aspects of the issue being discussed or studied generally characterizes the initial stage of intellectual investigation and production. "This is to ensure that reflection in later stages of the inquiry is not too narrow but has available to it a comprehensive array of data and varied but complementary perspectives, which can generate a holistic view" (Heron 1985, p. 129).

A second process follows generating ideas; networking or *idea linking*. Idea linking is associated with convergent thinking. Convergent activity, which follows divergent thinking, involves "reflecting on divergent aspects and perspectives, refining each and bringing out the common ground that they illuminate" (Heron 1985, p. 137). This stage includes identifying associations among ideas, and can be facilitated through networks, concept maps, and semantic webs which support idea linkages. Connecting new information in webs or maps of relations helps learners to understand and remember it in a variety of contexts and can encourage deeper, more meaningful learning of new material (Dansereau, O'Donnell, and Lambiotte 1988).

Computer conferencing currently offers few tools for this process. The online environment or architecture provides conferences and branches for various topical discussions, and limited searching mechanisms. However, the tools currently available are not adequate for identifying linkages or displaying nonlinear, spatial relationships among ideas generated within a conference. There are few tools for linking concepts and themes in order to frame and manage the personal and group information environment, or to make connections. Organizing and reordering ideas is difficult online. The lack of tools to help the user manipulate ideas online or with which to navigate the complex web of the proceedings and interactions is a major limitation for online education.

A third educational process I identify is *idea structuring*. Once ideas have been generated and relationships and linkages among these ideas are considered, organizing the ideas into some structure, either hierarchical and/or sequential, enables those ideas to be applied—to a problem-solving or decisionmaking activity such as producing a report or a paper. This process involves imposing order and structure as part of convergence to some objective. Organizing may involve hierarchy, the constructing of an integrated structure by abstracting and perceiving sub/superordinate relations, sequencing, proportion, and balance, a process which might be supported by system prompts (Smith et al. 1987). An online system might also aid the learner in integrating new ideas with previous ones, by structuring the learning environment using tools or prompts to suggest ways to hook new knowledge to existing information maps in our mind (Kozma 1987). In current conferencing systems, tools for structuring the ideas generated, in hierarchical or sequential form, or for defining the workspace, are weak or nonexistent. Nor are there decision-supports.

Current conferencing systems, then, offer adequate tools for one of the three educational processes, the idea-generating stage that involves divergent thinking in the group; but, they offer few, if any, tools for the second and third processes, idea linking and idea structuring, which involve convergent thinking and information management. The conferencing systems we have, in other words, provide support only for one stage of the learning process; this is a severe constraint on their use in the education context, and a considerable challenge for designers and implementers of online educational systems.

There are, however, related groups of software tools that support exactly these processes and could be used—at least as models—in educational applications of CMC. In particular, developments in hypertext and hypermedia suggest ways in which online education might develop for augmenting educational collaboration and amplifying intellectual activity.

Convergences

Hypertext and hypermedia systems were developed for linking, exploring, and navigating through large amounts of data stored in heterogenous media. These systems suggest themselves as potentially powerful tools to enhance the effective utilization of information generated in educational computer conferencing, and to expand the type of data that can be shared.

Hypertext in its fundamental form is reflective of a particular mode of thinking: exploring and linking concepts and conceptual material. Interfacing hypertext with computer conferencing could amplify the online educational environment: hypertext offers information management tools, enabling users to organize and link ideas generated in a computer conference. A hypertextual interface to computer conferences could enable associative structuring among ideas and thereby help both to manage the information as well as to make explicit to learners the importance of the interrelationship of ideas. It would also facilitate browsing through the database.

The convergence of hypermedia interfaces with computer conferencing systems would expand idea-linking capabilities by allowing authors and users the opportunity to link information from a variety of media, such as text, graphics, timelines, video, audio, and spreadsheets. Hypermedia interfaces would broaden the bandwidth of information available to online participants, to enable displaying and sharing graphics, video, sound, and voice. Tools to enhance exploring, linking, and organizing information, and transmitting graphical, video, and audio data could make online education an increasingly powerful environment. Nevertheless, there is a tremendous challenge to educators and researchers to learn how to design and benefit from such new environments. While linking hypertext with computer conferencing is potentially an attractive and viable direction for online education, it involves complex design issues (see Chapter 9 of this volume). There are other considerations as well. Such convergences might support idea generating and idea linking, but hypertext/hypermedia systems do not currently offer idea-structuring tools. They allow us to link ideas but do not assist us in deciding which ideas ought to be linked and how. There are no underlying models to organize an activity and to structure a particular process. Smith et al. (1987) note that "to be truly effective, hypertext applications must match additional power with additional control and structure." A similar view was expressed by Brown (1985b), who observed that the ability to store and manipulate huge amounts of information does not in itself build knowledge nor create an educational environment.

CONCLUSION

Computer conferencing systems offer a new environment for social and intellectual interaction and are being increasingly adopted by educators to facilitate course delivery and group learning. To study how new online environments can support and even amplify group knowledge building activities, this chapter proposed a collaborative learning perspective. The chapter explored five key attributes of the new online environment and then focussed on current system supports and needed additions for online group discussion and collaboration. Three educational processes (idea generating, idea linking, and idea structuring) were considered. Current computer conferencing systems were found to support idea generating, but new tools or convergences among existing tools such as hypertextual interfaces to computer conferencing, are required to facilitate idea linking and idea structuring. Decisions about the nature and degree of linking and structuring involve serious consideration. What tools and prompts should be available within new online educational environments? Research in the 1980s, for example, has shown that the application of text structures such as maps, frames, pattern guides, or advanced organizers to teaching practices has dramatically improved learner comprehension and recall (Taylor and Beach 1984; Hartman and Spiro 1989). However, such text structures may also impose reductive bias and rigid representations. These are critical concerns, central to defining the nature of the new educational environment. At issue is how to create a complex knowledge domain, especially how to build upon and retain the complexity of an environment like computer conferencing so that users learn to be critical thinkers by considering issues and ideas from many perspectives. Much work remains in developing approaches and tools to build upon the rich network of interconnections online in order to facilitate flexible, creative, and purposeful learning interactions. Such concerns are fundamental to guiding developments in the field and challenge us as educators, researchers, and developers of online education.

ACKNOWLEDGMENTS

This chapter has benefited from the thoughtful comments, critiques, and suggestions of several readers. I am grateful to Liz Burge, Catherine Chandler-Crichlow, Lynn Davie, Kate Hamilton, Jonathon Swallow, Lucio Teles, Geoffrey Thompson, and Judy Weinstein, who read and provided valuable feedback on various drafts. The responsibility for any errors, omissions, or problems of presentation is solely my own.

REFERENCES

Batson, T. (1988). The ENFI project: A networked classroom approach to writing instruction. *Academic Computing 2* (32-33): 55-56.

Bargh, J.A., & Schul, Y. (1980). On the cognitive benefits of teaching. *Journal of Educational Psychology, 72* (5): 593-604.

Bouton, C. & Garth, R.Y. (1983). Learning in groups. *New directions in teaching and learning. (no. 14)*. San Francisco: Jossey-Bass.

Brookfield, S.D. (1986). *Understanding and facilitating adult learning*. San Francisco: Jossey-Bass.

Brown, J.S. (1985a). Process versus product: A perspective on tools for communal and informal electronic learning. *Journal of Educational Computing Research, 1* (2): 179-201.

——— (1985b). Idea amplifiers---New kinds of electronic learning environments. *Educational Horizons, 63* (3): 108-112.

——— (in press, 1989). Towards a new epistemology for learning. In C. Frasson & J. Gauthiar (Eds.), *Intelligent tutoring systems at the crossroads of AI and education*. Norwood, NJ: Ablex.

Burge, L. (1988). Beyond andragogy: Some explorations for distance learning design. *Journal of Distance Education, 3* (1): 5-23.

Bush, V. (1945). As we may think. *Atlantic Monthly, 176* (1): 101-8.

Cohen, E.G. (1984). Talking and working together: Status, interaction, and learning. In P.L. Peterson, L.C. Wilkinson, & M. Hallinan (Eds.), *The social context of instruction*, pp. 171-187. New York: Academic Press.

Damon, W. & Phelps, E. (1989). Critical distinctions among three approaches to peer education. *International Journal of Educational Research, 13* (1): 9-19.

Dansereau, D., O'Donnell, A.M. & Lambiotte, A. (1988). Concept maps and scripted peer cooperation: Interactive tools for improving science and technical education. Paper presented at the American Educational Research Association, New Orleans, April.

Durling, R. & Schick, C. (1976). Concept attainment by pairs and individuals as a function of vocalization. *Journal of Educational Psychology, 68* (1): 83-91.

Engelbart, D. & Lehtman, H. (1988). Working together. *BYTE, 13* (13): 245-52.

Feenberg, A. (1987). Computer conferencing and the humanities. *Instructional Science, 16* (2): 169-186.

Greif, I. (1988). *Computer-supported cooperative work: A book of readings.* San Mateo, CA: Morgan Kaufman.

Harasim, L. (1986). Computer learning networks: Educational applications of computer conferencing. *Journal of Distance Education, 1* (1): 59-70.

———— (1987a). Teaching and learning on-line: Issues in computer-mediated graduate courses. *Canadian Journal for Educational Communication, 16* (2): 117-35.

———— (1987b). Computer-mediated cooperation in education: Group learning networks. In *Proceedings of the 2nd Guelph Symposium on Computer Conferencing, June 1-4* (pp. 171-186). Guelph, Canada: University of Guelph.

———— (1989a). Computer-mediated collaboration: New designs for learning. Paper presented at the American Educational Research Association, San Francisco, March.

———— (1989b). Online education: A new domain. In Robin Mason & T. Kaye (Eds.), *Mindweave: Communication, computers, and distance education.* Oxford: Pergamon Press, pp. 50-62.

Harasim, L. & Chandler-Crichlow, C. (1989). Tracking collaborative learning in online courses: Hypertextual analyses. Paper presented to the Canadian Educational Research Association, Quebec City, June.

Hartman, D.K. & Spiro, R.J. (1989). Explicit text structure for advanced knowledge acquisition in complex domains: A post-structuralist perspective. Paper presented at the American Educational Research Association, San Francisco, March.

Heron, J. (1985). The role of reflection in a co-operative inquiry. In Boud, D., Keogh, R., & Walker, D. (Eds.) *Reflection: Turning Experience into Learning.* London: Kogan Page, pp. 128-38.

Hiltz, S. R. (1986). The "virtual classroom": Using computer-mediated communication for university teaching. *Journal of Communication, 36* (2): 95-104.

Hiltz, S.R. & Turoff, M. (1978). *The network nation: Human communication via computer.* Reading, MA: Addison-Wesley.

———— (1985). Structuring computer-mediated communication systems to avoid information overload. *Communications of the ACM, 28* (7): 680-89.

Johnson, D.W. & Johnson, R.T. (1979). Conflict in the classroom: Controversy and learning. *Review of Educational Research, 49* (1): 51-70.

Johnson, D., Maruyama, G., Johnson, R., Nelson, D., & Skon, L. (1981). The effects of cooperative, competitive, and individualistic goal structures on achievement: A meta-analysis. *Psychological Bulletin, 89* (1): 47-62.

Keegan, D. (1986). *The foundations of distance education.* London: Croom Helm.

Kozma, R. (1987). The implications of cognitive psychology for computer-based learning tools. *Educational Technology, XXVII,* (11): 20-25.

——— (1989). Principles underlying the Learning Tool. Paper presented to the American Educational Research Association, San Francisco: March, 1989.

McGinley, W. & Tierney, R. (1989). Traversing the topical landscape: Reading and writing as ways of knowing. Paper presented to the American Educational Research Association, San Francisco: March.

Moore, M. (1973). Toward a theory of independent learning and teaching. *Journal of Higher Education, XLIV* (12): 661-79.

——— (1986). Self-directed learning and distance education. *Journal of Distance Education, 1* (1): 7-24.

Myers, D.G. & Lamm, H. (1976). The group polarization phenomenon. *Psychological Bulletin, 83* (4): 602-27.

Nelson, T.H. (1974). *Dream machines.* South Bend, IN: The Distributors.

——— (1987). *Literary machines.* South Bend, IN: The Distributors.

Rice, R. (1980). Impacts of organizational and interpersonal computer-mediated communications. In M. Williams (Ed.) *Annual review of information science and technology, 15*: 221-49. White Plains, NY: Knowledge Industry Publications.

——— (1982). Communication networking in computer conferencing systems: A longitudinal study of group roles and system structure. In M. Burgoon (Ed.) *Communication yearbook 6*: 925-44. Beverly Hills, CA: Sage Publications.

——— (1984). Mediated group communication. In R. Rice and Associates, Ed. *The new media: Communication, research, and technology.* Beverly Hills, CA: Sage Publications, pp. 129-54.

Sarin, S. & Greif, I. (1988). Computer-based real-time conferencing system. In I. Greif (Ed.) *Computer-supported cooperative work: A book of readings.* San Mateo, CA: Morgan Kaufmann.

Scardamalia, M., Bereiter, C., McLean, R.S., Swallow, J., & Woodruff, E. (1989). Computer-supported intentional learning environments. *Journal of Educational Computing Research, 5* (1): 51-68.

Sewart, D. (1981). Distance teaching: A contradictions in terms? *Teaching at a Distance* No. 19: 8-18.

Sharan, S. (1980). Cooperative learning in small groups: Recent methods and effects on achievement, attitudes, and ethnic relations. *Review of Educational Research, 50* (2): 241-71.

Sharan, S. & Sharan, Y. (1976). *Small-group teaching.* New Jersey: Educational Technology Publications.

Siegel, J., Dubrovsky, V., Kiesler, S., & McGuire, T. (1986). Group processes in computer-mediated communication. *Organizational Behavior and Human Decision Processes, 37* (2): 157-87.

Slavin, R.E. (1977). Classroom reward structure: An analytical and practical review. *Review of Educational Research, 47* (4): 633-50.

———— (1980). Cooperative learning. *Review of Educational Research, 50* (2): 315-42.

———— (1983). *Cooperative learning.* New York: Longman.

———— (1986). Cooperative learning: Where behavioral and humanistic approaches to classroom motivation meet. Paper presented to the American Educational Research Association, San Francisco, April.

Smith, J.B., Weiss, S.F., & Ferguson, G.F. (1987). A hypertext writing environment and its cognitive basis. In *Hypertext '87 Papers,* pp. 195-214. Proceedings of Hypertext '87, University of North Carolina, Chapel Hill, Nov. 13-15.

Stefik, M., Foster, G., Bobrow, D.G., Lanning, S. & Suchman, L. (1988). Beyond the chalkboard: Computer support for collaboration and problem solving in meetings. In I. Greif, (Ed.) *Computer-supported cooperative work: A book of readings.* San Mateo, CA: Morgan Kaufmann, pp. 335-66.

Stodolsky, S.S. (1984). Frameworks for studying instructional processes in peer work-groups. In P.L. Peterson, L.C. Wilkinson, & M. Hallinan (Eds.), *The social context of education* New York: Academic Press, pp. 107-24.

Taylor, B.M. & Beach, R.W. (1984). The effects of text structure instruction on middle-grade students' comprehension of expository text. *Reading Research Quarterly 19* (2): 134-46.

Thompson, G. (1989). Learner participation in online graduate courses. Unpublished MEd Thesis, Ontario Institute for Studies in Education, Toronto, Ontario.

Vygotsky, L.S. (1962). *Thought and language.* Cambridge, MA: MIT Press.

Webb, N.M. (1980). Group process: The key to learning in groups. *New Directions for Methodology of Social and Behavioural Sciences* No. 6: 77-87.

———— (1982a). Student interaction and learning in small groups. *Review of Educational Research, 52* (3): 421-45.

———— (1982b). Group composition, group interaction, and achievement in cooperative small groups. *Journal of Educational Psychology, 74* (4): 475-84.

──── (1989). Peer interaction and learning in small groups. *International Journal of Educational Research, 13* (1): 21-29.

Winkelmans, T. (1988). Educational computer conferencing: An application of analysis methodologies to a structured small group activity. Unpublished MA Thesis, University of Toronto.

Yankelovich, N. Meyrowitz, N. & van Dam, A. (1985). Reading and writing the electronic book. *IEEE Computer* (October): 15-30

Zuboff, S. (1988). *In the age of the smart machine: The future of work and power.* New York: Basic Books.

PART II
Design Perspectives

Chapter 4
Social Factor Research in Computer-Mediated Communications

Andrew Feenberg and Beryl Bellman

INTRODUCTION

This chapter introduces the idea of "social factors" as a new approach to the design of computer-mediated communication (CMC) environments, with special reference to education. The first part explains the idea of social factors and introduces the "social factors model" for the study of online communities. The second part offers case histories illustrating the links we find between the social needs of particular groups and specific program features. The third part is an example of the application of the social factors approach to drawing out the implications of organizational theory for program design.

SOCIAL FACTORS IN COMPUTER-MEDIATED COMMUNICATION

Social Factors in CMC Design

Computer networking as we know it today consists primarily in the sharing of software tools located on a central host machine. The development of these tools aims at the enhancement of individual effectiveness while achieving the efficiencies inherent in shared resources. But, since the network is a natural "meeting place" for its users, it is only a short step from these beginnings to a concern for enhancing group effectiveness through mediated activity. The technologies of computer conferencing and computer-supported collaborative work belong to a new class of "CMC" tools that convert the network into a social environment.

CMC is a sociotechnical system combining social and technical elements in a whole that is greater than the sum of its parts.[1] But conferencing systems are not yet designed to mediate social activities; they continue to be conceived as individual tools. Further, the needs of the imaginary "general user" have been anticipated on logical rather than social-psychological principles.

Groups are not just collections of individuals. They have specific characteristics of their own that transcend the individual level and that must be recognized by designers as social factors affecting the value of products at the level of both the group and the individual group member. "Human factors research" identifies generic constraints on product design relative to human nature; by analogy, research into social factors identifies socially specific constraints on the design of products for one or another social group or category. The existence of social considerations is generally known to product designers and marketing executives, but there is no one field that studies social factors systematically. As a result, they are more likely to be misunderstood or overlooked than human factors.

This is a matter of especially great consequence for CMC. Software designers are not typically communications specialists, and so create forms of community based on idealized and simplified models of human interaction. Often these programs confuse users by their complexity or impose arbitrary patterns of interaction. It is difficult for users to circumvent these structures; incorporating new patterns and special-purpose tools is virtually impossible in most systems.

In fact, CMC creates electronic social environments as complex and socially specific as the interiors designed to serve the different types of social activities that go on in face-to-face settings. Just as interior designers construct spaces in response to socially specific needs, so the designers of CMC systems must respond to the needs of the eventual users of their products. The social architecture, to the extent that it facilitates or impedes a given kind of communication, is as important a factor in determining the success of group communication as the location of chairs, tables, blackboards, podiums, and the like in more traditional forms of human interaction.

The software design process should therefore be based on an understanding of the social factors that affect group work. It should be responsive to the real-world demands of users interacting with each other. It should facilitate the easy integration of additional tools of whatever sort are appropriate for the task at hand. It should support a wide variety of social forms ranging from informal meetings through highly structured formal decisionmaking environments, from "virtual classrooms" to participatory newsletters, and should easily adapt to support new ones as they arise, ideally as easily as furniture is rearranged in a room. This is, in essence, the design of electronic community.

The Practice of Online Group Management

Individuals no longer enter the CMC environment primarily through private subscriptions to information utilities, but collectively, along with co-workers or fellow students in highly structured groups devoted to accomplishing common objectives. A new profession of social network design has arisen around the problems of organizing and leading these online groups.[2]

Social network designers possess a powerful body of practical knowledge that enables them to achieve an unusual measure of success in placing groups online. This practical knowledge supports the specific "social technologies" of CMC, which complete the technical apparatus and make it effective. Software designers can learn a great deal from studying online group management. This activity is at present the sole repository of most of what is known about the role of social factors in CMC (Feenberg 1986; Kerr 1986).

In what does the practical knowledge of network design consist? Some of the major elements are the following:

1. Selecting systems, training techniques, and materials adjusted to the proficiencies of groups

2. Selecting software and systems with the features best adapted to the needs of groups

3. Constructing effective conference architectures by breaking down the different concerns of the group into the optimal selection of conferences

4. Anticipating the leadership needs of online groups, providing leadership, and developing the moderating skills of members

5. Starting conferencing activities effectively, with all the members of the group clear on the agenda and procedures of the online exercise.

The practical knowledge of social network designers involves an unusual hybrid of insight into group processes and awareness of the technical features of communications systems. The social network designer needs these disparate skills because the electronic mediation of group activity requires building socially specific software structures out of available programs and features. Such structures are called groupware by Peter and Trudy Johnson-Lenz: "Groupware = intentional GROUP processes and procedures to achieve specific purposes + softWARE tools designed to support and facilitate the group's work" (Johnson-Lenz 1981).

The second part of this chapter contains numerous examples of groupware applied to solving many different types of the problems in education and related fields: the adaptation of interfaces to the needs of groups with poor computer skills, very different ways of organizing retrieval of items used by a group preparing a face-to-face meeting and a nuclear power station, ways for participants in an online educational program to protect themselves from information overload on various types of systems, and appropriate applications of synchronous conferencing in video teleconferencing and education, and so on. These examples illustrate the social network designers' attempt to overcome the limitations of existing systems, to diagnose the problems they cause, and to devise "fixes" for those problems with the means at hand. Such discoveries are prototypes of features that might usefully be integrated in new software.

The synergy between the practical knowledge of the social network designer and the technical knowledge of the software designer can provide the basis for developing a new generation of tailored conferencing systems that fully realizes the potential of the technology for increasing the effectiveness and productivity of online group activity.

Tailored Conferencing Systems

The basic CMC product must incorporate software tools that respond to all the standard user needs as well as to a wide variety of specialized needs. Each tailored version of the basic program will offer these constant features, and differ from others only in the variables it offers.

The value of software tools for different groups may vary widely. have little importance; for other groups, there may be one specific feature that makes the difference between success and failure.

Educational conferencing exhibits this difference clearly. Existing conferencing systems are fairly limited, for example, in their ability to handle mathematical symbols. Not surprisingly, educational applications of computer conferencing are almost entirely to be found on the nonmathematical side of the campus.[3]

Does this mean that the best system is the one that offers the most features? The most complex and powerful conferencing systems, such as the Electronic Information Exchange System, do in fact offer ways of meeting many group and task-specific needs, but their sophisticated features are too difficult for many classes of users to understand and learn easily. This problem is characteristic of powerful systems, which generally trade off ease of learning for additional flexibility (Goodwin 1987).

This is one of the most serious obstacles to the spread of CMC. There is no simple correlation between a group's needs and its level of proficiency. In fact, the most common profile is the user who needs an interface that is both extremely simple and optimized for group and task-specific functions. For such users, the power of an adaptable system is likely to be experienced as a weakness, a fatal design defect.

For most purposes a relatively simple interface must be designed that will orient users toward the constant and the variable features they are most likely to need. These features must be "foregrounded" by the interface, by being placed in routinely visible menus or help screens, while the others remain accessible in the background. The size of the foreground is determined by the typical skill with computers and available training time of the group for which the interface is designed.

The tailoring of computer conferencing programs is an essential design task because it is a critical success factor requiring an unusual combination of skills with both communications and computers. In most organizations computer skills are concentrated in a data-processing department that has no role in managing complex group activities in the organization at large. The habits of thought involved in solving group problems are quite different from those most commonly shaped by technical work. There is, furthermore, very little communication in most organizations between the computer department and those most skilled at organizing group activities. The day may come when the tailoring and installation of CMC is a routine administrative task, but for the moment it poses a challenge that few organizations are prepared to meet because it crosses one of the highest cultural barriers in organizational life today.

Assessing Group Needs

The knowledge gathered by social network designers from concrete experience is of great value in the implementation of conferencing activities, but far too unsystematic to serve as the basis for the design of tailored systems. We must apply to that knowledge more rigorous methods of analyzing group needs. This is essentially a research problem aimed at a very practical application.

The research in which we are engaged is designed to map the variety of social situations into a limited number of communication environments. Many types of groups and group activities will turn out to require identical designs. We conjecture that a half-dozen to a dozen distinct tailored configurations will cover most situations and needs. The difficulty of suiting everyone, while real, is thus manageable.

The key is the concept of "communications requirements," which stands at the pivot between sociological analysis of group behavior and the technical capabilities of CMC. Communications requirements are those group needs or problems which can be addressed specifically by the appropriate configuration of communication systems. Thus the need for immediate notification of waiting messages might be a communications requirement of one type of group; the need for secure communications, or for ways of sharing documents or graphs, might characterize other types of groups. Clearly, items that rank high on a user's list of communications requirements ought to be served conveniently by that user's communications system.

In the preliminary version of the Social Factors Model under preparation at the Western Behavioral Sciences Institute, communications requirements are classified under four main headings: conference production, retrieval of materials deposited in the conferences, pragmatics of the online communication process, and management of online groups. Under these headings are 12 main subheadings. Figure 4.1 presents these elements with examples or clarification in parentheses.

How can we use this concept of communications requirements to arrive at a few master profiles of typical user needs? There are essentially two directions in which to move:

Figure 4.1

```
                    private message
P                     |   group messages
                      |  /
R         ACCESS - public conference
                      |  \
O                     |    private conference
                    bulletin board
D

                    action support (decisionmaking tools, etc.)
U                           /    contextualizations
          GROUP PROCESS  ---
C                           \     leadership
                    rate of interaction (synchronous/asynchronous)
T

                conference architecture (group or topic centered)
I                       /
          RELEVANCE - overload protection
O                       \
                        norms of contribution
N
```

```
R              alarms
              /
E       TIME
              \
T               reminders

R         indices    key words
                     \ /  title displays
I       REFERENCE   -
                     / \  conference architecture
E       hypertext    search programs

V           data   programs
                    \ /
A       SHARING -
                 / \
L         lists    documents
```

Figure 4.1 (Continued)

```
                    syntax   learning
                         \ /
P           FRIENDLINESS - guidance
                         / \
R                  help   error control

A                     public (real name assignments)
                     /
G           IDENTITY - private (anonymous, pen names)
                     \
M                  subscriber information

A                  security
                  /
T           SAFETY - secrecy
                  \
I                  reliability

C                  mathematics
                  /
S           INPUTS - texts
                  \
                   graphics
```

```
                opening    grouping
                       \ /
M           ACCOUNTS   -  billing
A                      / \
N              updating   enrolling in conferences
A
G                     help files
E                    /   command prompts
M           TAILORING   ---
E                    \   opening screens
N                     system as a whole
T
```

1. Improved systems may come out of an empirical approach based on direct inquiry into the ideas and attitudes of actual online groups and prototyping of responses to their needs. The categories articulate the common knowledge that communicating subjects possess concerning their activities. One could elicit this knowledge by direct questioning or consulting with social network designers. The second part of this chapter offers examples of this empirical approach applied to groups in education and research.

2. A theoretical approach to improving CMC is also possible, based on social analysis and research in organizational theory. Communications requirements can be anticipated on the basis of careful study of the social characteristics of online groups in terms of a variety of theoretical frameworks for analyzing organizations. The third part of this chapter offers as an example one particular theoretical approach with suggestive results for education.

Our approach to research on social factors is to draw eclectically on many of these methods and to arrive quickly at hypotheses that are roughly testable through uncontrolled experiments and prototyping. In a field as neglected as this one, progress can be made in this manner, and need not await new theories or expensive controlled studies.

The Social Factors Model

The social factors model proposed below is an initial approach to giving a systematic order to research into the adaptation of CMC programs to the needs of different groups of users. It is important to note the self-imposed limitations of the model, which aims only at improving the program design process for group applications. Thus this approach differs from the existing literature on user acceptance in two respects: (1) it treats the user only as a group member and excludes all individual considerations, even such important ones as personal interest; and (2) it focuses only on user needs that can be served by modifications of CMC software and hardware, leaving aside other aspects of CMC that have nothing to do with design. The rationale for these limitations is to offer designers a clear picture of their particular piece of the CMC puzzle and to alert network designers and researchers to the role of software solutions.

The elaboration of the model posed several interesting methodological problems. At the outset we hoped to define the units of group analysis: were these markets, such as education; or professional activities, such as teaching; or some third, as yet unidentified, thing? We discovered that the larger units cannot be assumed in advance but need to be constructed around a detailed analysis of activities. Only the actual study and comparison of business-sponsored training programs and university courses can reveal whether they would be best served by the same CMC programs (insofar as they are both educational activities) or different programs (insofar as they occur in different markets).

Another major difficulty concerned the definition of group needs. These needs include many things irrelevant to the activities of CMC program designers. To avoid confusion, the natural tendency among people in the CMC field is to identify CMC-relevant needs with the program features that serve them. Thus, it is commonplace to talk about a group needing a search program, branching, or chatting. This way of thinking is not analytically precise, since such features as branching in fact fulfill a wide variety of different needs, and often a single need can be fulfilled by several different features. It would be more accurate to formulate CMC-relevant needs independently of the features that might fulfill them. A necessary stage of the analysis is to identify the group's communication requirements in terms general enough to study and test hypotheses about group needs, in relation both to the social characteristics of the group and to a variety of CMC program features.

With these methodological considerations in mind, we have developed a four-stage analysis of social groups and tasks.

Classification

First, the social field must be broken down by organization and activity. The logic of social interactions in business, government, educational, and other types of organizations is significantly different and may differentiate the implementation of similar activities. (For example, teaching in a business training program may differ enough from college teaching to require a somewhat different communications environment.) We will call the crossing of the two determinations, "organization" and "activity," the "social situation." The goal of the study, then, is to identify the appropriate communications environment for clusters of similar social situations. Figure 4.2 sketches typical determinations of "social situation." (In this, as in the following Figures, the categories falling under each heading are illustrative only.)

Figure 4.2

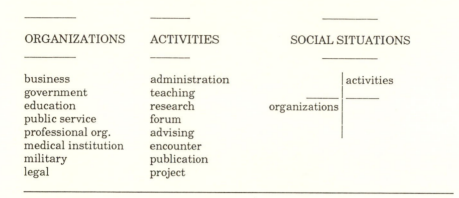

Analysis
Once social situations have been defined, the analysis can then study their typical social characteristics. These characteristics differentiate situations in terms of such things as the various roles played by participants, the structure of the groups in which they interact, their motivations, and the type of communication behavior in which they primarily engage, whether it be deliberation, decisionmaking, personal support, or whatever. Naturally, the analysis must focus on aspects of the subject most likely to generate communications requirements. This analysis will yield ideal-typical models of social situations.

Figure 4.3 presents the relation of social situations to social characteristics.

Simplification
The ideal types must then be matched against the communication requirements that follow plausibly from the study. At this point, one can imagine quite elaborate controlled studies that eventually refine the study of social factors. We do not now have many studies specifically concerned with the role of social factors, and so must attempt to fill the gap with the results of systematic observation, analysis, and structured interviews with participants and group leaders. This will make it possible to distinguish a limited number of "user profiles" that must be served by tailored interfaces (see Figure 4.4).

Figure 4.3

SOCIAL SITUATIONS   CHARACTERISTICS   IDEAL TYPES

business admin.   role |characteristics
business training   motivation   _____|_____
university research   sanctions   situations|
public encounter   proficiencies |
professional forum   group structure |
medical admin.   communication behavior
legal advising   etc.
military project
etc.

Figure 4.4

IDEAL TYPES   REQUIREMENTS   USER PROFILES

bus. admin. proficiency access |requirements
bus. training sanctions group process   _____|_____
univ. research motives   sharing   ideal types|
public encounter roles   friendliness |
prof. assoc. behavior   identity |
med. admin. structure   safety
legal advising roles   relevance
mil. proj. sanctions   time
etc.

Specification

The definition of user profiles is the expected outcome of the research program, so it is premature to list examples here. However, to complete the illustration of the model, we will fill out the chart with such likely user profiles as "distance learning," "deliberation," "project management," and so on. These must be matched to the precise class of features, options, and interface designs most likely to facilitate the work of online groups. The testing of prototyped systems must offer final correctives at this stage before the specification of tailoring schemes (see Figure 4.5).

Figure 4.5

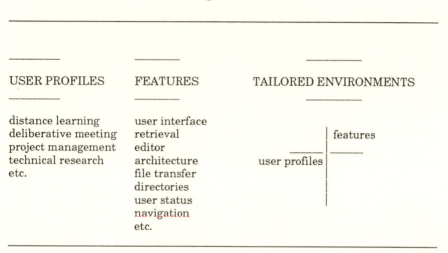

USER PROFILES	FEATURES	TAILORED ENVIRONMENTS
distance learning	user interface	
deliberative meeting	retrieval	features
project management	editor	
technical research	architecture	user profiles
etc.	file transfer	
	directories	
	user status	
	navigation	
	etc.	

Conclusion

CMC has great potential, but before that potential can be realized, programs must be adapted to the needs of users. This first part of the chapter has outlined an approach to that end through improved communication between computer conferencing organizers and researchers, and those who actually design the programs with which users must work. In the next two parts of the chapter, these ideas will be applied in examples drawn from group organization and theoretical research in the field of education.

CASE HISTORIES IN SOCIAL NETWORK DESIGN

Introduction

This section heading attempts to further the integration of two very different bodies of knowledge, the one technical and the other practical, by offering brief real-world examples, primarily from the fields of education and research, of ways in which specific conferencing interfaces or features are more or less adapted to the needs of various types of groups. The examples show the incredible variety of software solutions required in different circumstances and should make clear the impossibility of anticipating social needs a priori, without consulting the experience of online groups and their organizers.

The cases have been selected to highlight the relevance of software design to group activity in education, research, and related fields. Most of the cases recounted here end in success, in the sense that the organizers found a software solution to the problem they confronted. A few failures have been included to illustrate how things can go wrong when software is poorly suited to the needs of a group. The cases are arranged according to the categories of communications requirements laid out in the previous section of this chapter.

Friendliness: Interface Complexity

The first two examples show how different levels of proficiency and motivation interact with the complexity of the interface to affect group performance. The host in these cases was the Electronic Information Exchange System (EIES), a very powerful conferencing system that users unaccustomed to computers often find difficult to understand.

Case 1. The School of Management and Strategic Studies at WBSI
Problem: To network high level executives from around the world for a continuing education program.[4]
Summary: These executives live in widely scattered locations, but they can come together for training once every six months. This is fortunate, since using a computer, even for a very simple communications application, poses a formidable chal-

lenge to many of them. The first students had to be trained in EIES without the help of any special interface. Their training absorbed most of their energies for an entire week, an excessive burden for both students and technical trainers.

Solution: WBSI developed a standard terminal interface for the program, incorporating a simplified menu system, an easy word processor, and single key commands for signing on and for up- and downloading. This interface contains macro commands designed to interact with stored online commands on the host. Also incorporated in the system is an interactive tutorial that participants can employ to remind themselves of what they have learned in the brief training sessions they still require to get started. This system has other valuable features that help users find their way around the network. For example, they can do such things as call up rosters of fellow participants and conferences at will, either online or locally, and WBSI can update the rosters by remote procedures.

Case 2: FIPSE Technology Study Group

Problem: To network 50 project directors of U.S. Department of Education (FIPSE) programs on the application of new technology to college-level teaching.[5]

Summary: The organizers were confident that the project directors could learn the EIES interface without special help or training. The group was brought onto EIES without training, standard terminal software, or special online help screens. Many members complained of difficulties in using the system, especially with up- and downloading with a wide variety of computers, communications packages, and word processors.

Solution: The purpose of this program was to coordinate the wider dissemination of research project results, in the hope of receiving more generous future funding for the type of work the network members were engaged in. The learning difficulties encountered by many members were out of proportion to the motivation to participate supported by this purpose, and so the online forum ended up as a subset of the original recruitment to the program. Although conferencing made a contribution to the deliberations of this group, some of their work was ultimately transferred to conventional face-to-face meetings, where everyone could participate effectively.

Relevance

     Users of conferencing systems all complain about what they call "information overload." These systems expose users to overwhelming flows of information; the users quickly limit their involvement to relevant material, or drop out in despair. However, it is not always obvious what is relevant either to read or to write. Conferencing system software generally offers several tools for users to filter inputs; organizers can match these to group needs.

Case 3: The School of Management and Strategic Studies
Problem: To make it easier for the students to manage disruptions in their study schedule due to travel or other causes.
Summary: This is a nondegree continuing education program for executives in which the students are motivated primarily by curiosity and the pleasure of interaction with other members of the group. They travel frequently and are often too busy to participate for a month or two at a stretch. Since the program produces many hundreds of screens of material every month, when they reenter the discussion after a prolonged absence, they need to update their "markers" so as to receive only current items. Most participants found that they were unable to recall the EIES procedure for this operation from one trip to the next, and on EIES they were obliged to perform the operation separately for each of the many conferences in which they were enrolled, a time-consuming and tedious procedure.
Solution: The organizers decided to install the procedure in the standard terminal software as a menu option, prompted throughout and linked to online files and commands that automated it so that users had only to input the dates they had missed to skip over waiting items to current material.

Case 4: FULCRUM Office Automation Course
Problem: To facilitate a focus on different aspects of a discussion in an online course for consultants on office automation and sociotechnical issues.
Summary: The students in this case were using a Telemail conferencing software with a strictly linear structure in which each message was deposited chronologically in the same file. They found this software frustrating because they wanted to be able to follow each thread of the discussion to its conclusion separately, and to be able to begin new topics without interrupting ongoing discussions.

Solution: Several parallel conferences were set up to simulate "branching" and provide a place for new leader input and summaries. Participants could choose whether to participate in each topic and could segment their reading of the different topics (e.g., signing on to read only one conference).

Reference

One of the distinguishing features of social groups is the way in which they define and use their own past. There are groups, such as alumni of a college, that exist entirely through a shared past experience stored in memory. Some groups are legally obliged to keep careful written records going back many years, while others must access information about their own past quickly in a crisis. To each of these types of groups could be ascribed a different functional memory, a different type of retrieval system. Since computer conferencing makes available a written record of group interactions, it is possible to configure programs to provide for a wide variety of retrieval needs.

Case 5: Institute of Nuclear Power Operations

Problem: To ensure adequate access to safety information deposited in the "Nuclear Notepad" conferencing system over the years by a network of nuclear power utilities from around the world.[6]

Summary: Eight conferences, corresponding to such themes as control room design, radiological protection, and so on, were opened on the conferencing system. These were used to exchange safety information as it developed. The topical divisions were effective in organizing the day-to-day flow of messages, but not sufficiently fine to make rapid retrieval feasible in a crisis or to facilitate most effectively the documentation of claims before the Nuclear Regulatory Commission.

Solution: Retrieval by topic was clearly more important in this network than in most online groups. The organizers had experimented with freely branching structures and had concluded that this would be too confusing for most participants. Instead, a subject line option was added to improve retrieval of stored messages, but this did not fully satisfy the users. The organizers identified, but were unable to fulfill, this group's need for an elaborate indexing function and a "librarian" role, charged with rekeying the material in a standard format for instant access in an emergency.

Case 6: National Trade Productions INTECH Conference

Problem: To be able to retrieve specific names, facts, dates, and decisions from the accumulated text in a planning conference.

Summary: This need was identified by an advisory committee for a major computer exposition. The committee employed conferencing over a nine month planning period. As the time of the conference came closer, replacement speakers, logistical arrangement decisions, and other specific information needed to be retrieved quickly, but it was often difficult to remember "where" things had been discussed. The committee had no "librarian," and found that it could not work comfortably in a tightly structured communication environment (e.g., always put a new speaker's name in one conference, always talk about hotel arrangements in another).

Solution: The organizers made extensive use of the indexing and search features of the Confer II host software. The search program made it possible to find items no matter what fragment of information the user recalled as a starting point, whether it was content of topics, authors' names, item headers, or strings of characters.

Access

Access requirements are set on the basis of the answer to the question "Who needs to say what to whom?" CMC supports a variety of types of exchanges, including private and group messaging, private and public conferencing, read and write-only conferences, bulletin boards, and so on. Each of these options has a variety of possible applications to the needs of different groups.

Case 7: School of Management and Strategic Studies

Problem: To emulate the lecture/discussion section organization of large university classes online in order to increase the rate of participation.

Summary: As the School of Management and Strategic Studies grew, class size increased and the percentage of the group participating actively declined. Organizers reasoned that this was due to spreading a limited number of opportunities to intervene over a larger number of participants, on the analogy of the effect of size on face-to-face groups.

Solution: Participants were broken down into three conferences that were blind to each other and were expected to provide a favorable environment for discussion; all participants were enrolled as readers in a fourth conference, where the teacher was expected to address the whole group simultaneously. In reality, references in the teacher's conference to comments in the three subconferences awakened curiosity about the hidden material and provoked demands to "break down the walls." The subdivision of the group appeared finally so arbitrary that the solution was abandoned.

Case 8: McGraw-Hill

Problem: To provide a standard set of instructions or information to a group of people who would be "arriving" online at different times.

Summary: A network has been set up for teachers and members of the educational community that includes access to lesson plans, discussion on educational issues, and peer networking. An initial group of teachers was selected as participant moderators to get the network off the ground. Additional volunteer moderators were to join the group as the network grew. The sponsor wanted to use one of the conferences to provide the moderators with some basic information and "readings" about moderating online groups. It was also hoped that these moderators would share their experience with one another. But this would be difficult with the new moderators arriving late online to find the basic material buried under the discussion.

Solution: The CoSy conferencing system used by McGraw-Hill made it possible for the organizer to establish a public read-only conference for newcomers paralleling the interactive conference. The basic material was put in the read-only conference, and key notes and summaries from the discussion conference were added to the read-only conference from time to time.

Rate of Interaction

Synchronous and asychronous modes of communication have very different applications to different types of groups. The examples discussed above all concern asynchronous exchanges. Synchronous or "real-time" interaction has more specialized applications. In the commonest case, it is used in a "CB simulation" mode to build social contacts and a feeling of community. However, in some situations synchronous communication serves precise functional requirements of group activity.

Case 9: Institute for Networking Design (Tokyo) and Stanford University

Problem: To provide an effective medium in which to conduct a multimedia international teleconference.

Summary: The participating technical team members needed to exchange a great deal of logistical information (e.g., how the video pictures are coming across, changes in the schedule). Much of this information was connected to real-time comparisons and adjustments in the video segment of the program. They also wanted to "capture" this interaction for later analysis.

Solution: The organizers used the synchronous "chat" capability on Confer II, linked to conferencing so that the interaction would be retrievable for review.

Case 10: BESTNET

Problem: To supply an equivalent of office hours for students in a video course employing computer conferencing as its interactive component. Summary: BESTNET is a network of universities in the southwestern United States and Mexico that produce and share a series of video courses in the Spanish language on mathematics and the natural sciences.[7] Teachers or tutors are available to the students at the various institutions through a computer conferencing link on the Western Behavioral Sciences Institute (WBSI) VAX Notes system. Organizers decided that in addition to conferences and messages, some sort of real-time exchange with teachers was needed.

Solution: The DEC Phone utility offers a way of carrying on synchronous discussion with a small group with a split-screen capability that clearly separates the contributions of each member of the discussion. Teachers hold regularly scheduled "online office hours" using Phone, and students dial in to the service as needed.

A SYSTEMATIC APPROACH TO SOCIAL FACTORS:
GRID/GROUP ANALYSIS

Introduction

The social factors model suggests that the distinctive features of types of formal organizations are significant for the design of effective conferencing systems. Various theories identify the significant features of such organizations, and each offers insights into how to design conferencing programs tailored to different group needs. Yet so far no conferencing system has been designed specifically to accommodate the different needs of different kinds of organizations.

The difficulty is to connect the sociological treatment of organizations with the work of program design. The social factors model offers a way of accomplishing this, a procedure for passing from analysis to specification. The remarks that follow offer an example of how this might be done. We have taken here for illustrative purposes a particular theory of formal organizations, which we apply to education and use to indicate probable design requirements in terms of the social factors approach.

Grid and Group

Groups can be differentiated according to structural principles and by the type of social solidarity that bonds their members. By "structure," organizational theorists generally refer to the regular and patterned aspects of relationships among members of organizations. The degree of solidarity is indicated negatively by the weight of bureaucratic mechanisms in maintaining those aspects. In some groups these mechanisms are of little significance because members organize themselves on the basis of mutually recognized benefits or shared sentiments, and orient themselves towards commonly perceived goals. Other groups manifest rigid structures whereby virtually all activities are specified in some formal code of conduct.

Mary Douglas (1982) formulated a theory of organizations to understand and measure the relationship between these features. She proposes a four-cell matrix based on two variables, which she calls "grid" and "group." The former refers to structural principles of hierarchical organization, and the latter to social bonding or solidarity. Douglas' model provides us with a useful method for categorizing types of educational user groups and applications, as well as for analyzing how different forms of structure and solidarity can be taken into account in the design of conferencing systems.

Douglas distinguishes groups by the amount of formal structure they contain and social bonding they manifest. These variables are mapped in Figure 4.6.

Figure 4.6

Low Group High Grid	High Grid High Group
A high structure/low solidarity	C high structure/high solidarity
B low structure/low solidarity	D low structure/high solidarity
Low Grid Low Group	High Group Low Grid

The cells provide a typology of kinds of social organizations and of their subgroups. We can generally classify most postsecondary educational institutions under category D: a minimum of formal structures affect the daily life of the institution but there is a high level of social bonding between faculty, departments, students, and other groups within the university or college. By contrast, the military and naval academies, although sharing strong social bonds of solidarity, exhibit a greater bureaucratic structure because of their adherence to military hierarchical categories; they should be classed under matrix C.

The same method can be used to classify the educational environments within a postsecondary situation—large undergraduate lectures, teaching assistant sections, small lecture/discussion classes, independent study, graduate-level classes, graduate and honors seminars, laboratories, colloquia and panel discussions/symposia. Generally, the larger the course enrollment and the lower the grade level, the more structure and the less solidarity.

Figure 4.7

Low Group High Grid	High Grid High Group
A low division large-lecture sessions laboratories	C teaching assistant sections upper division lectures graduate courses
B independent study	D graduate seminars colloquia panels/symposia
Low Grid Low Group	High Group Low Grid

Each cell corresponds to a pedagogical method. Those in matrix A require features that reinforce structure and that do not depend on a great deal of student interaction. On the other hand, those in matrix C require features that simultaneously reinforce structure and take advantage of the social bonds between students and students and instructor. Those in matrix D do not require formal rules and deadlines, and assume mutual participation in an activity based on social bonding.

Application to Current Educational Programs

These categories are significant for designing conference architectures for educational environments. Most current uses of educational computer conferencing involve matrix C and/or D forms of discussion: participants manifest strong solidarity and contribute primarily out of their interest in experimenting with the medium. This is true for both voluntary postgraduate educational programs, such as the School of Management and Strategic Studies at WBSI and university credit courses that have a formal structure, like those of Connected Education at the New School for Social Research and the Virtual Classroom project at the New Jersey Institute of Technology.

WBSI's School of Management and Strategic Studies has no specific participation requirement. Although faculty direct the discussion in the computer conferences, participants are free to explore tangential topics and are rarely, if ever, disciplined for not directly addressing the theme of the conference. Normally over half of the participants read comments without contributing. Those who enter comments do so on the basis of their own motivation to play an active role in a loosely structured community with fairly strong bonds of solidarity.

Social bonding is also strong in the case of university credit courses, such as those conducted by Connected Education and Virtual Classroom. In both instances, students voluntarily choose to take their educational programs using conferencing in lieu of face-to-face classroom interaction, and this in itself tends to create strong bonds among the participants, who know themselves to be kindred spirits adventuring together on a technological frontier. Such students are also much more motivated and self-directed than their counterparts in traditional classroom settings. Although instructors will normally establish certain ground rules for participating in a CMC-based course, such as setting a deadline for turning in assignments, the instructor can trust in the students' willingness and initiative to an unusual degree. This has been especially noted in the Turoff and Hiltz studies of the Virtual

Classroom (cf. Turoff and Hiltz 1978; Hiltz 1984, 1987; Kerr and Hiltz 1982) which note that CMC works especially well for students who are self-motivated and inner-directed.

This conclusion gains support from instances where students with little solidarity among themselves have made poor use of the medium. This was the case, for example, in an unsuccessful experiment at the University of South Florida using EMAIL as an interactive component of a video telecourse on the judiciary produced by the Annenberg Foundation/Corporation for Public Broadcasting.

In this case the students were asked to interact without clear direction. The educational environment corresponded to matrix A, high structure with low solidarity, because the students were selected from a larger cohort who were able to take the course by watching videos without online interaction. Thus, no solidarity was established between students taking the course together, nor was there any real bond created with the faculty of record, with whom they were asked to correspond using the medium. The project evaluation concluded that unless computer communication is built into the course formally, as an interactive method to facilitate close discussion of topics, students will not avail themselves of the opportunity to utilize it.

Social Factors in Course Conversion

These examples raise important issues of course conversion. The notion that computer conferencing works best with highly motivated, self-directed students in a seminar setting may be an artifact of the existing method of course conversion and the accepted conferencing system configurations. It is unlikely that all courses can be converted in a similar manner. Each should be evaluated on the basis of structure and solidarity, and computer conferencing architecture should be designed in terms of where each falls within the grid/group matrix.

This should be a particular concern when designing courses that normally fall in the A cell of the grid/group matrix (high structure with low solidarity), such as the large lecture science and mathematics courses in most university curricula. These are lower division courses that normally have relatively high enrollments. Students in such courses rarely interact with each other, except perhaps socially, outside of the boundaries of the class. There are many different motivations for taking the courses, because the students have a variety of different majors. Competition for grades, in which each student is measured against all others on some sort of grading curve, may contribute to lower levels of solidarity in such courses. Consequently, study groups are infrequent, and when they are organized, they tend to be formed between students who share some outside social bond, such as membership in a fraternity or are established through extramural activities.

The lack of strong social bonds or solidarity in such classes contributes to low student performance and high attrition rates. These rates are attributed not only to the difficulty of the subject matter and to the students' inability to identify with the subject materials, but also to the typical anomie and lack of social bonding in such classes.

The preferred conferencing architectures and pedagogical methods employed in educational applications today were designed for courses in cell D of the matrix, such as graduate or upper division seminars, colloquia, and panel discussions or symposia. They rely on participants' motivations and solidarity to generate the bulk of the course material. Courses that would normally be taught with large lectures are at a real disadvantage when converted for computer conferencing delivery using these architectures and methods. To expand the range of applications in education, conferencing systems must respond to the requirements of different kinds of courses in the grid/group matrix, as well as to differences between types of user groups.

Similar considerations suggest that the application of conferencing to training programs in business may require significantly different procedures and architectures than those which have evolved in academe so far. The general lack of strong hierarchical structure in academe and its strong sense of solidarity contrasts sharply with the organizational structure of most large corporations, which may also exhibit strong solidarity but in the context of a clear structure. Business organizations fall well within the C cell of the grid/group matrix. Since the profiles of user groups within academe and large corporate bureaucracies are so very different, interfaces for education and training purposes within business must be configured differently as well.

An Experiment with Branching

These differences can be accommodated to a large extent by the tailoring of interfaces and conference architectures. We would like to conclude this discussion with a description of an experiment in which we are currently engaged, designed to test the usefulness of different conference architectures for different types of courses.

One general type of conferencing architecture, employed by such programs as Confer, Caucus, and VAX Notes, is based on item/reply branching. Each text designated by the author as an "item" can become the starting point for a sequence of "replies" addressed to the topic it raises. This makes it possible to create a subconference for each new topic entered into a conference. The item/reply interface prompts the user to choose, after reading each new text, whether to respond to it in a reply, to join it in replying to a previous item to which it is itself a reply, or to introduce a new topic in a new item. Texts are delivered marked as to whether they are items or replies, and in the latter case, the number of the item to which the reply is indicated.

This type of branching system can be used for two very different functions, which we will call "contextualizing" and "classifying." In the first case, each new item serves as a context for the replies attached to it. In this case, brief replies, such as comments and questions, delivered immediately on reading an item are most appropriate. As soon as users have passed on to new items, they cease to reply to the old ones, even if the same subject discussed in the old item is broached again. In the second case, where the item/reply structure is used as a means of classifying subjects of discussion, it is incumbent on each participant to use the structure to maintain a logical organization of the discussion by topic.

The usefulness of this form of branching is affected by the course type as defined by the grid/group matrix. In seminar courses, it does not seem to be of critical importance as a contextualizing tool, nor does it appear to be particularly effective as a means of classifying texts. Students may feel restricted by an overemphasis on the item/reply structure, and the discussions can be severely constrained by it. This was evident in an experimental course WBSI conducted on VAX Notes for the Harvard Alumni Association. Initially, the faculty member teaching the course determined that only he would be able to write items, and he asked participants to reply under the appropriate item to the issues he raised. However, very early on in the conference, participants opposed this structure and began adding items as well as replies.

Several were bothered by the reply branching, and could not figure out where to place their replies on the system. Although there were other factors involved in that confusion, it is important to note that all members of the conference were Harvard alumni engaged in a voluntary leisure activity, and several had status relatively equivalent to the faculty teaching the course. Consequently, this group was clearly in the D cell of the academic user matrix, and rebelled against a conference architecture that imposed excessive structure.

WBSI is now planning tests of the item/reply structure in a large lecture-type course of the sort that falls in the A cell of the grid/group matrix. For this experiment, the faculty member will be given exclusive control over the introduction of new items, with the students able only to reply. The students will be encouraged to make two different uses of replies: questions concerning topics raised by the faculty, and turning in assignments requested in an item.

In this experiment, the item/reply structure will be used in the contextualizing mode: students will not have to construct elaborate comments but merely tag their remarks onto an appropriate comment by the teacher. Each day or two the faculty will contribute a new item, advancing the discussion as in a lecture presentation. This may be an effective way of dealing with the lack of that self-confidence and solidarity required of students in online seminars but often absent in large lecture courses. This experiment will demonstrate methods for taking social factors into account in designing educational programs for delivery over computer networks.

Acknowledgments

This paper was prepared under a contract with the Digital Equipment Corporation. A great many people made important contributions to the development of the ideas presented here, especially Richard Farson, Darrell Icenogle, Oliver Vallee, Peter and Trudy Johnson-Lenz, Ulf Fagerquist, and George Metes. Several of the case histories were drawn from accounts by Jacques Vallee and Lisa Carlson. Mary Douglas suggested the application of organizational theory developed in the third part.

NOTES

1. For interesting examples of the effective and ineffective use of computer teleconferencing, see Johansen et al. (1979), pp. 59-84.   This book contains a valuable bibliography of early research in the field of computer conferencing.

2. Social network designers are involved in such projects as the development of conferencing and electronic messaging systems for local area networks within large, dispersed corporations, distance learning programs networking schools and universities, distance education training conferences for business and military, and more. For example, see Part II of this chapter.

3. One might conclude from this that conferencing is best suited to qualitative discussion, but that conclusion is premature so long as the systems are not well able to transmit graphics and mathematical symbols (Hiltz 1986).   There are several recent projects experimenting with the transmission of data compressed binary files to permit mathematical and other graphical symbols to be used in computer conference courses.   For example, WBSI is now involved in developing this capability on its VAX Notes conferencing system to transmit graphics for several calculus and physics courses in the BESTNET courses described below.

4. There have been several descriptions of the School of Management and Strategic Studies in books concerned with the innovative use of new technologies in education, including Rowan (1986) and Levinson (1988).   Apart from an experimental course using electronic mail (EMAIL) taught by David Hughes at Colorado College, there seems to have been no educational application of computer conferencing prior to the activities of the WBSI. Occasional experimental applications of EMAIL or conferencing to the discussion portion of residential classes may have occurred earlier, but I have not been able to find information about such experiments.   On the basis of an informal survey, we conclude that WBSI was the first institution to employ computer conferencing as the primary vehicle for delivery of an educational program.

5. The results of the FIPSE Technology Study Group's experiment with computer conferencing was published in a special edition of *Machine-Mediated Learning*, edited by Diane Belestri and Steven Ehrman (1987).

6. See Vallee (1984) for a discussion of these conferences.

7. See Arias and Bellman (1987) for a description of this project, and of implications of the medium for international cooperation between universities in the United States and Latin America.

REFERENCES

Arias, A., & Bellman, B. (1987). BESTNET: International coopera-
    tion through interactive Spanish/English transition
    telecourses. *Technology and Learning, 1* (3).
Douglas, M. (Ed). (1982). *Essays in the sociology of perception*.
    London: Routledge and Kegan Paul.
Feenberg, A. (1986a). Network design: An operating manual for
    computer conferencing. *IEEE Transactions on Professional
    Communications, 29* (1).
———— (1987). Computer conferencing and the humanities.
    Instructional Science, 16 : 169-86.
———— (1989). The planetary classroom: International applications
    of advanced communications to education. In E. Stefferud et
    al. (Eds.), *Message handling systems and distributed
    applications*. North Holland: pp. 511-524.
FIPSE Technology Study Group. (1988). Ivory towers, silicon
    basements: Learner-created computing in post-secondary
    education. Presented at Educom, Washington, DC.
Goodwin, N. C. (1987).   Functionality and usability.
    Communications of the ACM, 30 (3): 229-233.
Hiltz, S. R. (1984). *Online communities: A case study of the office of
    the future*. Norwood, NJ: Ablex Press.
Hiltz, S. R. (1986). The "virtual classroom": Using computer-
    mediated communication for university teaching. *Journal of
    Communication, 36* (2): 95-104.
Hiltz, S. R. (1987). College students' reactions to CAI in the social
    sciences. Submitted to *Computers and the Social Sciences*.
Hiltz, S. R., & Turoff, M. (1978). *The network nation: Human
    communication via computer*. Reading, MA: Addison-Wesley.
Johansen, R., Vallee, J. & Spangler, K. (1979). *Electronic meetings*.
    Reading, MA: Addison-Wesley.
Johnson-Lenz, P., & Johnson-Lenz, T. (1981). Consider the group-
    ware: Design and group process impacts on communication in
    the electronic medium.   In S. R. Hiltz & E. B. Kerr (Eds.),
    *Studies of computer-mediated communications systems: A syn-
    thesis of findings*.   Newark, NJ: NJIT Research Report no. 16.
    An abridged version is available in S. R. Hiltz & E. B. Kerr.
    (1982).   *Computer-mediated communication systems: Status
    and evaluation*. New York: Academic Press.
Kaye, T. (1987). Introducing computer-mediated communication
    into a distance education system. *The Canadian Journal of
    Educational Communications, 16* (2): 153-166.

Kerr, E. B. (1986). Electronic leadership: A guide to moderating online conferences. *IEEE Transactions on Professional Communications, 29* (1): 12-18.

Kerr, E. B., & Hiltz, S. R. (1982).

Levinson, P. (1988). *Mind at large: Knowing in the technological age*. Greenwich, CT: JAI Press.

Rowan, R. (1986). *The intuitive manager*. New York.

Vallee, J. (1984). *Computer message systems*. New York: McGraw-Hill.

Chapter 5
Cognitive and Technical Issues in the Design of Educational Computer Networking

Denis Newman

      Telecommunications technologies have been of growing interest to schools for instructional activities such as communication among students in different
parts of the world, collaborative science experiments among geographically distributed schools, and data gathering from online databases, to mention only a few (see for example, Chapter 8 of this volume). This kind of educational computer networking is to a large extent modeled on the use of technology by scientists and other adult professionals. Instead of providing an alternative medium for classroom discussion, the technology is providing an environment that engages students in authentic educational activities. In spite of the enormous potential for schools, the technology is only very slowly moving out of a marginal position. The technology and even the necessary phone lines have not been readily available in schools, and where they have been available, they have often been cumbersome and confusing for many teachers. Continuing changes in the hardware, software, and network design, particularly the enormous increase in the power of desktop microcomputers, may greatly improve the situation in schools because it simplifies the interactions with the technology. At the same time, the increase in local computing power can make the conversation over the long-distance network more remote and change some of the supports for the social cognition that is the basis for the shared dialogues the technology has made possible.

      Cognitive issues arise with respect to the social understandings of the mutual knowledge and shared objects that are central to discourse and, particularly, collaboration (Newman 1986). In this chapter, cognitive and technical issues are illustrated by four educational and academic networks, ranging from a local network within a sixth grade computer lab to a large-scale network linking educational researchers around the world. The central issue across these examples is the creation of a shared object as the basis of the computer-mediated conversation. The creation of a shared object distinguishes computer conferencing systems from other forms of computer-mediated communication (such as electronic mail systems). A conference, a bulletin board, or any of the kinds of conversations that fall under this category creates a single stream of discourse to which participants can refer. A message number is a shared reference within the structure of the conversation: there is a single object in the world to which the number refers, and there is a single conversation in which the numbered message has a specific place. For the members of the conversation, the topic structure provides objects, and references to them are mutually understood.

Nevertheless, the well-known computer conferencing systems, such as Electronic Information Exchange System (EIES) and Parti are not the only way that electronic group conversations can be conducted: electronic mail systems, although not designed specifically for the purpose, can also be used. In most conferencing systems, all messages within a particular conversation are saved in a single location on the central computer. People who are engaged in the conversation access that list in order to read new messages. In most electronic mail systems, by contrast, people's messages are stored in individual mailboxes: there is no central location where the history of the conversation can be reviewed. Unlike conferencing systems, the messages that constitute a conversation have no single numbering sequence that identifies them to all participants. Conferencing systems work best when a single computer is involved as the host; electronic mail works best when messages are passed from one computer to another. A group conversation can be conducted via electronic mail if, for example, people use aliases to send messages to a group of people engaged in the same conversation. However, when several host computers are involved, it is easy to lose the sense of a group conversation: past messages cannot be reviewed unless each participant has saved them, and there is no numbering system for the messages constituting the conversation that makes them easy to reference in later parts of the conversation. Despite these problems, electronic mail systems were used, either alone or in conjunction with conferencing systems, in the four systems discussed here because they were the only means available for communicating in the multihost environment.

This chapter explores the technical issues that arise in the educational environments that make the maintenance of a shared object difficult. It also examines the related cognitive issues involved in computer-mediated communication as applied to education, especially the education of children. Common to both these issues is the use of local computing power, that is, computers on the user's tabletop or within local phone-call range. When computer conferencing systems first began to be used, they ran on large computers that were accessed by terminals. Creating a shared object is relatively easy in such an environment, because there is only one computer, the host, that anybody accesses. Today, such large computers, if used at all, are not accessed with a terminal but with a personal computer running software that may emulate a terminal as one of its functions but that also provides important tools as well as an interface of its own. Bulletin board systems and fileservers on local area networks add to the microcomputer power base, making it increasingly unlikely that computer users will have direct, unmediated contact with a large central computer. The diversity that results has many advantages including empowering the ordinary computer user and allowing inexpensive computer-mediated conversations among a local group. Design issues arise, however, that were not anticipated in the original construction of conferencing systems. And the application to education becomes particularly interesting and problematic.

In this chapter, I discuss three design issues for educational applications that arise from the diversity we are faced with, illustrating these principles by examining four current network systems. Finally, I discuss cognitive issues in terms of the degrees of coordination that can be achieved in the face of diversity in local settings and over longer distances. Understanding the system in terms of both face-to-face and computer-mediated conversations is especially important in designing systems for education, where the nature of the educational activity may require coordination around immediate concrete objects.

THREE DESIGN PRINCIPLES FOR EDUCATIONAL NETWORKS

In the prototypical implementation of computer-mediated communication, people access a computer messaging system that is hosted by a large computer. Currently there is vast horizontal diversity represented by a multitude of parallel and only sometimes interconnected services. There is also a vertical diversity represented by small local systems, and larger systems that again are only occasionally interconnected. Group conversations organized around shared objects are not as easily managed within this diversity as they are when the conversation happens on a single machine. The situation calls for reassessing the principles that are critical to carrying on group conversations.

Our work with educational networking has led us to three principles for the design of networking systems. These are generalized principles: they apply to aspects of software design as well as to the overall connectivity of networks at a national level.

Group Conversation and Coordination

Networking must be thought of in terms of groups of people who have some common task or function around which they are conversing. Probably the most important and characteristic power of electronic networking is the ease of addressing a message to a group of people. The group conversation and the sense of group cohesion are central features. There are many kinds of conversations, of course. The tasks around which the group conversation revolves may require very different degrees of coordinated effort. Conducting a real-time distributed simulation requires a high degree of coordination; conducting a casual discussion of microchip technology may require little coordination in terms of temporal precision and response obligations. Different kinds of conversations demand different degrees of coordination. We are interested here in systems that provide for group conversation.

Local Communication

The second principle is to minimize the use of phone lines or data communication networks. Cost is a major factor in education: it makes sense to use expensive networks as little as possible. But regardless of cost, the most important communication in corporate and university experiences occurs on the local level (Eveland and Bikson 1986). When an electronic mail system connects workers in a building with workers in other buildings or parts of the country, most of the communication occurs among offices on the same floor, somewhat less among offices on different floors, and very little between sites in different cities. The same is true in schools: most communication happens within a school or district; there is far less need for communication at the state or national level. Long-distance communication is often both critical and highly motivating, but we should not use a national network for local communication. Similarly, we should not use a remote computer for text editing when a desktop microcomputer is available.

Diversity

The third principle is that it is unlikely there will ever be one monolithic network to which everybody belongs. The economics of the commercial networks, such as CompuServe and The Source, are very different from the university/research networks. In designing our networking systems in education, we have to assume that our users will want to communicate with a variety of people using a variety of systems. The solution for schools is not to try to get everybody on the same system but to find ways to move easily among systems. This may include creating ways that a local computer can pick up messages from a number of services, so that a user has to get messages from only one place. In general we have to try to make diversity easier to manage on a day-to-day basis.

I have used these three principles as a framework to examine four education networks and to elicit design suggestions for such networks. These principles also point to cognitive issues involved in conducting coordinated conversations around educational tasks.

International Research Cooperation

Since the mid-1980s there has been increasing interest in U.S.-Soviet joint research ventures. One such project focused on issues of computer use in schools. Researchers in Moscow and Pereslavl were in communication with researchers in San Diego, New York, and Cambridge. For the purposes of this chapter, the way the conversation was organized is more important than its content. The Soviet researchers were allowed access to the Parti conferencing system on The Source, through a European telecommunication link to Telenet. Although for the Soviet researchers political and technical conditions in the USSR somewhat restricted their access, they did manage to get onto The Source at least once a week. Several subconferences were set up for conversations about subprojects dealing with computers in education. Each of the Soviet and U.S. sites had a Parti name. The U.S. participants also had electronic mail addresses on the Internet, and most of the U.S participants used only their usual mail system, both for convenience and to save Source charges. The San Diego site acted as an intermediary between The Source and Internet, transferring messages from the conference to the Internet address, and forwarding replies from Internet to the conference.

The Parti system added an important level of coherence to the U.S.-Soviet conversation, which often referred to the the message numbers of earlier messages in the conference. The Parti system was also used for conversations among the U.S. participants (conversations which the Soviet researchers did not have access to). Even though the U.S. participants were all on the Internet and all messages had to be transferred to and from Parti, there was still an advantage of using Parti for this U.S.-only conversation, since it created a permanent record that otherwise would have been lost by the electronic mail structure of the Internet. Naturally, some side conversations occurred over the Internet that were not transferred to Parti as part of the permanent record of the group conversation. One of the U.S. sites even created an alias for themselves on the Internet in order to make it easy to conduct a local group "side" conversation for the purpose of local coordination. At the international level, the Parti conferencing system was very effective in creating a record of the group conversation. At the national level—within the United States—the Internet was the main medium of transmission, with the Parti system providing a shared object for the U.S.-only conversations. At the local level—among the researchers within a city—the Internet was the primary medium of conversation; the conversation on the Parti system was a somewhat remote topic of the local conversation.

This complex hierarchical arrangement is becoming more common, especially in education where a diverse set of people is engaged in a diverse set of conversations. Our other cases show how combinations of local and long-distance systems can be useful in coordinating educational activities.

National Exchanges of Student Writing

Several formative experiments on telecommunications have been conducted at Bank Street College of Education. Any telecommunication activity in education consists of both conversations in the classroom, where the primary education content lies, and the conversation over the wires. The long-distance conversation is often difficult to coordinate because of variations in schedules and resources at different sites. These examples of telecommunication activities show the appropriate level of coordination for various distances. They also show the interplay of local and long-distance conversations.

The Mathematics, Science and Technology Teacher Education (MASTTE) project (Quinsaat, Friel and McCarthy 1985; McGinnis 1986), had 12 sites around the country implementing Bank Street's multimedia science program, "The Voyage of the Mimi." Nine of these sites communicated with Bank Street and with each other via Parti on The Source. A "guest expert" series was very popular among a number of the sites and has elicited a large response. In this series, we announced over the network that experts (several of whom were featured on the TV show "Voyage of the Mimi") would be available to answer questions that are sent in. Teachers collected questions from their classes and sent them in via the network (or in some cases by phone). The expert wrote answers that were distributed over the network. Even this simple activity required a fair amount of coordination—phone calls, for example, to make sure the sites remembered the schedule of experts and submitted their questions. However, the value of the activity and the enjoyment of other sites were not affected if one site didn't respond.

Another project used the Bank Street Exchange, a bulletin board system running on an IBM AT at Bank Street, for the exchange of pen-pal letters and short essays between elementary classrooms in New York and San Diego. This project combined local and long-distance communication. To avoid expensive daytime rates on the commercial network system we were using, students relied on local communication facilities: the San Diego students used the U.C. San Diego (UCSD) electronic mail system, and the New York students used the Exchange. For example, in New York, children in classrooms (and sometimes from home) called the Exchange and wrote messages to other children. We downloaded those messages to an Apple II and then uploaded them to the commercial system after business hours, when the rates were lower.

An important observation from this and from other projects using long-distance communication is that electronic communication tends to be sporadic. This feature increases with the distance and organizational differences between the communicating sites. It is difficult to create tightly coordinated activities over distance because curricula, schedules, and holidays vary considerably. We ran into this problem continually with the pen-pal project. One classroom would become active while the other class was on vacation or engaged in other language arts activities. By the time the messages were answered, they were old news or the original senders had moved on to other interests. The portaging in some cases depended on undergraduate assistants, and so semester breaks also caused delays. Despite the technical speed of the medium, messages often took much longer to arrive than regular mail would have; and when they did arrive, it was often in bunches. A more complex cause of sporadic transmission was the relatively sparse amount of communication. New mail did not arrive each day, and so sites logged in less frequently. Alternatively, although messages may take only a few seconds to transmit, they may sit for a long time before being responded to.

Pen-pal letters seem like a simple application of the technology, but they actually require good coordination between sites. If the pen pals were corresponding from home, the situation would be simpler than at school because there would be no need to coordinate with the teacher's priorities for the use of the computer. But as we attempted to organize it, the writing activities of pen pals had to be coordinated. If one or the other failed to respond for a few weeks, the activity broke down, creating frustration on both sides.

This exchange of messages became more successful when an energetic UCSD undergraduate took it on as her course project, and modified the activity from personal letters to "editorials" about current events. The bombing of Libya took place the day before she began work with the group of San Diego students. The San Diego messages expressing their opinions about the event were answered relatively quickly by the New York students, and several exchanges ensued about this and other events. It is notable that the coordination in this case was facilitated by a dedicated undergraduate on one end and an enthusiastic computer coordinator on the other end. But their efforts were made easier by its being a class (group) project. Any student in either class could write an editorial: the success of the exchange did not depend on a specific student receiving a message from one other specific student on the other side of the continent.

Local Communication in a School

Local area networks (LANs) make it easy to communicate and share data within a building such as a school. In another Bank Street project, Earth Lab, we developed LAN technology for use in sixth grade science. Curriculum units in two earth science areas, weather and climate, and plate tectonics, provide the instructional context to test whether the LAN technology can help teachers to create a valuable environment for learning science (Brienne and Goldman 1989). Since September 1986, Earth Lab has been operating in the sixth grade of two schools.

We created or modified several pieces of Apple II software for use in these units. A network interface gives the teacher and students access to the programs, data, and text files. The interface makes it possible for a teacher to create a "workspace" for a group of students where data from a group project is kept or to create a "library" or common area for a class or for the school as a whole. A database management system, the Bank Street Filer, has been modified so that students can locate and contribute to a common database for group projects. We also created a special version of the Bank Street Writer, a word-processing program that is popular in elementary schools. The new Writer allows students to send electronic mail to anybody else in the school as well as to students at other schools. Teachers are also able to send messages to individuals or groups of children. A navigation simulation game, Rescue Mission, has been modified so that four groups of students can pilot their ships simultaneously.

Written communication is an important aspect of Earth Lab, and an important feature of the Earth Lab classroom environment is electronic mail. We use a very simple mail system created by adding a SEND MAIL function and an OPEN MAIL function to the Bank Street Writer (the word processor used for writing instruction by the schools we are working in). In this way, students are able to use their familiar writing environment for sending messages. Electronic mail within the classroom, and among classrooms using a common computer or science lab, simulates the way scientists use electronic mail within a scientific lab or on a single campus. We have devised activities that require groups of students to communicate with others. Text is composed jointly and shared over the LAN, for example, as contributions to a class research project on weather disasters. Students are encouraged, and sometimes required as an assignment, to send the teacher a short message describing their hypotheses about the outcome of an investigation. Since the Earth Lab activities involve a high degree of coordination among the science teacher, the computer coordinator, and the classroom teachers, staff use the network to help get their own work done.

We have designed science activities in which the task is divided among groups of children who use the local network technology to gather and share their information (Newman, Goldman, Brienne, Jackson and Magzamen 1989). One activity organized as a small-group collaboration was the collection of weather data from the rooftop weather station. Each day the computer lab teacher took one of the science groups up to collect data on temperature, barometric pressure, wind, and other weather conditions. The students returned to the computer lab and entered the data into a data base that grew to 64 entries. After the data were collected, the science groups each worked on interpreting the entire corpus of data in terms of relationships between the variables (for example, between air pressure and cloudiness). These investigations involving a coordination among the groups create data that are shared objects for the groups of students at two levels: within the group and among the groups. In both cases, the object—the data or other phenomena they are investigating—is physically present as the students work together around the computer or other objects.

While many of the Earth Lab activities occurred within the classroom, some involved communication with students in other parts of the country. From our experiences with long-distance networking, we have developed an efficient portage between the local classroom network and the networks available via modem connections. Each day the Earth Lab coordinator uses the modem to call out to the Bank Street Exchange, The Source, and other bulletin boards of interest. Messages are downloaded to the hard disk of the local network and then distributed to the directories of the individual students.

Through this portage system, we are beginning to solve two of the major problems we have found with networking applications in education. First, by having the children use the same software (in this case the Bank Street Writer) for all communication—papers, local messages, and long-distance messages—we will simplify the process: it will be necessary to know only one method of entering text. Second, we have reduced the problem of sporadic long-distance communications by providing a single source for all communication. If all communication comes over one channel, children are less frustrated by long delays in the long-distance networks. Each day, the probability of getting some message is high enough to maintain interest. When long-distance messages arrive, they provide an additional motivator. The use of local power where possible (the second design principle) as part of a system that integrated diverse networks (the third design principle) avoided many frustrations.

COMPONENTS OF A NETWORKING SYSTEM

In each of the preceding examples, the network system consisted of at least two levels. Assuming that our third principle is correct—that we will be working with diverse systems in education—a scheme for fitting the parts together is necessary. The levels involved in the preceding examples are (1) the individual microcomputer, (2) the local area network or the local bulletin board, and (3) the national or international network. Each of these components is currently in use in education, but the connections among the levels require considerable development before they function as an integrated system.

Microcomputers

A microcomputer connected to a modem and phone line or to a local area network is the starting place. Microcomputers are becoming increasingly powerful. Even the standard workhorse of the classroom, the Apple IIe, has sufficient power to do a range of work that in the past was done by host computers accessed by terminals. Software—for example, Apple Computer's Applelink—is now available that allows the user to rapidly upload and download information from the host, and then to read and write messages while no longer connected. Microcomputer software can also be programmed to send and receive messages automatically at night, when the transmission rates are lowest. Microcomputer software such as MacEmail, developed by Dan Tappan at BBN, provides a complete Macintosh interface to the host, making it unnecessary to learn the obscure commands of the host, and provides for the local storage of information obtained from the host. Our electronic mail system for Earth Lab was built into the local word processor: it was not necessary to learn a new writing system just for the purpose of communication. This kind of software is consistent with our second principle of keeping processing as close to home as possible and minimizing connect time. The new generation of software also can deal automatically with a variety of services, saving time and trouble for the user.

Local Area Networks and Bulletin Boards

One piece of the networking system we envision, although currently the least developed, has the greatest importance and potential: a small electronic mail or conferencing system that people can reach with a local phone call or on a local area network. Systems reached by a local phone call are generally called bulletin boards because they were originally very rudimentary systems on which users could post public messages. In recent years, however, they have become more sophisticated. Common microcomputers such as the IBM AT can now support multiple simultaneous users and conferencing software as sophisticated as the Parti system. Likewise, LAN fileservers can play the role of communication center as well as coordinating many instructional activities through common access to data on the server. These systems will play a pivotal role because they can both serve the needs for local communication and mediate the use of larger national or international networks.

For local communication, LANs and bulletin boards (I will continue to use this outmoded term) can serve a school district or school very well. Current systems provide conferencing structures for group communication and other methods of maintaining coherent threads of conversation. The role of bulletin boards and LAN fileservers in long-distance communication is being developed to solve some problems teachers have in this area. These systems can play a potentially powerful role as an intermediary between the local user and the long-distance services. Using the kinds of automatic log-on capacities already found in microcomputer communication software, the bulletin board could itself call services like CompuServe or Parti, collect any waiting messages for local users, and log off. The board would automatically distribute those messages to the various local users. Likewise, a user could leave a message on the board for an alias corresponding to a person on another system. The board could automatically send that message out to the other system at night, when the rates are cheapest. As demonstrated by Earth Lab, these functions do not have to be automated; a system operator can do these tasks for local users, making it unnecessary for each local user to log onto several different services. In this way, communication is enormously simplified: the local user has to use only one system for all levels of communication.

It would also be feasible for local bulletin boards anywhere in the country to form a network by all participants getting accounts on the same nationwide service, such as CompuServe or a Parti system. The network we envision could link any kind of bulletin board with any other, and would take advantage of the convenience and lower rates of data communication networks. Each school or district can set up a board for the local teachers and students and obtain a single account on the Parti system. Teachers and students can send messages to any of a number of conferences on the nationwide system, and each of the sites will have access to it. A system operator at each site can transfer the messages back and forth from the local board to the Parti system, by downloading them from Parti to a microcomputer and then uploading them to the board, or vice versa. Teachers and students will be able to communicate with their counterparts in other districts without ever having to "leave" their own board.

This local system, whether operated manually or automated, will satisfy the three design principles I began with. It provides group conversations both within the local area and via a nationwide conferencing system: it provides for local communication, and it can deal with a variety of nationwide services without complicating the lives of the local users. We have found that teachers accept local boards more readily than they accept long-distance services. The cost, both for normal usage and for getting to know the system, is far lower. Bulletin boards are also simpler, and so have far fewer layers of menus.

Long-Distance Network Services

As we attempt to move as much communication as possible to the local level, the structure of the larger services becomes less critical. From the point of view of the local bulletin board, the difference in structure between CompuServe and Parti makes less difference. Probably the local system will have to learn to deal with both because not all the teachers will use the same one.

A weakness found in the Parti system, CompuServe, and other large information utilities is that there is no provision for direct interservice communication. A person on Parti cannot send a message directly to a person on CompuServe or to people using any of the university computers. In contrast, there are several interconnecting networks that allow people at universities to send messages anywhere in a vast system of university computers. Unfortunately, school districts typically cannot get access to this kind of network unless they own, at least, a substantial minicomputer and hire a systems programmer to get the network connection operating. It is more likely that schools will continue to use public-access network services that tend to be self-contained.

A process we are calling a "portage" is a simple solution to the isolation of network services. (In some circles the process is called "porting," but we prefer "portage" because the image of lifting a canoe out of the water, carrying it over a hill and putting it back in the water provides a nice metaphor.) A message can be portaged from CompuServe to Parti by downloading it from CompuServe to a microcomputer and then uploading it to Parti. Compared with the computerized "gateways" (more akin to the locks on a canal system) that connect networks in the university, business, and military realms, a portage can be slow and cumbersome. Its tremendous advantage, however, is its flexibility. Just about any network can be connected with any other. Programmable communication software will also help to automate the process so that a portage can more nearly resemble an inexpensive gateway. At least for the near future, schools will continue to use microcomputers or bulletin boards as portage sites, downloading and uploading information as a method of crossing from one network service to another.

Many groups, including state departments of education, are currently experimenting with ways to connect their groups with computer networks. On the basis of the three principles, recommendations for network system design emphasize local control and diversity. It will be most useful to build up local capacity, using the larger network to coordinate local users. District-level people will be critical in this endeavor because they will form the mediating link between the needs for local and long-distance communication. Statewide networks that plan to involve only one service may actually restrict communication, especially for district people who would benefit from communication with, for example, people in other states implementing similar programs.

In general, the design of systems intended for group conversations needs to break away from the single-host approach. Distributed conferencing systems, which allow any computer to "host" a conversation and which distribute messages as electronic mail, may begin to replace the older generation of conferencing systems, merging their functions with electronic mail. The most critical feature of such systems will be their relations with other systems. Unlike the older generation, they will be suited for receiving messages from, and sending messages to, the world outside themselves. These systems will become feasible for education when they are available on smaller machines that can be operated by a school or school district. For the schools, network design should start in the classroom and work outward, adding the power to carry on distant conversations without adding to the complexity of the student's communication tool.

COGNITIVE ISSUES

The design and implementation of the technology is only a small part of the whole conversation. Cognitive issues arise when we begin to consider the people involved in the conversations and the tasks around which they are conversing. If we take the local environment seriously, the question of the mixture of face-to-face and computer-mediated conversation is of considerable interest. And when we begin to consider children, the issue arises of how abstractly we can represent the shared objects that are the basis for the conversation. While children can very early understand mutual knowledge (Newman 1986), and sixth graders have little trouble understanding the function of a fileserver as storing shared data (Newman 1988), the activities are very often coordinated around immediate concerns and concrete materials that are difficult to integrate into this abstract form.

In moving from the design of technology to the design of educational activities that make use of it, issues about how the conversation is maintained take on broader meaning because assistance in maintaining it comes from the technology, the people who are organizing the activity, and the nature of the activity itself. There are complex relationships among the distance to the shared object of the conversation, the amount of coordination required in the activity, and the cognitive resources of the communicators. The cognitive resources available include the expertise and knowledge base (perhaps roughly related to amount of schooling) as well as the other people in the context, such as teachers, who can help to structure the activity that provides a frame of reference for understanding the conversation.

Greater cognitive resources are needed to maintain coordinated activities over a long distance. But the activities themselves, in providing a frame of reference, make the coordination easier. If the group has a preexisting task and the group members have a relationship to each other, coordination is easier. But where a group of individuals or sites have no intrinsic functional relationship to each other, a considerable amount of extrinsic coordination is necessary in order to use long-distance networks for highly coordinated activities. Networks, such as the Intercultural Learning Network (Levin, Riel, Miyake and Cohen 1987) that have successfully implemented coordinated activities among distant classrooms have relied on supervision by university-based researchers who form a functional research community with purposes beyond the implementation of classroom activities. We also have found in earlier work that a group of district people from around the country could very successfully use the network to plan a conference (Newman and Rehfield 1985). In this case, the group had a common purpose outside the network activities for which the network was instrumental.

Classrooms in distant cities that join a common network activity often have no connection with one another outside the network activity itself. In these cases, it may be more appropriate to design activities in which sites contribute to a common database of material or information but the contribution of any one site is not critical. The "guest expert" activity, described above, meets this description, as do "telecourses" in which geographically scattered students take part in "class discussion" using computer conferencing. Joint data collection activities in which data from every site are critical to the experimental outcome will probably require a considerable amount of extrinsic coordination among distant, unrelated classrooms.

The situation is quite different at the local level of the classroom or school. At this level, planning a science curriculum is not hindered by differences in schedules. Planning meetings are not necessary within a classroom; but even where the activity involves, for example, other teachers in a grade level or the school's computer coordinator, face-to-face meetings are relatively easy to arrange. Within a science class, for example, aspects of a single activity can be assigned to different children who then come together for discussions. Using a local area network with a common disk storage device makes that coordination easier and, perhaps, more enjoyable for students. But the critical conversation in this case is the teacher-led class discussion. Computers mediate even here because the data around which the conversation centers were compiled by the computer, and the activity of data collection was assisted by the technology (Newman, Goldman, Brienne, Jackson, and Magzamen, 1989). Electronic mail interactions in a classroom can be commented on in person simultaneously with the electronic transmission (Goldman and Newman, in press). While professional groups who have a firm understanding of the shared project can, for example, relate to a shared conversational object that has been portaged from a distant network, it may be more reasonable to organize classroom discussion around more immediate objects. In Earth Lab, for example, students worked in groups of four where the shared object of conversation was the single computer screen (and the books, notes, and other materials) at their work table.

There are many factors involved in maintaining an educational conversation around some shared object. These are cognitive issues in the sense that the student must maintain a representation of the object. We cannot, however, separate the cognitive representation from the social supports provided by the structuring activities of other people, both online "moderators" and teachers, and students in the immediate situation. Learning takes place in the context of this whole conversation (Newman, Griffin and Cole 1989). Young students will likely require a greater level of support to maintain an educational conversation than will adults. The support can come both from a technology that helps display the structure and process of the shared activity and from the other people who provide the structuring and interpretation of the students' activities.

CONCLUSION

The central concept underlying computer conferencing systems is the idea of a conversation as a shared object for a group of people. These conversations can have a variety of purposes, but in all cases a sense of community arises from the interactions by virtue of the shared common history. The original design of these systems relied on a shared computer that all participants accessed through a terminal. The rapid change in technology resulting from the rise of the microcomputer has altered these initial designs. Yet the notion of a group conversation remains the goal for new systems.

The concept of a computer-mediated conversation has been extended from its initial implementations on large computers. The main extension involves moving toward local communication systems in which the computer-mediated conversation is mingled with face-to-face conversations. People have available an array of conversations: some face-to-face, others entirely mediated by computer; some in the local setting, others over long distance. A hierarchy of systems is available for these conversations, and education can use systems at all these levels. In reconceptualizing the notion of a computer-mediated group conversation, the whole conversation, including the nature of the activity itself, the needs for coordination, the opportunities for mixing media must be considered. The whole conversation is seldom captured entirely in the numbered notes of a computer conference. The whole conversation is the basis for elaborating new tools for working and learning together in the current computer environment.

REFERENCES

Brienne, D., & Goldman, S. V. (1989). Networking: How it has enhanced science classes in New York schools...and how it can enhance classes in your school, too. *Classroom Computer Learning, 9* (7): 45-53.

Eveland, J.D., & Bikson, T. K. (1986). Evolving electronic communication networks: An empirical assessment. Paper presented at the Conference on Computer-Supported Cooperative Work, Austin, TX, December 3-5.

Goldman, S. V., & Newman, D. (in press). Electronic interactions: How students and teachers organize schooling over the wires. *Discourse Processes*.

Levin, J. A., Riel, M. M., Miyake, N., & Cohen, M. (1987). Education on the electronic frontier: Teleapprentices in globally distributed education contexts. *Contemporary Educational Psychology, 12*: 254-60.

McGinnis, M. R. (1986). Supporting science teachers through electronic networking. Paper presented at the New England Educational Research Organization, Rockport, ME.

Newman, D. (1986). The role of mutual knowledge in perspective taking development. *Developmental Review, 6*: 122-45.

—— (1988). Sixth graders and shared data: Designing a LAN environment to support collaborative work. Paper presented at the Second Conference on Computer Supported Cooperative Work, Portland, OR, October.

Newman, D. & Rehfield, K. (1985). Using a national network for professional development. Paper presented at the Annual Meeting of the American Educational Research Association, Chicago, April.

Newman, D., Goldman, S. V., Brienne, D., Jackson, I., & Magzamen, S. (1989). Peer collaboration in computer-mediated science investigations. *Journal of Educational Computing Research, 5* (2): 151-66.

Newman, D., Griffin, P., & Cole, M. (1989). *The construction zone: Working for cognitive change in school*. Cambridge: Cambridge University Press.

Quinsaat, M., Friel, S. & McCarthy, R. (1985). Training issues in the teaching of science, mathematics, and the use of technology. In L. Loucks (chair), *"Voyage of the Mimi": Perspectives of teacher education*. Symposium at the annual meeting of the American Educational Research Association, Chicago, April.

Chapter 6
Three Behavioral Models for Computer-Mediated Communication

Elaine K. McCreary

INTRODUCTION: NEW ROLES

The realm of computer-mediated communication (CMC) into which the human species has begun to migrate imposes new social roles that still lack clear protocols for fulfillment. As town planners have laid out the settlements, highways, and byways for embodied communities, so the authors of CMC architectures are delineating the settlement work zones and conduits of the new online communities. In both cases we must ensure that the designers we employ have the professional refinement to build material and virtual spaces that are in harmony with human nature and culture.

Three roles will be given special attention here: the individual participant, who will be newly defined as a "CMC collaborator"; the now familiar "conference moderator"; and a role that will be introduced in this chapter, the "diffusion manager." For some time to come, one of the most fertile knowledge creation frontiers in CMC will be the quest for models to guide our experimentation with these new social roles.

This chapter presents three long-standing models previously derived from direct observation of human behavior, and examines their heuristic potential as tools to guide our indirect observation of human behavior in online communities. Each of the following sections begins by discussing the nature or demands of one of these new social roles, cites a model with some apparent relevance to the online role, and then examines how the model can be applied to CMC to elucidate what is observed, to train people for the role, or perhaps to be transformed into a new model, more representative of CMC phenomena.

THE ROLE OF DIFFUSION MANAGER:
EXPANDING THE COMMUNITY OF USERS

Nature of the Role

An intentional online community (as opposed to a spontaneous one) comes into being when a large organization such as a university, a corporation, or a governmental bureaucracy decides to move its people into online communication. The diffusion manager's contribution is essential to the success of intentional online communities. The diffusion manager must entice members of the organization to engage each other via online communication. There are two aspects of this predicament the manager can consider. One is the set of perceptions members entertain before they have "taken the plunge." This line of research, developed over 50 years, is found under the rubric of technology transfer, adoption of innovations, adoption/diffusion process, and the adoption decisions process. A second way to view the situation is in terms of the activities or preoccupations of those who are already "in the pool." What are their goals, purposes, activities? What is their driving interest in continued involvement? This approach (referred to as "motivational orientations for participation") has been applied to research on voluntary participation in continuing adult education activities. A model by Houle, who conducted early studies on motivational orientations, offers insight into CMC adopters.

Houle's Model of Motivational Orientations

Houle began with a qualitative study of certain midlife adults, exemplary for the extent and fervor of their continuing education, in order to discern variations in their motivation for engaging in this voluntary activity. His study produced a three-part typology that identified goal-oriented, activity-oriented, and learning-oriented voluntary participants.

For Goal-oriented Participants
These people engaged in the new activity because of a desire to get ahead on their job, or to fulfill social roles or external expectations. Houle found that their engagement was sporadic and took place in response to specific needs. Their interest in the new activity was its immediate practicality.

For Activity-oriented Participants
These people engaged in continued education for reasons unrelated to the apparent purpose or content of the activities themselves. The activity provided fellowship and escape from the limitations of their immediate environment. Some of these people found a success or satisfaction that eluded them in their local work environment. They began sustained participation when their problems or needs for a change of scene became sufficiently pressing.

For Learning-oriented Participants
Learning and participating were constants in these people's lives from as early as they could remember, not an activity undertaken in adulthood. They were driven by a desire to know and, in every case, to seek out activities that provided them with an opportunity to extend their knowledge. Almost all these people were aware of their preoccupation with learning, and some displayed an urgent sense of their difference from the majority of their co-learners.

Applying "Participant Orientations" to CMC

Models created to describe participant orientations to taking part in adult education programs have something to tell us about participant orientations for involvement in CMC. Both contexts, continuing education and CMC, offer alternative social environments to the regular places that people live and work. Second, both continuing education and CMC environments further offer subsets of activity: for continuing education, this would be separate programs, courses, conferences, or workshops; for CMC, it's separate conversations and conferences. Third, both continuing education and CMC are more or less voluntary activities. The participant can disengage at will, although both contexts have exceptional instances in which people are in some way formally required to participate. But the general rule of continuing education still holds: if the participants are not getting what they want from the activity, they will leave. Finally, there is a similarity in that the collective activities of both continuing education and CMC involve participants who have personal agendas. Whatever the group purpose, each person has their own personal motives or reasons for participating and their own expectations.

Houle placed the following caveats on his typology: all people demonstrate each of these motives to some extent; no one orientation is innately better than any of the others; and this classification probably does not hold true for those who participate only occasionally. What the typology does assert is that an individual can be typed as engaging primarily through one of these three motivational orientations.

The diffusion manager should recognize that each of the basic approaches appeals to certain reluctant adopters of CMC. There is a goal-oriented appeal to those who have a managerial or administrative purpose to fulfill and who will perceive in CMC a way of keeping the edge, of staying current, of using state-of-the-art instruments to achieve what they already understand to be their goals and purposes.

Second, there is an activity-oriented appeal to aficionados who cannot resist online activity. Human communities are bound together by those members who thrive on social interaction. In the CMC context, there are two distinct subsets of these participants who are inherently "exploration-oriented." There are the "techies," who tirelessly explore the capacity of CMC programs, services, and networks. Then there are the social explorers who "mix," "mingle," and "gate-crash"—delighting in reaching and conversing with another human being who is geographically far away. The diffusion manager should gratefully acknowledge such enthusiastic activity. These people enrich the capacity of the system to benefit participants of the other two types.

Third, the diffusion manager will find, especially in educational organizations, those people who have a "knowledge orientation" to participation in CMC. In any large CMC network there will be those compelled to seek knowledge; in an educational CMC system there will be those who particularly want to understand "knowing and learning." These will be professional educators and researchers, people who want to link CMC to database searching, videotext teaching, online testing, library searching, and so on.

For a large organization moving online, the diffusion manager will serve an important liaison function between the system authors and managers, on the one side, and the diverse community of potential users, on the other side, who will require appropriate system adjustments to accommodate their "efficiency," "exploration," and "knowledge" orientations.

THE ROLE OF THE CONFERENCE MODERATOR

Nature of the Role

The moderator is like the lead player in a jazz ensemble. Participants do not know in advance what roles they will play in relation to the others: they begin the ensemble in pursuit of a theme; but how that pursuit will progress, the contributions to be made by each member, and how it is to be resolved to a satisfactory conclusion remain to be discovered. It is the moderator who organizes and leads each participant to create an ensemble. Through experience we have begun to gather inductively some guidelines for conference moderators. Brochet (1985) refers to special skills or functions of moderators at four stages of conference development: (1) successful beginnings, (2) nurturing the introductory stages, (3) maintaining the mature conference, and (4) wrapping up the conference. Brochet's work, which synthesizes advice from experienced moderators, emphasizes the moderator's role in assisting participants with the conferencing software and with focusing activity toward task completion. Least emphasized was the moderator's contribution to successful social dynamics of the conference. However, social dynamics should be viewed as essential to productive conferencing.

Conferences differ along several dimensions. Their membership may be restricted to a certain number of participants or open to anyone who has technical access. They vary in their purpose between clearly defined tasks and vague general reasons for being; and they vary in the domain they are addressing between managerial purposes, educational purposes, strictly social interactions, and the special case of research or intensely creative work. The remarks in this section are directed especially to moderators of conferences that have (1) a closed membership, all of whom begin to participate at more or less the same time; and (2) are given a demanding task. The model to be presented here is relevant to the process of moderating groups that aspire to the highest degree of synergistic productivity. The success of such conferences is determined by more than the structure of the CMC software and the nature of the task. Success will be predicated on achieving a dynamic structure of human beings in configuration—on the emergence of a single social entity from a collection of individuals.

Tuckman's Stages of Group Development

Tuckman (1965) produced a classic review of 50 articles dealing with stages of group development. The study encompassed
research on groups formed for personal therapy, human relations
training, professional projects, and laboratory exercises. Throughout, two realms of group functioning—its interpersonal relations
and its task activity—were compared. While the two realms are
distinct, it was found that over time their underlying dynamics
were similar. Across the 50 studies, Tuckman found that
whatever the group settings or length of group life, each group ex-
hibited close approximation to a four-phase pattern of group
development that is summarized below.

Phase 1:   "Forming"
Group structure in this phase is typified by individuals testing which behaviors will be acceptable in the group. They seek
boundaries for the situation in a manner dependent on the apparent authority figure. Members attempt to work out authority
problems by quick acceptance of and dependence on the most
readily available structure and rigid arbitrary norms. Tuckman
found this to be so even in an interdisciplinary professional group.
Task activity in this phase is typified by questions and behaviors aimed at identifying the task and how group experience
will be used to accomplish it. Members are seeking ground rules
for the task. There tends to be a quick initial acceptance of the
group's goals and a subsequent orientation to implementation
techniques to be used.

Phase 2:   "Storming"
Group structure in this phase is characterized by conflict,
frustration, and disruption at the group level and by anxiety,
threat, and resistance between individuals. Infighting is common.
Key issues polarize the group between those members who are
more active, experimental, and minimally defensive, and those
who are more passive, security seeking, and self-defensive. The
underlying current is a leadership struggle to determine whether
control will be monopolized, shared among a subset, or equally
shared among all group members.
Task activity in this phase is overshadowed by resistance to
the demands of the task. Far more emotionality about the task is
displayed than actual work on it. Task definition and analysis
provoke experimental aggression and hostility.

Phase 3:   "Norming"

Group structure in this phase becomes a reality for the first time as the group becomes an entity by virtue of the members' acceptance of it. The phase is characterized by the development of cohesion evidenced in mutual support. There is a notable reduction of conflict, resolution of the polarized issues, and a resolution of relations during which time tailored group norms and values emerge. Reforming and repair take place, and a flexible organization emerges. Members begin to conceive of the group as a unit and may show this with the emergence of a "team dialect." Members explicitly express concern for their integration, mutuality of interaction, and maintenance of interpersonal relationships.

In this phase, the group finally settles down. Task activity is characterized by openness and a free exchange of opinions in which information is acted on so that alternatives can be evaluated.

Phase 4:   "Performing"

Group structure in this stage attains a task-oriented role relatedness. One sees strong but flexible norms and the use of personal differences in the collaborative process. The group structure is functional rather than viewed as an end in itself (as in the preceding stage). Groups at this stage of development illustrate a positive interdependence. Members show a simultaneous autonomy and mutuality—that is, they can operate in any combination or as a unit.

Task activity at this stage reaches its fulfillment as solutions emerge and constructive action is undertaken. Remaining issues are dealt with in a less excited way. What is observed is a unified group applying itself to the task.

Applying "Stages of Group Development" to CMC

Thus far in the development of online social roles, our advice to conference moderators has stressed their function in the first phases of group formation. Members require and even demand guidelines, structure, parameters, assurance of what their contribution is to be. Our natural tendency as task-directed groups seems to have been to skip as quickly as possible from the first phase, getting oriented and organized, to the fourth phase, achieving the goal, tending to look on any digressions or objections as aberrations. Tuckman's model directs us to the fact that disruptions are an important and natural stage of true group formation. The real challenge lies at the level of learning how to work and even how to "be" together, rather than simply to focus on getting the job done.

Tuckman qualifies the model at the second level, called "storming," by saying that when the task does not deal with the self at a penetrating level, then extreme emotionality in the task area is not expected. But with the most creative aspects of academe—art, theater, engineering, anywhere a personality is a mark stamped on the product—it's difficult to separate the final product from the personhood of those who engaged in its creation. There are two kinds of threat operating at this second phase of group development. One has to do with the self-esteem tied up in task completion, and the other has to do with the self-concept tied up in one's relations to other members of the group as a social entity.

What is assumed in nurturing the process of group development is that the best product will be achieved when each member makes a full contribution; and, further, that personal agendas will be achieved when members can successfully navigate this second phase and come to terms with each other's idiosyncracies, arriving at a collectively defined set of new norms in Phase 3. In other words, group synergy for the highest level of task performance will follow from successful creation of a group through each member's acceptance of the others' place in the scheme of things.

It follows that one of the moderator's principal functions is to see that Phase 2 gets a full airing. The moderator can sanction the expression of alternatives and objections to the social structure as it is first presented in Phase 1, and then can facilitate the group moving on to Phase 3 by testing consensus and by trying to formulate for group approval the new social and operational norms that are emerging. Unless the group moves successfully through these two interim phases, it will not achieve the highest degree of productivity in Phase 4.

THE ROLE OF THE CMC COLLABORATOR

Nature of the Role

Conferences have participants: conference participants are so often engaged in making decisions, drawing conclusions, setting policies, and so forth that it might be desirable to refer to such people as "citizens," for if we call the new online collectives "communities," surely these communities have citizens. This section addresses the special communication demands that the medium directs to participants as online citizens and collaborators.

Among CMC users there has developed a kind of "folk wisdom" about what happens online. One example is an awareness that some participants are very much themselves online while others show marked differences between their face-to-face and their online personas. Another is that there seems to be more equally distributed air time in online meetings. It is also recognized that visual image prejudice is absent online: we speak of CMC tending to equalize status. On the other hand, we note dangers associated with the use of sarcasm, humor, irony, and other forms of double entendre online. Failure to answer a question or acknowledge a comment is taken more seriously than a simple lack of confirmation: neglect online can have the impact of negation for communicators new to the medium.

What seems to underlie these experiences is the threat to human communication when proximity precedes compatibility. In face-to-face meetings larger than three persons, it is not possible to sit side by side with every other person in the group. In CMC, however, this is precisely what happens. Every participants sits closely enough to whisper visually (screen-to-screen) with every other participant. Conference mode makes absolute proximity universal and unavoidable. This produces a contracted social space that does not allow for variable distance in accord with variable compatibility.

Furthermore, everyone is watching: each exchange is observed by every participant. A slip in courtesy can become a serious faux pas; a casual comment may be taken as an insult; a disagreement could be viewed as an argument. Intentions can be misconstrued and blown out of proportion.

However, certain insights generated by the term "online collaboration" remind us that communication is far from a natural thing for us; it is, in fact, intensive work undertaken together. The privacy and individuality of our internal, mental worlds make human communication highly problematic. William Perry describes how these mental frameworks affect our capacity to interact successfully.

Perry's Model of Cognitive and Ethical Development

Perry's Map of Cognitive and Ethical Development (1981) contains nine "positions" or stances a person can take, perspectives from which to view the world, to interpret and judge what others are saying and doing. These nine positions are sequenced through four larger phases labeled Dualism, Multiplicity, Relativism, and Commitment.

Each of the positions is illustrated below with a few phrases of subliminal self-talk characterizing a person in that cognitive and ethical development condition. Notice that Perry uses a change of voice from "we" the ignorant, in early stages, to "you" (meaning everyone) at position 5, and finally an active, self-responsible "I" beginning at position 6.

Dualism is a state of contrasted polarities wherein all that is not Good is Bad, all that is not Right is Wrong, all that is not Success is Failure, and so forth. Right answers exist somewhere for every problem, and authorities have the answer.

1. Authorities know, and if we work hard, read every word, and learn Right answers, all will be well.
2. True Authorities must be Right; all others are frauds. Good Authorities give us problems so we can learn to find the Right Answer by our own independent thought.

Multiplicity is a state of atomistic, free-floating, arbitrary personal opinion. It continues to assert that for some questions the Right Answers are known; for the remaining questions any opinion is as good as any other.

3. Some uncertainties are real and legitimate temporarily, even for Authorities. They're working on them to get to the Truth.
4a. Where Authorities don't know the Right Answers, everyone has a right to his/her opinion; no one is wrong.
4b. Authorities are not asking for the Right Answers; they want us to think about things in a certain way, supporting opinion with data.

Relativism is a state that accepts the existence of irreducible uncertainty and yet acknowledges that a procedure of disciplined metathought is possible whereby the diversity of opinions can be analyzed and judged for their relative merit.

5. Even for them, everything is relative but not equally valid. You have to understand how each context works. Theories are not Truth but metaphors to interpret data with. You have to think about how you are processing data.
6. I see I'm going to have to make my own decisions in an uncertain world with no one to tell me I'm right.

Commitment is a state in which the individual experiences that the capacity to act, including to make choices and affirmations, resides within oneself, not outside in the certainty once granted by Authorities.

7. Well, I've made my first Commitment (to a career, or marriage, or values). Transition: Why didn't that settle everything?
8. I've made several Commitments.   I've got to balance them—how many, how deep? how certain, how tentative?
9. This is how life will be.   I must be wholehearted while tentative, fight for my values yet respect others, believe my deepest values right yet be ready to learn.

Perry notes that there are several ways a person can try to avoid progressing along these frameworks. These include "temporizing" or postponement of movement until some condition has changed; "escape" through alienation or abandonment of responsibility; exploiting Multiplicity or Relativism in order to avoid Commitment; and "retreat," whereby one avoids complexity and ambivalence by regression to Dualism colored by hatred of otherness (Perry, 1981, pp. 78-80).

Applying "Interpretive Frameworks" to CMC

Successful human communication resides with the listener. Far from being a matter of broadcasting oneself to others, communication, as a process of engaging with one's environment in order to understand it, is principally and predominantly a matter of observing and listening.   CMC enhances the listener/observer's capacity to review and probe what has been said in order to interpret and understand it.   The nature of CMC lends itself to communication entailing more careful explication and understanding. Messages are read in a sequential (albeit rather plodding) way; there are no traffic jams like those in face-to-face discussion where excited conversation leads to "overwriting."   Second, the permanent written memory allows one to go back over, review, rethink, reinterpret the speaker's meaning. Third, the protracted nature of CMC allows one to seek clarification, to check the accuracy of one's explication of the speaker. Because CMC removes visual cues that identify speakers with a priori characteristics such as age, gender, socioeconomic status, or race, it causes participants instead to build up a composite picture of speakers from their statements: it refocuses attention from the speakers to the substance of their statements.

Participating in a CMC environment with Perry's model in mind enables us to go even further, to look beyond the substantive differences between statements, in order to analyze the cognitive and ethical assumptions underlying the way people may be thinking as they make their statements. The model also serves moderators well when they must analyze why seemingly insolvable conflicts arise in online discussion.

Perry's full model offers benefits for every participant who aspires to be collaborative, to help others learn as well as to help him/herself. At the very least you may be able to understand why another discussant will not engage further when you feel a satisfactory resolution has not been reached; and/or you may come to understand why your position is being maligned when you have only the best of intentions. The most encouraging feature of the model is that an individual can be propelled from one position to the next by those anomalies unaccounted for by the lesser position, making growth at least a possibility if not an inevitability. Researchers will be able to advance our understanding of these phenomena by studying them in CMC transactions.

Perry's model, relating as it does to each and every communication of each and every communicator, is for me the most significant one to consider because it is the most salient. Very few of us will serve as diffusion managers; from time to time we may serve as conference moderators; but every time we touch a CMC keyboard we collaborate in the new human culture that is emerging online. It is to this collaboration at the level of metathought that I will address concluding remarks.

CONCLUSION

This chapter began by suggesting that our species is migrating from local, embodied communities of interest to nonspatial, computer-mediated communities of interaction. In this migration we should not underestimate the consequence of shedding our distracting visual layer. In direct face-to-face dialogue, the visual aspect entertained the listener, embellished the message, and qualified and clarified communications. It also dissembled and camouflaged intended meanings. Without the visual, and with the permanent written record, we are directly confronted with the necessity to engage with our collaborators at some levels of metathought. We no longer need to, nor can we, avoid perceiving the coherent interpretive frameworks from which our collaborators are working.

The upper limits of this increasing mental intimacy are almost unimaginable. Teilhard de Chardin projected a far distant future in which

> Forced against one another by the increase in their numbers and the multiplication of their interrelations —compressed together by the activation of a common force and the awareness of a common distress—the men of the future will form, in some way, but one single consciousness. (Teilhard de Chardin 1964, p. 321)

From where we stand today, Teilhard's vision of the future is an inconceivably long way off. Yet with our present crude technology for eliminating the space/time between us, we have begun the move. Over time, as we accustom ourselves to mental proximity with collaborators whom we see and understand and accept with a thoroughness not usually accorded our co-workers, we may find ourselves—rather than disoriented by the experience—to be more than ever "at home."

REFERENCES

Brochet, M. (Ed.). (1985). *Effective moderation of computer conferences: Notes and suggestions.* Guelph, Ontario: Computing Support Services, University of Guelph.

Houle, C. O. (1961). *The inquiring mind.* Madison: University of Wisconsin Press.

—— (1977). "Motivation and participation with special reference to non-traditional forms of study." In O.E.C.D. *Learning Opportunities for Adults*, Vol. 3, (the nonparticipation issue). Paris: OECD, pp. 8-34.

———— (1980). *Continuing learning in the professions*. San Francisco: Jossey-Bass.

Perry, W. G. (1981). "Cognitive and ethical growth: The making of meaning." In A. W. Chickering and Associates (Eds.). *The modern American college: Responding to the new realities of diverse students and a changing society*. San Francisco: Jossey-Bass.

Teilhard de Chardin, P. (1964). *The future of man*. (Translated from the French by Norman Denny). London: Colins.

Tuckman, B. W. (1965). Development sequence on small groups. *Psychological Bulletin, 63* (6): 384-99.

PART III
Methodological Perspectives

Chapter 7
Evaluating the Virtual Classroom

Starr Roxanne Hiltz

EVALUATING THE VIRTUAL CLASSROOM

The Virtual Classroom® is a specially tailored and enhanced CMC system for learning and communicating. Students in the Virtual Classroom share their thoughts, questions, and reactions with professors and classmates, using computers and software that enables them to send and receive messages, interact with professors and classmates, read and comment on lecture material, take tests, and receive feedback without having to attend scheduled classes. Learning can take place at any location and at any time—using a computer on campus, at home or in the work place.

The primary goal of the project "Tools for the Enhancement and Evaluation of a Virtual Classroom" is to explore whether it is possible to use communication systems to improve access to and the effectiveness of postsecondary educational delivery. The most important "product" of the project is knowledge about the advantages and disadvantages of this new technology, as they may be influenced by variations in student characteristics and implementation techniques and settings. Evaluation is as important as software development for the Virtual Classroom project. The two key questions are the following:

1. Is the Virtual Classroom a viable option for educational delivery? That is, are outcomes, on the whole, at least as good as outcomes for traditional face-to-face courses?
2. What variables are associated with especially good and especially poor outcomes in this new teaching and learning environment?

This chapter presents the major methods of data collection that were developed, and discusses problems that arose and the relative fruitfulness of the different methodologies. Other aspects of the project will be only very briefly referred to (for full reports see Hiltz 1986a, 1987, 1988a, 1988b).

Overview of the Project

From 1985 to 1987, with major funding from the Annenberg/CPB Project, the New Jersey Institute of Technology (NJIT) constructed a prototypical virtual classroom, offering many courses fully or partially online. Students and professors, using personal computers, communicate with each other through a larger, centralized computer that runs a computer-mediated communications system called EIES® (Electronic Information Exchange System) enhanced with special software to support educational delivery. EIES runs only on a computer that is made by Perkin-Elmer Corp. and resides at NJIT. Subsequent versions of the Virtual Classroom on systems called TEIES® which operate on IBM mainframes and EIES2, which operates in the UNIX environment, are available for lease to other educational institutions.

The project has included iterative development of both software and teaching techniques. We implemented innovations, collected data to provide feedback, and then modified the software or the teaching techniques to try to take better advantage of the potentials of the medium. We hope that others can learn from our experiences. In particular, the evaluation instruments developed are available to others to use (with attribution, please), as appendices in the full research reports. If other investigators use some of the same indicators to explore some of the same issues that we did, this would aid in the building of a cumulative body of knowledge about online education.

Software Innovations
Conceptually, we divided these into (1) a set of structures, called Branch Activities, that could be attached to a class conference in order to support special types of assignments or delivery of material for activities that were to involve the whole class; (2) a set of teaching support tools to help the instructor manage assignments and grading of quizzes for individual students; and (3) microcomputer-based software for the integration of graphical information with text information.

An "activity" is an executable program rather than ordinary text. For example, initial activity types include reading of long documents, examinations, conditional question and response delivery, compiling and running Pascal or Fortran programs, and selection of choices from a list (see Hiltz 1986c). Instructional management tools include an electronic grade book and routines to collect and track the handing in of assignments (see Gleason 1987). Another major tool is "Personal TEIES®," which allows the composition, display, and communication of mixed text and graphics elements (see Foster 1987).

Collaborative Learning Strategies
Computer-mediated communication is particularly suited to the implementation of collaborative learning strategies or approaches. Collaborative learning means that both teachers and learners are active participants in the learning process; knowledge is not something that is "delivered" to students in this process, but something that emerges from active dialogue among those who seek to understand and apply concepts and techniques. All courses in this project attempted to include collaborative learning elements (see Johnson and Johnson 1975; Bouton and Garth 1983; Whipple 1987).

An Overview of the Research Methods

In order to explore our key research questions, it was necessary to observe a variety of types of courses, students, and implementation environments. The primary research design rests upon matched but "nonequivalent" sections of the same course taught in the Virtual Classroom (VC) and in the traditional physical classroom. The same teacher, text and other printed materials, and midterm and final exams were used; the classes are "nonequivalent" because the students were able to select the delivery mode. The matched courses included introductory sociology at Upsala College, freshman-level computer-assisted statistics at Upsala, introduction to computer science at NJIT, and an upper-level course in statistics at NJIT. The two colleges provided very different implementation environments. Upsala is a small liberal arts-oriented college with one microcomputer laboratory and little prior integration of computing into the curriculum; NJIT is a technological university where, for the last three years, incoming freshmen have been issued IBM-PC compatible microcomputers to take home, and computers are used in all freshman-level courses.

Three online courses were repeated, to allow the instructors to improve them, based on experience, and to increase the number of subjects in the study. In addition, some courses were taught with mixed modes of delivery (partially online and partially face-to-face). One section of NJIT's management course for majors in other fields (OSS 471) conducted its management laboratory exercises in the traditional manner (offline), and another used the VC as a "virtual laboratory." Other courses that used VC in a mixed or adjunct mode included organizational communication, a freshman writing seminar, an anthropology course on North American Indians, and a course in business French (all at Upsala). In addition, the project included some data collection on courses offered online to distance education students by other institutions: the media studies program offered by the New School through Connected Education on EIES, and a graduate-level course offered by the Ontario Institute for Studies in Education (OISE) on the PARTIcipate system. Altogether, we collected data from a total of 150 students in completely online courses, 111 in mixed-mode courses, and 121 in traditional or "control" courses.

Most of the data used in the study were collected with a pre- and post-course questionnaire. However, we also have behavioral data (including grades, when appropriate or available, and amount and type of online activity), and qualitative observations and interviews.

EDUCATIONAL TECHNOLOGY AND EDUCATIONAL EFFECTIVENESS

There is extensive literature on the effects of the medium of communication on learning; on educational innovations in general; and on the instructional uses of computers in particular. In addition, there are many publications in the area of computer-mediated communication, and a few on the use of computer-mediated communication to support educational delivery. Each of these areas of previous research has relevance for predicting problems, opportunities, and effects in implementing a "virtual classroom."

Communication Medium and Educational Outcomes

Previous studies of courses delivered by television or other noncomputer media tend to indicate "no difference" in basic outcomes. For instance, Schramm (1977, p. 28) states:

Overall, there is no basis in the research for saying that students learn more or less from television than from classroom teaching. This does not mean that under some conditions of teaching some students do not learn more of a certain subject matter or skills from one medium or channel of teaching than from the other. But the results of the broad comparisons say that there is, in general, no significant difference.

Each medium has advantages and disadvantages. Outcomes seem to be related more to the particular implementation of an educational use of a medium than to the intrinsic characteristics of a medium. Implementations that capitalize on the strengths of a medium, and that adjust for or circumvent its limitations, can be expected to be successful. Certainly, we know that some courses offered in the traditional classroom are more successful than others, and that this can be related to variations in the teaching skill and style of the instructor. Thus, it is not that "media do not make a difference," but that other factors may be more important than, or interact with, the medium in affecting educational outcomes for students. A primary goal in studying a new medium of communication for educational delivery must be the identification of effective and ineffective ways of using it. Clark and Salomon (1986, p. 10), discussing past research on the instructional impact of new media, summarize the lesson as follows: "Even in the few cases where dramatic changes in achievement or ability were found to result from the introduction of a medium such as television...it was not the medium per se which caused the change but rather the curricular reform which its introduction enabled."

The "curricular reforms" that the VC approach may enable are greater utilization of "active learning" and of "group learning."

The Computer and Active Learning

Development of the computer as an aid in the educational process has thus far focused on computer-assisted instruction

(CAI). In CAI, the student is communicating with a program in the computer that may provide a tutorial, drill and practice, or simulation and modeling exercises. At least for certain types of students and instructional goals, CAI can be more effective than traditional methods alone. In their comprehensive review of CAI, Chambers and Sprecher (1980) conclude that it has many advantages when used in an adjunct or supplementary mode within a regular classroom, with class discussion following. Learners are forced to be actively involved in the learning process, and each may proceed at his/her own pace. Feedback tailored to the student provides reinforcement that aids learning. However, as the sole or primary mode of instruction for distance learning, CAI appears to be effective only if there is also "significant" communication between teacher and student: "Primary CAI, and distance learning in general, may achieve results similar to those for adjunct CAI as long as there is sufficient human interaction accompanying the use of the CAI materials" (Chambers and Sprecher 1980, p. 336).

Bork (1981) has been prominent among those who advocate the use of the computer as a "responsive learning environment." Creating an "active learning situation" (Bork 1985) is the prime consideration in computer applications to education, from this point of view. The "drill-and-practice" CAI approach has been a limiting and negative influence upon developing the educational potentials of the personal computer. Too often, people using computers "tend to transpose books and lectures, and so they miss the component of active learning which is so important" (Bork 1985).

Instructional Strategies: The Concept of Collaborative Learning

Computer-mediated communication (CMC) is particularly suited to the implementation of collaborative learning strategies or approaches. Literally, to collaborate means to work together (co-labor). Teachers and learners are active participants in the learning process; knowledge is not "delivered" to students, but emerges from active dialogue among those who seek to understand and apply concepts and techniques. In the collaborative learning model,

Education does not consist merely of "pouring" facts from the teacher to the students as though they were glasses to be filled with some form of intellectual orange juice.

> Knowledge is an interactive process, not an accumulation
> of Trivial Pursuit answers; education at its best develops
> the students' abilities to learn for themselves.... Another
> way to say this is that collaboration results in a level of
> knowledge within the group that is greater than the sum
> of the knowledge of the individual participants. Col-
> laborative activities lead to emergent knowledge, which
> is the result of interaction between (not summation of)
> the understandings of those who contribute to its for-
> mation. (Whipple 1987, p. 5)

For example, most online courses included one or more
"seminar" segments in which the students became the teachers.
Individuals or small groups of students were responsible for reading material not assigned to the rest of the class; preparing a written summary for the class of the most important ideas in the
material; and leading a discussion on the topic or material for
which they were responsible. Seminar format is generally
restricted to small classes of very advanced students in the face-to-
face situation, because it is too time-consuming to have more than
about 15 students doing major presentations. Second, less advanced students may feel very embarrassed and do not present
material well in an oral report to their peers, and are even worse
at trying to play the role of teacher in conducting a discussion. In
the written mode, they can take as long as they need to polish
their presentations, and they are judged on the quality of their
work and ideas, not their public speaking skills. Other students
can read material in much less time than an oral presentation
takes. If the material is poorly presented, they may hit the "break"
key, whereas etiquette in the face-to-face situation dictates that
they must sit and suffer through a poor student presentation.
Finally, it is easier for students to "play the role" of teacher in this
medium, which is more egalitarian than face-to-face communication. Seminar style presentations and discussions are thus an example of a collaborative learning activity that is often difficult in
the traditional classroom, but that tends to work very well in the
Virtual Classroom environment, even with fairly large classes of
undergraduates.

Another example is the role-play or the simulation. In the
"Virtual Management Lab," NJIT management students applied
the theories and techniques they were studying to a simulation of
the first fiscal year of a hypothetical corporation. They decided
how to organize the corporation, selected the individuals to play
roles such as president and vice president for finance, and
developed a product plan, a marketing plan, an information

management plan, and all of the other management tools that would need to be developed in a "real" organization. The instructor, Enrico Hsu, played the role of the market, the government, and other event-generating entities in the environment.

Another form of collaborative activity is peer learning groups. In a freshman writing seminar, for instance, groups of six students formed an online writing group. Each student entered his/her first draft of a paper for others to see and comment on. Each writing group member was required to make constructive suggestions on the drafts of each of the others, responding to specific questions provided by the instructor (e.g., How can the opening be improved? What suggestions can you make to improve the organization of the essay?).

THEORETICAL FRAMEWORK

This study builds upon previous work on acceptance of computer-mediated communication systems and on teaching effectiveness, in conceptualizing the variables that can be expected to affect the process and outcome, and measuring them.

"Acceptance" or "success" of computer systems is sometimes assumed to be unidimensional. For instance, if students use an interactive computer system, then it may be defined by promoters or implementers of computing in education as "successful." "Technicists" (see Mowshowitz 1981) or "systems rationalists" (see Kling 1980) may assume that if a system is implemented and being used, then the users must like it, and it must be having the intended beneficial impacts. However, many social analyses of computing do not assume that use alone implies success (see, for instance, Keen 1981; Attewell and Rule 1984; Strassman 1985).

In one study of the users of four systems, three components of acceptance of CMC systems were found to be only moderately interrelated: use, subjective satisfaction, and benefits (Hiltz, Kerr, and Johnson 1985; Hiltz and Johnson 1987). These three dimensions of "success" were used in the present study. It was expected that there would be positive but only moderate correlations among the amount and type of use of the system made by a student; subjective satisfaction with the system itself; and outcomes in terms of the effectiveness of learning. We have several key measures of amount and type of use: total hours of connect time, number of log-ins, number of conference comments composed, number of private messages sent, and number of different addressees to whom private messages were sent. Measures of the effectiveness of learning or "outcomes" and of subjective satisfaction with the system are described in detail below.

Theoretical Framework and Independent Variables

Four major approaches to studying the acceptance and diffusion of computer technology and its impacts on society were identified: technological determinist (characteristics of the system); social-psychological (characteristics of the users); human relations (characteristics of the groups and organizations within which systems are implemented); and interactionist or systems contingent. This classification uses theoretical perspectives presented in the work of Kling (1980) and Mowshowitz (1981), and empirical approaches from the work of Zmud (1979) and others on the effects of individual differences on the adoption of MIS and other technologies.

Technological Determinants

Rob Kling, in his review of theoretical approaches (1980), identifies "systems rationalists": those who tend to believe that efficiently and effectively designed computer systems will produce efficient and effective user behavior. Mowshowitz's typology of theoretical approaches to the study of computing issues has a parallel category: the "technicist," who "defines the success or failure of particular computer applications in terms of systems design and implementation" (1981, p. 148). From the viewpoint of technological determinism, characteristics of the system or technology determine user behavior. Applying this approach to prediction of success of the Virtual Classroom, we would expect to find "uniform impacts" (Ehrmann 1986) of the same system on different students and among different classes. This perspective would lead one to ask, "What are the central tendencies or average outcomes in the Virtual Classroom?"

The psychological or "individual differences" approach to predicting human behavior when confronted with a new technology emphasizes individual characteristics: attitudes and attributes, including "personality type," expectations, beliefs, skills, and capabilities (Zmud 1979). Attitudes consist of an affective dimension involving emotions ("Computers are fun") and a cognitive dimension based on beliefs ("Using this system will improve my education"). In the context of this study, this approach predicts that student characteristics and pre-use expectations about the specific system will be strongly correlated with actual use of and reactions to the system. Among the individual attributes that we expected to affect success are ability (measured by SAT scores), sex, and ethnic group or nationality. We did not expect age, previous use of computers, or typing skills to affect use or outcomes, but we included them in order to check for these influences. Measures of these variables are straightforward.

The personality-level attributes that we expected to affect educational outcomes in the Virtual Classroom have to do with self-discipline, which may be related to perceived sphere of control; we predicted a moderate relationship between measures of sphere of control and acceptance.

Work on the conceptualization and measurement of "locus of control" built for many years on the work of Rotter (1966), who devised a single scale to measure internal vs. external locus of control. Paulhus (1983; see also Paulhus and Christie 1981) devised a new set of 30 items based on a theory of 3 separate "spheres of control" (SOC) that could vary independently. Personal Efficacy as a sub-scale measures control over the nonsocial environment (is personal achievement a result of one's effort, or of "luck"?). Interpersonal control measures control over people in dyads and groups. Sociopolitical control refers to control over social and political events and institutions. A confirmatory factor analysis, correlations with measures on other scales, and experimental research that predicted behavior on the basis of SOC subscale scores supported the reliability, validity, and utility of the three subscales. For this study, the personal efficacy and interpersonal control scales were mixed in the baseline questionnaire.

The human relations approach "focuses primarily on organizational members as individuals working within a group setting" (Rice 1986). The small groups of which an individual is part are seen as the most powerful determinants of behavior. From this perspective, participation in the decision to use the Virtual Classroom, user training and support, the nature of existing ties among group members, and the style of teaching or group management (electronic or otherwise) are crucial determinants of the acceptance and impacts of a new computer or communications technology. This theoretical perspective predicts large differences among the courses in which the students are enrolled, corresponding with differences in social interaction among the groups and in skill and level of effort of the teacher.

In the interactionist (Markus 1983) or systems contingency (Hiltz 1988c) approach to the social impacts of computing, all of the above three classes of variables are expected to affect outcomes in the VC. This approach was adopted for the present study. The variables are not simply additive; they interact to form a complex system of determinants. For example, student ability and attitudes are presumed to interact with educational technology: favorable outcomes are contingent on certain levels of student ability and motivation. This theoretical perspective can be equated with what Kling (1980) calls the "package" or interactionist approach to the social impacts of computing. In Mowshowitz's classification, we are termed "pragmatists," taking the position that "the use made of computers is determined in part by the social or organizational settings in which they are introduced" (Mowshowitz 1981, p. 150).

EDUCATIONAL OUTCOMES TO BE MEASURED

Educational outcomes of a delivery medium can be looked at for students or for faculty members. The quantitative data we collected focus upon outcomes for students; qualitative or anecdotal data document the effects on the instructors. (Only a handful of faculty members participated, making statistical analysis unsuitable.)

Eleven hypotheses guided the data collection and analysis strategies. Extensive analyses of data tested the hypotheses. Since these represent a voluminous amount of material, they are not presented in this report (see Hiltz 1988).

Mastery

Shavelson et al. (1986, p. vi.) state:

Telecourse evaluations must ultimately focus on outcomes and address the exchangeability of these outcomes with those attained by students in traditional courses. By "exchangeability" we mean the extent to which the knowledge, skills, and attitudes acquired by students from a telecourse are interchangeable with the knowledge, skills, and attitudes that are: (a) valued by faculty and administrators, and (b) acquired by students enrolled in the same course offered as part of the traditional curriculum.

The most basic of the desirable outcomes for a course is mastery of the fundamental facts, concepts, and skills that the course is designed to teach. Such mastery is usually tested by examinations and assignments that are graded. Of course, a score for a ten-minute quiz or a one-hour essay question is only a proxy measure for student mastery of the content of a course. Students can also be asked to report their impressions of the extent to which a course improved their mastery of concepts, skills, or facts. For this purpose we used postcourse questionnaire items drawn from widely used measures of teaching effectiveness. In our analyses both instructor-assigned grades and student self-reports measure achievement of learning goals in a course. If there is no difference in test scores for material presented online vs. material presented in traditional face-to-face courses, we may consider this a criterion for minimal "success" of the Virtual Classroom.

Given that previous studies of courses delivered by television or other noncomputer media tend to indicate "no difference" in this basic outcome, (e.g., Schramm 1977), we do not expect significant differences in grade distributions between VC and TC (traditional classroom) sections of a course. Though there may be some variation from course to course, depending upon the nature of the subject matter and the characteristics of the students, we expect that overall:

Hypothesis 1: There will be no significant differences in scores measuring mastery of material taught in the virtual and traditional classrooms.

Measuring Improved Writing

Since all communication in the VC is in writing, and students will see one another's writing, practice in written communication may improve skills. Good writing in fact combines a number of skills, including organization, sentence structure, grammar, and the almost indefinable elements of "voice" and "style" that make it interesting or engaging. Thus, improvements in writing skill are very difficult to measure.

    Computers in the form of text processors and spelling check-
ers have been used from elementary school on up to try both to
speed up and to improve the writing process. As Daiute (1985)
points out, if electronic mail or computer conferencing is added to
the word processing capabilities, one can expect some additional
possible improvements, because, after all, writing is supposed to be
a "social" process, a process of communication. Using the computer not only to assist in the manipulation of text but also to communicate it to others may help to provide motivation, a source of
collaboration or constructive criticism, and a defined "audience."
"Setting writing in a wider communication context can help students express themselves more naturally, even when they are
writing formal essays" (Daiute 1985, p. 5). Moreover, "The computer conference can be a tool for consolidating and transmitting
ideas in writing at a time when the writer feels most communicative, most excited, or most confused" (Daiute 1985, p. 25).
    As Daiute (1985, p. xiv) explains:

> With the computer as the instrument, writing is more
> like talking. Writers interact with the computer instru-
> ment, while the pen and the typewriter are static tools.
> The computer enhances the communication functions of
> writing not only because it interacts with the writers but
> also because it offers a channel for writers to communi-
> cate with one another and because it can carry out a
> variety of production activities. Writing on the computer
> means using the machine as a pencil, eraser, typewriter,
> printer, scissors, paste, copier, filing cabinet, memo pad,
> and post office. Thus, the computer is a communication
> channel as well as a writing tool. The computer is a lan-
> guage machine.

    Freed from the need to constantly recopy when revisions are
made, the student using a word processing program can sup-
posedly revise more easily and thus produce a better final version.
However, using the computer in the writing process can have disadvantages as well as advantages. (For some case studies and
reviews, see Bridwell, Sirc, and Brooke 1986; Collins 1982; Daiute
and Taylor 1981; Kiefer and Smith 1984; Malone 1981.) Nontypists
may be able to write much faster by hand than by using a
keyboard. In addition, in order to write using a computer, the student has to access and "power up" the equipment and software,
and learn to use the commands of the text-editing system as well
as of the larger computer system in which it is embedded. The few
studies of comparative writing quality have shown that writing on
the computer is sometimes rated lower than writing done by the

same people with traditional tools. It may be more "sloppy," because it is more like talking. Spoken sentences often are loosely constructed, and there tend to be more grammatical errors in speech, and more use of phrases such as "sort or" and "kind of." Computer drafts also tend to have more spelling errors (which may be "typos") and syntax errors caused by omitted and repeated words. Finally, "this research is not conclusive, because none of the studies have been done after the writers have become as comfortable with the computer as they are with pen or typewriter" (Daiute 1985, p. 113).

The major objective of the writing seminar at Upsala College is to improve writing. The students in one of these classes had the Virtual Classroom available for part of their work. All of their writing assignments were done in small groups online, and the students were asked to critique one another according to guidelines provided by the instructor. The impact on their ability to write clearly and well was assessed, using data generated by standard before-and-after testing procedures at Upsala. Every freshman is given a "holistically graded" written essay exam upon entrance, and again in the spring semester, after the writing course has finished. We took advantage of this existing data to attempt to compare changes in writing scores for the experimental online section with changes for students in the other sections.

Hypothesis 2: Writing scores will improve more for students in a writing course with access to the VC than for students in similar courses who do not use the system.

Other factors may affect the validity of these data. Students are not randomly assigned to the various sections, and the teachers and specific topics used for writing assignments vary. There is a methodological question as to whether a single "holistic" assessment of writing quality captures specific types of improvement that may occur. Moreover, there is a serious question as to whether any single semester-long course can significantly improve writing. However, since the data were already being collected, we felt it was worth examining whether there would be within-score differences associated with system use.

Other Outcomes

A high examination score is only one of the many goals related to educational process and outcomes. Less tangible or higher-level changes may actually be of greater long-term value than the ability to score well on a test that covers a specific set of subject-matter material at a particular point in time. The italicized words in the list below are used in the remainder of this document to refer to the indicated outcome. The variables are given a brief conceptual definition below; their operational definitions are specified in later sections of this report.

Hypothesis 3: VC students will be more likely than TC students to report each of the following:
    3.1   *Convenient access* to educational experiences.
    3.2   Increased *participation* in a course. This may be due to convenience or ease of participating, and may be reflected in the regularity and quality of their assignments, reading, and contributions to class discussion. Though this may be considered a "process" rather than an "outcome" variable, student participation in the activities of a course is usually considered a desirable objective in and of itself.
    3.3   Improved ability to apply the material of the course in new contexts and *express* their own independent *ideas* relating to the material.
    3.4   Improved *access* to their *professor*.
    3.5   Increased level of *interest* in the subject matter, which may carry beyond the end of the course.
    3.6   Improved ability to *synthesize* or "see connection among diverse ideas and information" (Davis, Dukes, and Gamson 1981). Kraworth et al. (1984) define "synthesis" as "the putting together of elements and parts so as to form a whole, arranging and combining them in such a way as to constitute a pattern or structure not clearly there before."
    3.7   *Computer comfort*—improved attitudes toward the use of computers and greater knowledge of the use of computers. This was measured by repeating questions on attitudes toward computers before and after the course, and by directly asking the students if they have improved their computer competence.
    3.8   Improved ability to communicate with and cooperate with other students in doing classwork (group *collaboration*).

3.9   Improved overall *quality*, whereby the student assesses the experience as being "better" than the TC in some way, involving learning more on the whole or getting more out of the course.

Collaborative Learning as an Intervening Variable

Group collaboration experience is listed as a desirable objective in itself, because in "later life" people will often have to work together on team projects, rather than carrying out separate competitive efforts. "Group" or "collaborative" learning is also conceptualized for the VC environment, as a key means or process that may aid in achieving other objectives, such as mastery of the material. For instance, it is much easier to encourage students to look at and learn from one another's work when all students are entering their assignments online, compared with the TC, where this would require massive amounts of photocopying. However, some students may not take advantage of these opportunities to learn from their peers.

Group learning was measured for all participating students with a set of four items included at the bottom of the "general information" page of the postcourse questionnaire. In addition, for those students using the system, a number of items on the section labeled "comparison with traditional classrooms" were used as indicators.

Hypothesis 4: Those students who experience "group" or "collaborative" learning in the VC are most likely to judge the outcomes of online courses to be superior to the outcomes of traditional courses.

There may be conflict or inconsistency among some of the goals and processes in the VC. For example, self-pacing may conflict to some extent with collaborative learning. Irregular patterns of participation, though convenient for the individual learner, may make it difficult for groups to complete collaborative projects within a set time frame. In addition to examining measures of each of the individual processes and outcomes of interest, the project assesses the extent to which they are mutually supportive (positively correlated), independent (not correlated), or incompatible (negatively correlated).

Correlates of Outcomes

The theoretical framework adopted anticipates that many factors in addition to collaborative learning experiences will be associated with outcomes.

Hypothesis 5: Differences among students in academic ability (e.g., as measured by SAT scores or grade point average) will be strongly associated with outcomes in the Virtual Classroom. High-ability students will report more positive outcomes than low-ability students.

Good reading and writing skills are a precondition for collaborative learning in this environment. Since three of the courses have a mathematical foundation (the two statistics courses and the computer science course), basic quantitative or computational skills may also be necessary. An online course replaces all oral explanation with a writing-based discussion. Learning depends on asking questions and receiving responses from the instructor and the other students. Students who lack basic communication skills are likely to be unable or unwilling to formulate questions about any difficulties they are having.

Another set of personal characteristics that is likely to be related to outcomes is attitudes and expectations. Students must be motivated in order to discipline themselves to sign on regularly and to participate actively. The relevant expectations include attitudes toward computers, toward the system that will be used, and toward the course.

Hypothesis 6: Students with more positive pre-course attitudes toward computers in general and toward the specific system to be used will be more likely to participate actively online and to perceive greater benefits from the VC mode.

As discussed in the section on theoretical perspectives, the personality attributes related to self-discipline and achievement motivation that are expected to be correlated with student behavior in the VC may be tapped by measures of "sphere of control."

Hypothesis 7: Students with a greater "sphere of control" on both the personal and the interpersonal levels will be more likely to regularly and actively participate online and to perceive greater benefits from the VC mode.

Students do not actually take courses online within a homogeneous context. They take a particular course, which develops a social structure, heavily influenced by the style and skill of their instructor in conducting the course. According the the "human relations" approach, we would expect process and outcomes to differ among these groups or courses.

Hypothesis 8: There will be significant differences in process and outcome among courses, when mode of delivery is controlled. (Another way of stating this hypothesis is that there will be an interaction effect between mode and course.)

Implementation Issues

Adoption of this innovation is not likely to be strongly influenced by findings on comparative outcomes of traditional and virtual classes. It is more likely to be decided on "political" and practical economic grounds.

As Shavelson et al. note:

The telecourse is a controversial, emotionally charged issue in higher education. To some it represents a threat—indeed, the greater the sophistication of the course, the greater the competition and threat to traditional educational institutions, their curricula, and instructors. (1986)

Case study methods were used to document implementation issues. In particular, opposition to the experiment was recorded as well as dealt with. The practical problems of implementing the courses, and the costs in terms of time and hassles to faculty and staff, were described. This recording of largely qualitative aspects of the implementation can be used to suggest problems and solutions for future implementations.

The qualitative data on course implementations were obtained in three ways. The evaluator was an observer in each of the online classes (participant observation). In faculty workshops, held both online and face-to-face, implementation problems were discussed. Finally, each instructor offering a completely or partially online course was asked to produce a course report that included the following:

1.   Description of the topics covered in the course, with a syllabus or outline of what was covered week by week.
2.   Description of the materials and activities provided for the on-line class (type, length, frequency). How did these differ from TC class materials, activities, and scheduling, and why?
3.   Description of what worked well in terms of students seeming to learn and to participate, and the major problems (things that did not go over well). Included here might be problems with procrastination (uneven and delayed participation); software or hardware inadequacies; and getting students to actively ask questions or discuss issues. Also requested was a section on any "group" or "collaborative" learning activities; how these worked and how they did not.

Implementation issues were therefore treated in a mostly qualitative manner. Material from the course reports and the transcripts of online courses has been used to illustrate and explain the data obtained from questionnaires, grade distributions, and measures of online activity.

Two aspects of implementation can be explored with our quasi-experimental design and examined using quantitative rather than purely qualitative data. These are the effect of course repetition and the effect of the nature of the educational environment, as it varies among colleges.

Because the VC is a new approach, we expected that instructors would learn from their first attempts and improve their skills for teaching online with practice.

Hypothesis 9: Outcomes for the second offering of a VC course by an instructor will be significantly better than those for the first attempt at teaching online.

In addition, the Virtual Classroom was implemented within two very different educational environments. It was not possible to disentangle which differences between Upsala and NJIT explain differences in outcomes. However, it was expected that these outcomes would be influenced by differences in access to equipment, skill level, and computer experience of the students, and the general "educational environment" within which the experiment took place.

Hypothesis 10:

There will be significant differences between the Upsala and NJIT implementations of the VC, in terms of both process and outcomes of the online courses.

Two Modes or Three?

In the hypotheses above, mode of delivery is dichotomized: courses using VC versus those conducted totally in a TC environment. The initial design for this field study anticipated only two modes of delivery. In fact, as actually implemented, we had three modes of delivery: totally VC, totally TC, and mixed. Is the mixed mode some sort of average of the other two modes? We have no prior studies to draw on, but we suspect that it is not.

Hypothesis 11:
> Results for the "mixed" mode will not represent a simple "average" of results for totally VC and totally TC modes, but will represent a distinctive set of strengths and weaknesses.

This is admittedly vague. What it means is that in each of the preceding hypotheses, we were aware that there may be significant differences between VC courses offered totally online and those offered in a mixed mode.

RESEARCH DESIGN

The standard experimental design of random assignment to matched sections of traditional and experimental courses cannot be used for evaluation of the VC: it is neither practical, ethical, nor particularly relevant. Students cannot be randomly assigned to sections of a course meeting at different times, given the constraints of their other obligations, and the same instructor obviously cannot teach two sections of the same course at the same time. It is not ethical, because this is an experiment; there is some risk that the outcomes will not be favorable, and students should voluntarily agree to assume the risk of using an experimental form of delivery for an entire course. Finally, it is not methodologically sound in terms of estimating future impacts. Students who choose telecourses, especially telecourses delivered via computer, are likely to differ from students choosing traditional courses in non-random ways. They are more likely to have out-of-class obligations that make it difficult for them to attend regularly scheduled classes, for instance, and to have more positive attitudes toward computers. Random assignment is also not methodologically sound when one of the objectives is to explore variations among on-line classes. For many online courses there simply are no "face-to-face" equivalents, because they are designed specifically for distance education; and many traditional classes, such as biology or chemistry, require laboratory equipment for which no online equivalent is possible at present.

Shavelson et al. (1986) identify three designs relevant to evaluating student outcomes from telecourses:

1. "Uncontrolled Assignment to Form Nonequivalent Groups," in which students self-select into tele-courses or traditional courses. "Before" and "after" knowledge and skills are measured. This is the primary evaluation design chosen for this study.
2. "Patched-up Design" is "appropriate when institutions regularly cycle students through the same course, such that students from one cycle can serve as a control group for students from another cycle." Unfortunately, this is not the case at NJIT or Upsala, and the design can be used only to a very limited extent: to compare first vs. second VC offerings by the same instructor.
3. "Case Study Methods" provide narrative (descriptive and qualitative) accounts. Elements of the case study method were included.

This set of research design choices, however, ignores the important question of variation in success within telecourses. In examining the question of "assessing interactive modes of instruction," Davis, Dukes, and Gamson reach the following conclusion:

> Low priority should be given to conventional evaluation studies that compare a control group using a conventional classroom with an experimental group using some interactive technique.... We doubt that fruitful, context-free generalizations can be found demonstrating that one technique is uniformly better than another, even for specific learning objectives.
>
> Our alternative approach accepts the fact that these techniques show no evidence of general inferiority to conventional techniques.... The focus should be on the conditions under which given interactive techniques are most and least appropriate. We need to know the contextual variables that maximize the effectiveness of a given method. (1981, pp. 321-22.)

The Virtual Classroom is a new educational technology: we think it still necessary to prove that it is just as good as a traditional classroom for mastery of facts and information. For this purpose, we performed a traditional evaluation of experimental and quasi-experimental design. For each of five target undergraduate courses, we matched the same course with the same teacher, texts, and tests in TC mode with a mode employing the VC. Examination scores and other outcomes are compared for the two sections. At the core of the evaluation design, then, is a 2 x 5 factorial design, with each of five courses offered in two modes of delivery (see the top of Table 7.1).

This basic design was supplemented with data from other courses that used the VC in a variety of ways. Three analyses involved the following:

1. The online courses that are repeated fall and spring, analyzed as a quasi-experimental factorial design with 4 (course) by 2 (first vs. second offering) conditions (middle display of Table 7.1).
2. Differences among modes in terms of totally online courses vs. traditional classroom courses vs. mixed-mode courses: one factor, three levels of treatment. This gives us the largest number of subjects; the number for whom at least some data are available is shown at the bottom of the diagram for "design 3."
3. Contextual factors related to the conditions under which VC was most and least effective. These include differences among courses and organizational settings, and differences related to student characteristics, attitudes, and behavior. One of the major contextual variables considered was the institution within which a course is conducted. The third display in Table 7.1 shows the basic 3 (modes) by 4 (colleges) design for this analysis.

EVALUATION INSTRUMENTS AND PROCEDURES

Data collection and analysis were (and are) conducted under "protection of human subjects" guidelines, whereby all participating students are informed of the goals and procedures followed in the project and the confidentiality of the data is protected. Various methods are used for data collection, including questionnaires for students, automatic monitoring of online activity, participant ob-

Table 7.1 Quasi-experimental Designs for Assessing Differences in Outcome by Mode

Number of Students for Whom
Data Are Available Shown in Cells

Design 1
COURSE BY MODE

COURSE	ONLINE	FTF
CIS 213	13	18
MATH 305	12	22
MANAGEMENT	28	24
INTRODUCTORY SOC	16	19
STATISTICS	11	15
TOTAL	80	98

Design 2
REPETITION OF ONLINE COURSES

COURSE	FALL	SPRING
CIS 213	13	19
MATH 305	12	24
MANAGEMENT	28	30
STATISTICS	11	11
TOTAL	64	84

Design 3
SCHOOL BY MODE

	ONLINE	MIXED	FTF	TOTAL
UPSALA	41	38	26	105
NJIT	71	58	63	192
CONNECT-ED	13			13
OISE	7			7
TOTAL	132	96	89	315

servation in the online conferences, use of available data (such as grade distributions or test scores) for participating students, descriptive case reports by the instructor for each course, and a small number of personal interviews.

Questionnaires

Pre- and postcourse questionnaires completed by students are the most important data source. The pre-course questionnaire measures student characteristics and expectations. The postcourse questionnaire focuses on detailed evaluations of the effectiveness of the online course or course segments, and on student perceptions of the ways in which the VC is better or worse than the TC.

The pre-course questionnaire was administered and collected at the beginning of the first "training" session in which EIES comprised or supplemented the instructional delivery mode. For Connected Education students and OISE students, the pre-course questionnaire was included with the mailed system documentation, with immediate return requested.

Postcourse questionnaires were distributed about a week before final exams, then the instructor collected each questionnaire when the exam was handed to each student. If the questionnaire was not completed, the instructor handed a new one to the student and asked her/him to complete it after finishing the exam. Students were told that they could stay extra time if necessary to complete the questionnaire. A student might refuse to complete a questionnaire, under the protection-of-human-subjects regulations; this did not affect the course grade in any way.

For courses in "mixed" mode, the postcourse questionnaire was distributed and collected in class, toward the end of the semester. A mailing with two follow-up requests was used for Connected Education students and for students who were absent during the in-class administration.

Measuring Course Effectiveness

The postcourse questionnaire included items used to measure students' subjective assessments of courses. These items were developed on the basis of a review of the literature on teaching effectiveness, particularly Centra's (1982) summary. Copies of the available student rating instruments described in that book, and permission to use items from these standard questionnaires, were obtained. Effectiveness was conceptualized as being related to four dimensions: course content, characteristics of the teaching, course outcomes, and comparisons of process in the virtual and on-line formats. These dimensions are presented as separate sections in the postcourse questionnaire, with the hope that the responding students might keep the dimensions separate in their ratings.

Not all institutions were willing to give permission to use items from their teaching effectiveness instruments. Among those from whom permission to use items for measuring effectiveness were obtained and from which items were used are the following:

- Center for Research on Teaching and Learning, University of Michigan (many items borrowed from their "catalog" of questions available for instructor-designed questionnaires)
- Evaluation and Examination Service, University of Iowa, Student Perceptions of Teaching (SPOT) test item pool (many items used or adapted)
- Endeavor Instructional Rating System, Evanston Ill. (a few items adapted)
- Instructor and Course Evaluation (ICE), Southern Illinois University at Carbondale (a few items adapted).

Almost all of these items from standard teaching effectiveness questionnaires suffer from the potential methodological problem of response bias. Likert-type items are worded positively, and the semantic differential-type items are arranged so that the most positive response constantly occurs on the same side of the page. Though rewording was considered for approximately half of the items, it was decided to leave them in their original forms so that the results might be more directly comparable with those for other studies using the same items.

Course evaluations by students are admittedly a controversial means of measuring course outcomes. They have been observed to vary with many factors in addition to teacher competence and student learning, such as an interaction between faculty status and class size (Hamilton 1980). Student evaluations are strongly related to grades received in the course. There is argument about which is the cause and which is the effect. If grades are "objective" measurements of amount of learning, then we would expect that students with higher grades in a course would subjectively report more positive outcomes. However, it may be that a student who has a good grade in a course rates that course and instructor positively as a kind of "halo effect" of being pleased with the course because of receiving a good grade. If so, we would expect student ratings on various dimensions to be somewhat homogeneous, with little discrimination among items measuring different aspects of the process or outcome. For example, students with a D or F would rate everything about the course as poor, while students with an A would rate everything about a course as excellent. Such distortions of teaching evaluations are probably more prevalent when the student raters know that their responses are being used as input for evaluating faculty in personnel decisions.

In this case, the participants knew that their ratings were used only for this research project, and the ratings were made before final grades were received. Despite the limitations of subjective ratings, the students were probably in a better position than anyone else to report on the extent to which they had or had not experienced various positive or negative outcomes from a course.

Survey of Dropouts

All students who dropped an online course or who requested transfer to the traditional sections were surveyed with a special questionnaire designed for this purpose. The questionnaire probed whether the action by the student was a "rejection" of the technology (e.g., dissatisfaction with the software or with response time, or inadequate access to equipment) or was unrelated to mode of delivery (e.g., personal problems, dislike of the subject matter in the course, or the work load required).

We had initially planned to have dropouts interviewed personally, either when the student saw an instructor about dropping a course or shortly after. However, this proved not to be practical. Though official regulations say that students dropping a course should see the instructor and that the registrar should inform an instructor promptly of drops, this in fact does not happen. Students "disappear" without formally dropping until the deadline for withdrawal, right before the end of the semester. They apparently also forge instructors' signatures on course withdrawal forms. In sum, our information on course withdrawals has proven to be so delayed that an immediate personal interview could not be conducted.

Dropouts who did not respond to the mailed questionnaire (with two mailed follow-ups) were contacted several times in order to try to interview them by telephone. They turned out to be very hard to reach; we were able to obtain only one such interview.

Automatic Monitoring of Use

We were using and refining software built into the current EIES system for measuring the amount and type of online activity by participants. A routine on EIES called CONFerence ANalysis (CONFAN) permits the tabulation and display of the number and percentage of lines and items contributed by each member of a conference, either for a specified part of the conference or for the entire conference. This automated analysis was run for each class conference. We will need to extend this capability in the future so that measures of participation in the "branches" can also be gathered and displayed. For this study, branch responses were manually counted and included in the results of the CONFAN.

Monthly "billing group" data available for each member of a billing group during the previous calendar month were recorded for the following:

- Total number of conference comments contributed. This is not a complete measure of student activity related to the class, since it excludes contributions made in "branches" (which were numerous for some courses), notebooks, or private messages. The latter is measured separately (see below)
- Total hours online
- Total number of log-ins to the system
- Total number of private messages sent
- Number of different addressees for private messages sent during the last full month. This is a rough measure of the number of different communication partners with whom students are exchanging information online.

By recording these data monthly, we can aggregate to obtain the total for the whole course, and examine the extent to which these measures of activity change during the course.

Other Types of Data

In addition to the standard questionnaires, the monitored data on participation, and grades on tests and the final grade for the course, several other types of data were gathered.

Institutional Data

During the 1986-1987 academic year, measures of general verbal and mathematical ability (the SATs) and level of academic performance (the grade point average) were obtained from college records for each student, if the student agreed and signed a formal release.

Feedback from Faculty

An online conference for faculty, messages exchanged with the project director, and two day-long face-to-face faculty workshops were used to exchange information about experiences conducting classes in the virtual classroom. All faculty members also produced descriptions of their experiences in teaching online. This, together with direct observation of the online classes, was used to generate the mostly qualitative data that served as the basis for the guide to teaching online included in Volume 2 of the final report (Hiltz 1988b).

Interviews with Students

Personal or telephone interviews were conducted with 10 students. Most of these students were selected from a list of 30 who had given the most positive or the most negative ratings of VC on the postcourse questionnaire, or who had dropped out and had not responded to the "dropout" questionnaire. A few "moderately negative" or "moderately positive" students were included in the personal interview sample, to fill the spectrum of reactions. The purpose of the interviews was to probe the reasons underlying the students' evaluations, and to explore the full context of experiences and circumstances that resulted in their opinions of the VC.

Content Analysis

Initially, we planned to do extensive content analysis of the transcripts of online courses, and to record sample sessions of matched traditional sections, and use the same content analysis techniques on them. The objective was both a content coding scheme applicable to this mode of communication, and a quantification of how differences in process would be related to differences in outcome. However, the content coding proved to be extremely time-consuming and expensive, and not very fruitful for our purposes. The initial target selected was a set of courses offered by the Western Behavioral Sciences Institute. The students in these courses take approximately one course a month for two years. We had them fill out a questionnaire rating the quality of six specific courses, hoping to correlate differences in subjectively assessed quality with differences in process. However, we discovered practically no variance in the proposed dependent variable: all the courses were graded as As.

A very rudimentary kind of content analysis employed the automated counts of the number and length of comments in class conferences by each participant. We hypothesized that "student-centered" courses, in which most of the content was contributed by the students, would be rated better than "teacher-dominated" online courses. This did not turn out to be true. Among the highest-rated courses some were "student-centered" and some were "teacher-dominated," according to our counts of relative proportions of contributions.

MEASURING THE VARIABLES

Many of the independent and dependent variables in this study are fairly simple and straightforward, such as age or gender, and were measured with single questions on the questionnaires. Others measure complex concepts, and were conceived from the beginning as composed of a number of dimensions, represented by a series of questions.

For all courses in all modes, a set of postcourse questionnaire items was used to measure student perceptions of general characteristics of the course content, the quality of the instruction, and course outcomes. An additional extensive set of items was used to measure student perceptions of the nature and quality of the online courses as compared with traditional courses. The first two sets of dependent variables (items dealing with course content and quality of the teaching) were treated only in terms of a combined index in this study, since they were not conceived of as being substantially influenced by mode of delivery. The two sets of variables measuring course outcomes and VC ratings were treated both individually and in combined indexes.

Constructing Indexes

Many of the conceptual constructs used in this study are multidimensional. It is more valid to use several items, each measuring a slightly different aspect of the variable, and then combine them, than to rely on one question. In building these indexes, items were included in the questionnaires that appeared to have "face validity": conceptually, they appear to measure some attitude or behavior that is included in the concept. Data from these intended scales were subjected to an item analysis to see if they were indeed correlated. A reliability analysis was conducted that computed Cronbach's alpha as an overall measure of the reliability of the composite measure. In this procedure, (provided by SPSSX but not by SPSS-PC), each designated component is left out of the total index and the alpha level is computed for an index without that item. In arriving at the final indexes, we omitted items that did not correlate well with the index as a whole, and/or items that substantially lowered the alpha value if they were included.

Composite independent variables include the Personal Efficacy and Interpersonal Control scales devised by Paulhus and Christie (1981) for measuring a person's perceived "sphere of control." The standard scaling items and scoring was used.

The set of items on "current feelings about using computers" were combined into a Computer Attitudes index (Table 7.2). The same items were repeated on the postcourse questionnaire, with that index labeled Computer Attitudes-2. Similarly, the items on "expectations about the EIES system" were combined into an EIES Expectations index (see Table 7.3).

In the Computer Attitudes index, an item on perceived reliability of computers was originally included. It did not correlate well with the other items, and lowered the reliability of the scale, so it was omitted. Apparently, people who otherwise have positive attitudes toward computers may nevertheless feel that they are unreliable.

Indexes formed by combining items from the "course rating" and "instructor rating" portions of the postcourse questionnaire are shown in Tables 7.4 and 7.5. Because all of these items were worded the same way on the questionnaires, with 1 or "strongly agree" the most positive response and 5 or "strongly disagree" the most negative, scores were not reversed on any items in constructing the index. This results in indexes for these two constructs for which the highest total scores correspond to the worst ratings. Key course-rating questions with high intercorrelations, chosen from both the Characteristics of the Course and the Course Outcomes section, were included in the Course Rating Index. All of the items on the instructor were included in the Instructor Rating Index.

Multiple items measuring the course outcomes of increased interest in the subject matter and in ability to synthesize material were combined into interest and synthesis indexes (see Table 7.6). The other items in the postcourse questionnaire section on course outcomes were used individually.

In the Collaboration Index (Table 7.7) we had initially included an item in the "individual vs. group learning" section of the questionnaire that asked the student to rate the degree of competitiveness among the students in the class. This item was not highly correlated with the other items that we thought indicate collaboration, such as making friends and working cooperatively. Apparently, collaborative work can proceed within a competitive environment. Perhaps when a competitive situation is perceived, students collaborate to form a team that can compete more effectively than an individual.

Four of the items asking the students to directly compare the VC with the TC were used for a composite "VC Overall" index (Table 7.8). An item on preferring traditionally delivered courses was omitted because it was used only in the spring; its inclusion would have lowered the number of cases greatly.

EVALUATION PROBLEMS AND FAILURES

We have already alluded to problems encountered in using content analysis in the examination of how communication processes in the VC differed from those in the TC, and how those differences might be related to outcomes. Several other methodological problems were encountered. These included the following:

- Failure to recruit the desired number of students for the VC sections, despite posters, brochures, and material with registration information
- Failure of the method used for measuring writing improvement. There was no difference between the VC section and the TC sections of the writing course in the postcourse holistic writing scores, or in the change in scores between the pre-test and the post-test.

However, there also was no significant difference for all of the sections combined in the pre- vs. post scores. A much more sensitive, detailed, and reliable measuring technique would be needed to capture changes in writing as the result of a single course

- Impossibility of rigid experimental control that "holds everything constant" except the medium of course delivery. This will be discussed in more detail below.

Relaxing Experimental Controls

The initial quasi-experimental design called for the "matched" sections of four courses to be "the same" in every way except that one section would be completely online (meeting face to face only for training, the midterm, and the final) and the other section would be completely face to face. They were to have the same content and the same assignments. The assumption that this could be done without crippling the potentials of the medium or raising ethical issues turned out to be incorrect. In fact, in all of target courses, adjustments had to be made.

Even before the semester started, the instructors pointed out that to require the same assignments in the matched sections would severely limit their ability to make use of the unique characteristics of the medium. The VC supports collaborative assignments and in-depth discussions, whereas the TC does not. So, though the offline reading assignments and the exams remained the same, the assignments given students were quite different for the two modes. This was true even for the Upsala statistics course, for instance, where the online section began with students filling out a questionnaire in the class conference, and then using the data provided by the other class members to carry out a statistical analysis. The offline section did this assignment using a presupplied data set.

The instructor for the NJIT statistics course found that many of the students wanted to work together in parallel, taking the opportunity to ask questions of her or the other students face to face, while working online. She scheduled a once-a-week, two-hour period when she was available in the NJIT microlab. About a third to half of the class seemed to show up each week (unfortunately, we did not keep records of which ones). Generally, there were periods of one or two students working silently at each of the terminals in the lab; periods where subgroups were in animated discussion around a terminal, pointing at the screen; and short periods when several or all of them were conferring with the instructor about a question raised by the online material. We had not anticipated this "group lab" adaptation of the medium, but the instructor felt that it worked well for her and her students.

In computer science, the instructor found that the students could read through and understand the written version of his lecture material in a much shorter time than was required to cover the same material by talking and listening and taking notes. Therefore, he supplemented the online section by adding some activities and material not included in his traditional section.

In sociology, the online assignments were totally different from those for the matched face-to-face section. The online assignments involved role-playing and discussions. However, the midterm exam was based mainly on the textbook. There were many more failures on the midterm in the online section. The instructor felt that perhaps this was not fair to the students, since they had been tested on material that was not similar to the assignments they had been doing. Therefore, two optional face-to-face exam review sessions were held, and those who attended were given the opportunity to retake the midterm. This incident underscores the impossibility of complete "matching." The two media are suited to very different types of learning and assignments, and it does not make sense to try to test the students using the same examination. Nevertheless, for this study, we stuck rigidly with the use of the same midterm and final in all courses.

Additional Methodological Hindsight

The personal interviews with students proved very valuable. It was extremely time-consuming to reach the students, conduct and record the interviews, and then transcribe them. However, they provided a great deal of insight into the personal experiences that underlay the statistical results.

On the other hand, the "sphere of control" indexes failed utterly to produce statistically significant relationships with use, satisfaction, or outcomes. The correlations were weak and generally not significant. It does not appear that they were worth the page of space they occupied on the pre-course questionnaire.

SUMMARY OF FINDINGS

Despite implementation problems, the results of this field experiment are generally positive, in terms of supporting the conclusion that the VC mode of delivery can increase access to and effectiveness of college-level education.

Results of statistical analysis of data relating to the major hypotheses are listed below. Findings related to the hypothesis that the mixed mode results would not simply represent an "average" of the VC and TC modes are included in reviewing other hypotheses.

H1:   There will be no significant differences in scores measuring mastery of material taught in the virtual and traditional classrooms.

Finding: No consistent differences. In computer science courses, VC final grades were significantly better.

H2:   Writing scores will improve for students with access to VC.

Finding: Writing score changes were not significantly different for the section that used VC. There were no detectable changes in scores for either mode. We do not know if this is because of the inadequacy of the holistic scoring method used, or because there was in fact no improvement in writing as a result of a one-semester course.

H3:   VC students will perceive VC to be superior to TC on a number of dimensions:

3.1   Convenient access to educational experiences (supported)

3.2   Increased participation in a course (supported)

3.3   Improved ability to apply the material of the course in new contexts and express their own independent ideas relating to the material (rejected: increased confidence in expressing ideas was most likely to occur in the mixed-modes courses)

3.4   Improved access to their professor (supported)

3.5   Increased level of interest in the subject matter, which may carry beyond the end of the course.

Finding: This is course-dependent. Though the averages for measures of increased interest are higher for both the

VC and mixed modes, the overall scores are not significantly different. Interest Index scores are highest for the VC mode at NJIT and for the mixed-mode courses at Upsala.

3.6   Improved ability to synthesize or "see connection among diverse ideas and information" (no significant differences overall; mode interacts with course).

3.7   Computer comfort—improved attitudes toward the use of computers and greater knowledge of their use (supported).

3.8   Increased levels of communication and cooperation with other students in doing coursework (group collaboration).

Findings: Mixed and course-dependent. For example, although 47 percent of all students in VC and mixed-mode courses felt that they had communicated more with other students than in traditional courses, 33 percent disagreed. The extent of collaborative learning was highest in the mixed-mode courses.

3.9   Improved overall quality, whereby the student assesses the experience as being "better" than the TC in some way, involving learning more on the whole or getting more out of the course (supported).

General Findings: Though the "average" results supported most of the above predictions, there was a great deal of variation, particularly among courses. Generally, the above outcomes depend more on variations among courses than on variations among modes of delivery. The totally online upper-level courses at NJIT, the courses offered to remote students, and the mixed-mode courses were most likely to result in student perceptions of the VC as "better" in any of these senses.

H4:   Those students who experience "collaborative learning" in the VC are most likely to judge the outcomes of online courses to be superior to the outcomes of traditional courses.

Finding: Supported by both correlational analysis of survey data and qualitative data from individual interviews. Students who experienced high levels of communication with other students and with their professor (who participated in a "collaborative learning" approach to their coursework) were most likely to judge the outcomes of VC courses to be superior to those of traditionally delivered courses.

H5 and H6: Outcomes are related to student characteristics.

Finding: In many cases, results of the quantitative analysis are inconclusive in determining which is "better," the VC mode or the TC mode. The overall answer is "It depends." Results are superior for well-motivated and well-prepared students who have adequate access to the necessary equipment and who take advantage of the opportunities provided for increased interaction with their professor and with other students, and for active participation in a course. Students who lack the necessary basic skills or who begin with a negative attitude will do better in a traditionally delivered course.

H7:   Students with a greater sphere of control will be more likely to participate in and perceive benefits from the VC mode.

Finding: There were no consistent associations with sphere of control. However, qualitative data gathered in student interviews indicate that the self-discipline to regularly set aside time to take part in online courses is a crucial determinant of success for the student.

H8:   There will be significant interaction between course and mode of delivery (supported).

H9:   Outcomes for second offerings of courses online will be better (supported; but not all differences were statistically significant).

H10:   There will be differences in outcomes related to differences between the NJIT and Upsala settings (supported; outcomes were better at NJIT, where equipment access was much better).

    The VC is not without disadvantages, and it is not the preferred mode for all students (or all faculty). Students (and faculty) report that they have to spend more time on a course taught in this mode than they do on traditional courses. Students also find it more demanding in general, since they are asked to play an active part in the work of the class on a daily basis, rather than just passively taking notes once or twice a week. For some students, the VC can be perceived as an imposition rather than an opportunity.

CONCLUSION

The VC is a viable option for postsecondary educational delivery. On the average, outcomes are at least as good as outcomes for traditional face-to-face courses. The average student who participated in this experiment felt that both access to and the quality of the educational experience were improved. However, improved outcomes are contingent upon providing adequate access to equipment, faculty effort and skill in teaching with this new tool, and student characteristics. Students who are motivated to explore the VC, are self-disciplined, and have average or better quantitative and verbal skills (as measured by tests such as the SAT) are likely to experience superior outcomes, compared with traditional courses. Students who lack this motivation and basic college-level skills, or who must travel to use a computer terminal for access, are more likely to drop out of an online course, to participate more irregularly, and to perform more poorly than they would in a traditional course.

Table 7.2 Items Combined into the Computer Attitudes Index

ITEMS IN THE COMPUTER ATTITUDES INDEX

For each of the following pairs of words, please circle the response that is closest to your CURRENT FEELINGS ABOUT USING COMPUTERS. For instance, if you feel computer systems in general are completely "stimulating" to use and not at all "dull," circle 1; 4 means that you are undecided or neutral, or think they are equally likely to be stimulating or dull; 3 means you feel that they are slightly more stimulating than dull, etc.

									X	SD
DULL-1 [R]										
Stimulating	1	2	3	4	5	6	7	Dull		
	23%	24%	21%	21%	5%	2%	3%		2.8	1.5
DREARY-1 [R]										
Fun	1	2	3	4	5	6	7	Dreary		
	22%	27%	23%	15%	8%	2%	3%		2.7	1.5
DIFFICULT-1 [R]										
Easy	1	2	3	4	5	6	7	Difficult		
	7%	15%	18%	27%	16%	12%	5%		3.8	1.6
IMPERSONAL-1 [R]										
Personal	1	2	3	4	5	6	7	Impersonal		
	6%	10%	13%	36%	11%	13%	11%		4.2	1.6
HELPFUL-1										
Hindering	1	2	3	4	5	6	7	Helpful		
	4%	2%	5%	15%	16%	31%	27%		5.4	1.6
UNTHREATENING-1										
Threatening	1	2	3	4	5	6	7	Unthreatening		
	4%	6%	6%	26%	12%	21%	26%		5.0	1.7
INEFFICIENT-1 [R]										
Efficient	1	2	3	4	5	6	7	Inefficient		
	38%	30%	15%	10%	2%	2%	2%		2.2	1.4
OBLIGING-1										
Demanding	1	2	3	4	5	6	7	Obliging		
	12%	12%	13%	40%	11%	8%	4%		3.6	1.5
UNDESIRABLE-1 [R]										
Desirable	1	2	3	4	5	6	7	Undesirable		
	25%	26%	16%	23%	3%	3%	4%		2.8	1.6

Notes: [R] indicates item was reversed for scoring; range = 7 (least favorable) to 70 (most favorable); alpha= .82.

Table 7.3 Items Comprising the "EIES Expectations" Index

Indicate your expectations about how it will be to use this system by circling the number which best indicates where your feelings lie on the scales below.

```
EASY-1
     4%        6%        14%       25%       19%       20%       11%
 :   1   :    2    :    3    :    4    :    5    :    6    :    7    :
Hard to                                                  Easy to
  learn                                                   learn
                         (Mean=4.5, Std Dev= 1.6)


FRIENDLY-1
     4%        7%        8%        24%       28%       20%        9%
 :   1   :    2    :    3    :    4    :    5    :    6    :    7    :
Impersonal                                              Friendly
                       (Mean= 4.6, Std Dev= 1.5)


NOT FRUSTRATING-1
     4%       10%        16%       24%       21%       21%        9%
 :   1   :    2    :    3    :    4    :    5    :    6    :    7    :
Frustrating                                             Not
                                                        frustrating
                     (Mean= 4.3, Std Dev= 1.6)


PRODUCTIVE-1
     2%        1%        5%        18%       24%       34%       16%
 :   1   :    2    :    3    :    4    :    5    :    6    :    7    :
Unproductive                                            Productive
                     (Mean= 5.3     Std Dev= 1.3)
```

EFFICIENCY-1 [R]

Do you expect that use of the system will increase the efficiency of your education (the quantity of work that you can complete in a given time)?

```
    19%       21%        14%       24%       15%        5%         2%
 :   1   :    2    :    3    :    4    :    5    :    6    :    7    :
 Definitely                          Unsure              Definitely
    yes                                                     not
                     (Mean=3.2   Std Dev= 1.6)
```

Table 7.3 continued

QUALITY-1 [R]

Do you expect that use of the system will increase the quality of your education?

```
     21%       22%       18%       25%       6%       4%       3%
 :    1   :    2    :    3    :    4    :    5   :    6   :    7    :
  Definitely                       Unsure                   Definitely
     yes                                                        not
                                (Mean= 3.0   Std Dev= 1.6)
```

RESENT-1

I resent being required to use EIES for this course.

```
     4%        3%        6%        19%       7%      17%       43%
 :    1   :    2    :    3    :    4    :    5   :    6   :    7    :
  Definitely                       Unsure                   Definitely
     yes                                                        not
                                (Mean= 5.5   Std Dev= 1.7)
```

OVERALL-1 [R]

Overall, how useful do you expect the system to be for online classes?

```
     23%       27%       20%       19%       6%       3%       2%
 :    1   :    2    :    3    :    4    :    5   :    6   :    7    :
     Very                                                 Not useful
   Useful                                                   at all
                                (Mean= 2.8   Std Dev= 1.5)
```

EXPECTED TIME

While you are part of an online course, how much time in the average week do you foresee yourself using EIES in relation to your coursework?

```
     (1)        4%     Less than 30 minutes
     (2)       12%     30 minutes to 1 hour
     (3)       43%     1 - 3 hours
     (4)       29%     4 - 6 hours
     (5)        7%     7 - 9 hours
     (6)        5%     10 hours or more
```

Notes: Range = 9 (worst expectations) to 62 (highest); Cronbach's alpha= .82.

Table 7.4 Items Included in the Course Rating Index

WASTE OF TIME [R]
This course was a waste of time   SA A N D SD

COURSE OVERALL
How would you rate this course overall?

(1)Excellent   (2)Very good   (3)Good   (4)Fair   (5)Poor

MORE INTERESTED
I became more interested in the subject   SA A N D SD

LEARNED FACTS
I learned a great deal of factual material   SA A N D SD

CONCEPTS
I gained a good understanding of basic
  concepts   SA A N D SD

CENTRAL ISSUES
I learned to identify central issues in this
field   SA A N D SD

COMMUNICATED CLEARLY
I developed the ability to communicate
clearly about this subject   SA A N D SD

Notes: [R] indicates item was reversed for scoring; range = 7 (best) to 35 (worst); alpha= .88.

Table 7.5 The Instructor Rating Index

WELL ORGANIZED
Instructor organized the course well   SA   A   N   D   SD

GRADING FAIR
Grading was fair and impartial   SA   A   N   D   SD

ENJOYS TEACHING
Instructor seems to enjoy teaching   SA   A   N   D   SD

LACKS KNOWLEDGE [R]
Instructor lacks sufficient knowledge
  about this subject area   SA   A   N   D   SD

IDEAS ENCOURAGED
Students were encouraged to express   SA   A   N   D   SD
  ideas

PRESENTED CLEARLY
Instructor presented material clearly
  and summarized main points   SA   A   N   D   SD

OTHER VIEWS
Instructor discussed points of view
  other than her/his own   SA   A   N   D   SD

PERSONAL HELP
The student was able to get personal
  help in this course   SA   A   N   D   SD

INSTRUCTOR BORING [R]
Instructor presented material in
  a boring manner   SA   A   N   D   SD

HELPFUL CRITIQUE
Instructor critiqued my work in
  a constructive and helpful way   SA   A   N   D   SD

TEACHER OVERALL
Overall, I would rate this teacher as

(1)Excellent   (2)Very good   (3)Good   (4)Fair   (5)Poor

Notes: [R] indicates item scoring was reversed for the scale; range = 11 (best) to 55 (worst); alpha= .88.

Table 7.6 Components of the Interest and Synthesis Indexes

Index of Increased Interest in the Subject

MORE INTERESTED [R]
I became more interested in the subject   SA   A   N   D   SD

DID ADDITIONAL READING [R]
I was stimulated to do additional reading   SA   A   N   D   SD

DISCUSS OUTSIDE [R]
I was stimulated to discuss related topics
   outside of class   SA   A   N   D   SD

Notes: [R] indicates response values reversed for index scoring; range = 3 (least interest stimulated) to 15; alpha= .66.

Items Included in the Synthesis Index

CENTRAL ISSUES [R]
I learned to identify central issues in this   SA   A   N   D   SD
   field

GENERALIZATIONS [R]
My ability to integrate facts and develop
   generalizations improved   SA   A   N   D   SD

RELATIONSHIPS [R]
I learned to see relationships between
   important topics and ideas   SA   A   N   D   SD

Notes: [R] indicates scores were reversed for index construction. Range= 3 (low synthesis) to 15; alpha= .80.

175

Table 7.7 Items Comprising the Collaboration Index

I developed new friendships in this
class [R]   SA A N D SD

I learned to value other points of
view [R]   SA A N D SD

Individual vs. Group Learning

Some courses are essentially a very INDIVIDUAL experience; contact with other students does not play an important part in
your learning. In other courses, communication with other students plays a dominant role. For THIS COURSE, please circle
the number below that seems to be what you experienced.

```
    1         2         3         4         5         6
Individual                                      Group
experience                                      experience
```

The help I got from other students was   [R]

```
    1         2         3         4         5         6
Crucially important                             Useless or
  to me                                         misleading
```

Students in my class tended to be

```
    1         2         3         4         5         6
Not at all                                      Extremely
cooperative                                     cooperative
```

How often did you communicate with other students outside of
class, by computer, "face-to-face," or on the telephone?

```
    1         2         3         4         5         6
Never                                           Constantly
```

Notes: Items marked [R] reversed for scoring; range = 6 (least collaboration) to 34
(most collaboration); alpha= .74.

Table 7.8 Items Comprising the VC Overall Index

INCREASE QUALITY [R]
Did use of the system increase the quality of your education?

```
:   1   :   2   :   3   :   4   :   5   :   6   :   7   :
  Definitely              Unsure                  Definitely
     yes                                             not
```

NOT CHOOSE ANOTHER
I would NOT choose to take another online course.

```
:   1   :   2   :   3   :   4   :   5   :   6   :   7   :
  Strongly                                          Strongly
  Agree                                             Disagree
```

BETTER LEARNING [R]
I found the course to be a better learning experience than
normal face-to-face courses.

```
:   1   :   2   :   3   :   4   :   5   :   6   :   7   :
  Strongly                                          Strongly
  Agree                                             Disagree
```

LEARNED MORE [R]
I learned a great deal more because of the use of EIES.

```
:   1   :   2   :   3   :   4   :   5   :   6   :   7   :
  Strongly                                          Strongly
  Agree                                             Disagree
```

Notes: [R] indicates item was reversed for scoring; range = 4 (worst) to 28 (best);
alpha= .85.

Acknowledgments

Major funding for this project, "Tools for the Enhancement and Evaluation of a Virtual Classroom," was contributed by the Annenberg/CPB Project. In addition, contributions were made by the Department of Higher Education of the State of New Jersey, the New Jersey Governor's Commission on Science and Technology, IBM, NJIT, and Upsala College.

Among the many people who have contributed to this project, the author is particularly grateful to Steve Ehrmann, John Foster, Ronald Rice, Ellen Schreihoffer, Murray Turoff, and all of the faculty members who gave their time and creativity to the project. The project is a team effort, and the editorial "we" is used in this report to allude to the collective nature of the implementation and research. For further information write to the Assistant Project Director, Ellen Schreihoffer, NJIT, 323 King Blvd., Newark NJ 07102.

EIES, TEIES, Personal TEIES, and Virtual Classroom are registered trademarks of New Jersey Institute of Technology. All questions are copyrighted by the author.

REFERENCES

Attewell, P. & Rule, J. (1984). Computing and organizations: What we know and what we don't know. *Communications of the ACM, 27* (12): 1184-1191.

Bork, A. (1981). *Learning with computers*. Bedford, MA: Digital Press.

———— (1985). Advantages of computer based learning. *Journal of Structured Learning, 8* : .

Bouton, C. & Garth, R. Y. (1983). *Learning in groups. New directions in teaching and learning.* (no. 14) San Francisco: Jossey-Bass.

Bridwell, L. S., Sirc, G., & Brooke, R. (1986). Revising and computers: Case studies of student writers. In S. Freedman (ed.), *The acquisition of written language: Revision and response.* Norwood, NJ: Ablex.

Carey, J. A. (1980). Paralanguage in computer-mediated communication. *Proceedings of the Association for Computational Linguistics* : 61-63.

Centra, J. A. (1982). *Determining faculty effectiveness.* San Francisco: Jossey-Bass.

Chambers, J. A., & Sprecher, J. W. (1980). Computer assisted instruction: Current trends and critical issues. *Communications of the ACM, 23* (6): 332-42.

Clark, R. E., & Salomon, G. (1986). Media in teaching. In M. C. Wittrock (ed.), *Handbook of research on teaching* (3rd ed.). New York: Macmillan.

Clement, D. E. (1971). Learning and retention in student-led discussion groups. *Journal of Social Psychology, 84* : 279-86.

Collier, K. G. (1966). An experiment in university teaching. *Universities Quarterly, 20* : 336-48.

———— (1980). Peer-group learning in higher education: The development of higher order skills. *Studies in Higher Education, 5* (1): 55-62.

Collins, A. (1982). *Learning to read and write with personal computers*. Cambridge, MA: Bolt, Beranek, and Newman.

Costin, F. (1972). Lecturing versus other methods of teaching: A review of research. *British Journal of Educational Technology, 3* : 4-31.

Culnan, M. J., & Markus, M. L. (1987). *Information technologies: Electronic media and intraorganizational communication. Handbook on organizational communication.* Beverley Hills, CA: Sage.

Daiute, C. (1985). *Writing and computers*. Reading, MA: Addison-Wesley.

Daiute, C., & Taylor, R. (1981). Computers and the improvement of writing. *Proceedings of the ACM*.

Davie, L. E. (1987). Facilitation of adult learning through computer conferencing. In *Proceedings of the Second Guelph Symposium on Computer Conferencing, June 1-4*. Guelph, Ontario: University of Guelph, pp. 11-22.

Davie, L. E., & Palmer, P. (1984). Computer teleconferencing for advanced distance education. *Canadian Journal of University Continuing Education, 10* (2): 56-66.

Davis, J. A., Dukes, R. & Gamson, W. A. (1981). Assessing interactive modes of sociology instruction. *Teaching Sociology, 3* (3): 313-23.

Duranti, A. (1986). Framing discourse in a new medium: Openings in electronic mail. *The Quarterly Newsletter of the Laboratory of Comparative Human Cognition, 8* (2): 64-71.

Ehrmann, S. C. (1986). Two views of innovation, two views of evaluation: The "best uses" paradigm. Working paper. Washington, DC: the Annenberg/CPB Project, Corporation for Public Broadcasting.

Erskine, C. A., & Tomkin, A. (1963). Evaluation of the effect of the group discussion method in a complex teaching programme. *Journal of Medical Education, 37* : 1036-42.

Farson, R. (1987). The electronic future of executive education. Unpublished paper. La Jolla, CA.: Western Behavioral Sciences Institute.

Field, B. O. (1973). In D. E. Billing, and B. S. Furniss, (Eds.), *Aims, methods and assessment in advanced scientific education*. Heyden.

Foster, J. (1987). *Final design specifications for personal TEIES: Text and graphics composition system and personal communications manager*. Technical Report 87-15.2. Newark, NJ: Computerized Conferencing and Communications Center, New Jersey Institute of Technology.

Gleason, B. J. (1987). *Instructional management tools on EIES*. Technical Report 87-12. Newark, NJ: Computerized Conferencing and Communications Center, New Jersey Institute of Technology.

Goldschmid, M. L., & Goldschmid, B. (1976). Peer teaching in higher education: A review. *Higher Education, 5* : 9-33.

Hamilton, L. C. (1980). Grades, class size and faculty status predict teaching evaluations. *Teaching Sociology, 8* (1): 47-62.

Harasim, L. (1986). Computer learning networks: Educational applications of computer conferencing. *Journal of Distance Education, 1* (1): 59-70.

———— (Spring 1987). Teaching and learning online: Issues in computer-mediated graduate courses. *Canadian Journal of Educational Communication, 16* (2): 117-35.

Heimstra, G. (1982). Teleconferencing, concern for face, and organizational culture. In M. Burgoon (Ed.), *Communication Yearbook* 6. Beverley Hills, CA: Sage.

Hiltz, S. R. (1986a). *Branching capabilities in conferences: A manual and functional specifications*. Technical Report 86-1. Newark, NJ: Computerized Conferencing and Communications Center, New Jersey Institute of Technology. (Revised 1987).

———— (1986b). Recent developments in teleconferencing and related technology. In A. E. Cawkell (Ed.), *Handbook of information technology and office systems*. Amsterdam, North Holland, pp. 823-50.

———— (1986c). *The virtual classroom: Building the foundations*. Research Report 24. Newark, NJ: Computerized Conferencing and Communications Center, New Jersey Institute of Technology.

———— (1986d). The virtual classroom: Using computer-mediated communication for university teaching. *Journal of Communication, 36* (2): 95-104.

———— (1988a). Learning in a virtual classroom: Volume 1 of A Virtual Classroom on EIES, Research Report 25, Center for

Computerized Conferencing and Communications, NJIT, Newark, NJ.

———— (1988b). Teaching in a virtual classroom: Volume 2 of A Virtual Classroom on EIES, Research Report 25, Center for Computerized Conferencing and Communications, NJIT, Newark, NJ.

———— (1988c). Productivity enhancement from computer-mediated communication: A systems contingency approach. *Communications of the ACM,* December, 31 (12): 1438-1454.

Hiltz, S. R., & Johnson, K. (1987). Measuring acceptance of computer-mediated communication systems. Paper presented to the International Communication Association, Montreal, Canada. Revision in press *JASIS.*

Hiltz, S. R., Johnson, K., Aronovitch, C., & Turoff, M. (1980). *Face to face vs. computerized conferences: A controlled experiment,* Vol. 1, *Findings.* Research Report No. 12. Newark: Computerized Conferencing and Communications Center, New Jersey Institute of Technology.

Hiltz, S. R., Johnson, K., & Turoff, M. (1986). Experiments in group decision making, 1: Communications process and outcome in face-to-face vs. computerized conferences. *Human Communication Research, 13* (2): 225-52.

Hiltz, S. R., Kerr, E. B., & Johnson, K. (1985). *Determinants of acceptance of computer-mediated communication systems.* Research Report 22. Newark: Computerized Conferencing and Communications Center, New Jersey Institute of Technology.

Hiltz, S. R., & Turoff, M. (1978). *The network nation.* Reading, MA: Addison-Wesley.

———— (1985). Structuring computer-mediated communication systems to avoid information overload. *Communication of the ACM, 28* (7): 680-89.

Huber, G. P. (1982). Organizational information systems: Determinants of their performance and behavior. *Management Science, 28* (2): 138-53.

Johansen, R., Vallee, J., & Spangler, K. (1979). *Electronic meetings: Technological alternatives and social choices.* Reading, MA: Addison-Wesley.

Johnson, D. W., & Johnson, R. T. (1975). *Learning together and alone: Cooperation, competition, and individualization.* Englewood Cliffs, NJ: Prentice-Hall.

Keen, P. (1981). Information systems and organizational change. *Communications of the ACM, 24* (1): 24-33.

Kerr, E. B., & Hiltz, S. R. (1982). *Computer-mediated communication systems: Status and evaluation.* New York: Academic Press.

Kiefer, K., & Smith, C. (1984). Improving students' revising and editing: The Writer's Workbench system at Colorado State University. In W. Wresh (Ed.), *A writer's tool: The computer in composition instruction*. Urbana, IL: National Council of Teachers of English.

Kling, R. (1980). Social analyses of computing: Theoretical perspectives in recent empirical research. *Computing Surveys, 12* (1): 61-110.

Kraworth, D. R. et al. (1984). Taxonomy of educational objectives: The classification of educational goals. Handbook II. Affective domain}. New York: David McKay.

Malone, T. (1981). Toward a theory of intrinsically motivating instruction. *Cognitive Science, 5* (4): 333-69.

Markus, M. L. (1983). Power, politics, and MIS implementation. *Communications of the ACM, 26* (6): 430-44.

McCreary, E. K., and J. Van Duren. (1987). Educational applications of computer conferencing. *Canadian J. of Educational Communication, 16* (2): 107-15.

Mowshowitz, A. (1981). On approaches to the study of social issues in computing. *Communications of the ACM, 24* (3): 146-55.

Paulhus, D. (1983). Sphere-specific measures of perceived control. *Journal of Personality and Social Psychology, 44* (6): 1253-1265.

Paulhus, D., and Christie, R. (1981). Spheres of control: An interactionist approach to the assessment of perceived control. In H.M. Lefcourt (Ed.), *Research with the locus of control construct*, Volume 1. New York: Academic Press.

Quinn, C. N., Mehan, H., Levin, J. A., & Black, S. D. (1983). Real education in non-real time: The use of electronic messaging systems for instruction. *Instructional Science, 11* : 313-27.

Rice, R. (1980). Computer conferencing. In B. Dervin and M. Voigt (Eds.), *Progress in communication sciences*, Vol. 1. Norwood, NJ: Ablex, pp. 215-40.

Rice, R. & Associates. (1984). *The new media: Communication, research, and technology*. Beverley Hills, CA: Sage.

Rice, R. (1986). Applying the human relations perspective to the study of new media. *Computers and Society, 15* (4): 32-37.

Rice, R., & Love, G. (1987). Electronic emotion: Socio-emotional content in a computer-mediated communication network. *Communication Research, 14* (1): 85-108.

Rotter, J. B. (1966). Generalized expectancies for internal vs. external control of reinforcement. *Psychological Monographs, 80* (whole issue).

Rudduck, J. (1978). *Learning through small group discussion.* Guildford, England: Society for Research into Higher Education.

Schramm, W. (1977). *Big media, little media: Tools and technologies for instruction.* Beverley Hills, CA: Sage.

Shavelson, R. J., Stasz, C., Schlossman, S., Webb, N., Hotta, J. Y., & Goldstein, S. (1986). *Evaluating student outcomes from telecourse instruction: A feasibility study.* Santa Monica, CA: Rand.

Short, J., Williams, E., & Christie, B. (1976). *The social psychology of telecommunications.* London: Wiley.

Sproull, L., & Kiesler, S. (1986). Reducing social context cues: Electronic mail in organizational communication. *Management Science, 32* (11): 1492-1512.

Steinfield, C. W. (1986). Computer-mediated communication systems. In M. E. Williams (Ed.), *Annual review of information science and technology*, Vol. 21. Washington, DC: American Society for Information Science, pp. 167-202.

Strassman, P. A. (1985). *Information payoff: The transformation of work in the electronic age.* New York: Macmillan.

Turner, J. A. (1984). Computer-mediated work: The interplay between technology and structured jobs. *Communications of the ACM, 27* (12): 1210-17.

Turoff, M. (1972). "Party Line" and "Discussion" computerized conferencing systems. In S. Winkler (Ed.), *Computer communication—Impacts and implications. Proceedings of the International Conference on Computer Communications.* Washington, DC, pp. 161-70.

Uhlig, R. P., Farber, D. J., & Bair, J. H. (1979). *The office of the future: Communication and computers.* Amsterdam: North Holland.

Welsch, L. A. (1982). Using electronic mail as a teaching tool. *Communications of the ACM, 25* (2): 105-8.

Whipple, W. R. (1987). Collaborative learning: Recognizing it when we see it. *Bulletin of the American Association for Higher Education, 40* (2): 3-7.

Zmud, R. W. (1979). Individual differences and MIS success: A review of the empirical literature. *Management Science, 25* (10): 966-79.

Chapter 8
Analyzing Instructional Interactions on Electronic Message Networks

James A. Levin
Haesun Kim
Margaret M. Riel

INTRODUCTION

More and more schools are starting to explore the uses of electronic message systems for instruction. Networks have been used in social science instruction (Cohen, Levin, and Riel 1986), in science instruction (Levin and Cohen 1985; Newman 1986; Katz, McSwiney, and Stroud 1987; Levin, Waugh, and Kolopanis 1988), for writing (Riel 1985), and in other domains. Research has started to focus on the impact of this sort of long-distance instruction based on the interchange of electronic text messages in "nonreal time" (Hiltz and Turoff 1978; Quinn, Mehan, Levin, and Black 1983). One obvious question that arises is whether instruction on electronic networks is more or less effective than face-to-face instruction.

We have been focusing on a different, more interesting question: In what ways is instructional interaction on electronic networks different from face-to-face instruction and in what ways is it similar? Once we have a more detailed understanding of the nature of the interaction, we will be in a good position to address the issue of which medium is more effective and for what purposes. We can also learn new aspects of the more familiar instructional medium by contrasting it with instruction in a very different medium.

Research on instruction conducted on electronic networks has the advantage that the interactions are self-transcribed. Also, because of current limitations of the media, interactions are largely text-based, avoiding the difficult problems of interpreting nonverbal communication. Finally, the data can be collected without the intrusiveness of video cameras or human observers. Despite these advantages, however, one soon ends up with a massive number of pages of messages, without established methodologies for analyzing a mass of messages.

In this chapter we describe a number of techniques we have developed for analyzing messaging on electronic mail networks, and we point to some of the conclusions we have reached based on these analyses.

THE INTERCULTURAL LEARNING NETWORK

The analytical techniques presented here are illustrated by applying them to the interaction that occurred on the Intercultural Learning Network (ICLN). The ICLN has a loosely organized set of participants, including elementary, middle, and high school students and teachers, junior college, undergraduate, and graduate students and faculty, and a few participants from outside the educational system. It has included participants from California, Illinois, Connecticut, Alaska, Hawaii, and other states in the United States, from Puerto Rico, from Tijuana and Mexico City in Mexico, from Tokyo, and from Jerusalem. Participants typically write messages on a microcomputer using a word processor, and then send these messages to the other participants through the electronic mail system on The Source, a commercial computer system available from all of the sites on the network. Group communication was maintained through the use of "memo lists," so that a message sent to a group name went to each of the participants on that list.

Since the ICLN was created as part of research projects to explore the nature of instructional networking, the number of sites has remained fairly small. Nevertheless, it has been a fairly active network since it was established in 1983. In the analyses below we analyze in depth various "time slices" of the ongoing interaction in messages sent between March 1986 and March 1987.

Interaction on this network has been organized around "activities," proposed by different participants on the network, and then pursued by the subset of participants that volunteer to join in. To give a better feel for the type of activity pursued, below is a message that was part of an activity called the Moon Observation Project. In this project, students in different locations first drew pictures of what they thought the first quarter moon looked like, the full moon, and the last quarter moon. Then they went out to observe and draw the moon that night. The message that follows is one of the early, organizational messages:

```
From: BCF302 (TOKYO)      34 Lines
On: 27 APR 1986  At: 12:24
To: STK148   To: BBW928   To: TCM869   To: BDR323
Dear Jim,

I did the moon exp. to 9 nonnetworking students of my
college.  Here come the results.

First quarter crescent: 2 correct; 7 incorrect.
Last quarter crescent: 2 correct; 7 incorrect.

Correctness is only counted by the direction of the
horns.  Somehow, all the drawn moons are, what should
I say, standing upright on one of their horns.  None
drew a slanted crescent.

Full moon figures:
     clear rabbit 2 (one drew two facing each other)
     fuzzy rabbit 2 (one is lying down on the bottom)
     meaningless shapes 4; "rock" 1.

Clear rabbits have pestles.

In addition, I asked them what Americans/Israelis see
when we see the full moon in Japan.
```

# of answerers	U.S.	Israel
2	full	full
2	half	half
1	crescent	dark (no moon)
1	half	crescent
1	waning	waxing
1	crescent	NA
1	dark	half

```
I got good variety, didn't I?  So this question appears
to be more difficult than we thought.  Naomi
```

This message, the sixth in a set of interchanges, was followed by a long series of other messages stretching over five months that led the conduct of the project in which a number of

different sites involved students in the actual observational and
message. These Moon Observation Project messages are among
those analyzed later in this chapter. At the same time this interchange was taking place, there were numerous other activities
taking place in parallel, as illustrated by our analyses.

PARTICIPANT STRUCTURES ANALYSIS

Interaction in educational settings has been analyzed in
terms of "participant structures" (Philips 1972, 1982). Participant
structures provide a way to compare interaction in different educational settings. Used in efforts to compare home and school interactive patterns, participants structures have helped explain why
students from certain cultures systematically function poorly in
the conventional Western classroom setting (Florio 1978; Mehan
1979; Au 1980). The following list of participant structures was
used to contrast teacher-student interactions and students' interactions with computers (Mehan, Moll, and Riel 1985):

1. Organization of the work group
2. Task organization
3. Response opportunities
4. Response obligations
5. Evaluation.

These same participant structures, with some modification,
provided a schematic frame for comparing interaction on a range of
different networks (Riel and Levin 1985). It helped isolate features
that contribute to more and less success in the development of networks.
Participant structures modified for examining network interaction are as follows:

1. Organization of the network group: its size, common
   knowledge, experiences, or interests, the physical location of
   the participants
2. Network task organization: the types of activities that participants engage in over the network
3. Response opportunities: ease of access to the interaction, including social and technical resources for sending and receiving
   messages

4. Response obligations: the tacit or formal requirements for responding to messages
5. Evaluation and coordination: the assessment of the quantity or quality of the exchanges on the network and efforts to facilitate group interaction.

Riel and Levin (1985) reviewed efforts to develop a number of network communities. The participant structures provided a framework for the comparison of successful and unsuccessful efforts. This analysis pointed to a set of factors that were more likely to result in a functioning network community. The following descriptions are of participant structures most likely to lead to success:

1. A group of people who work together or share interest in a task, but who find it difficult to meet in the same location and/or at the same time
2. A well-specified task to be accomplished by this group
3. Ease of access to a reliable computer network
4. A sense of responsibility to the group and/or task
5. Strong leadership and final evaluation of the group task

While these features make the task of building a networking community much easier, there does not need to be a perfect overlap of all features to succeed at network building. It is important to note that all of the successful networks that were described by Riel and Levin (1985) deviated from this pattern by only a single feature. All the networks that failed to sustain interaction differed from this pattern on two or more of these features.

This analysis of participant structures was used to frame the development of the ICLN. They give a descriptive profile of the network that provides the background for more detailed methods of message analysis that we will introduce in the next section.

Organization of the Network Community

The organization of the group is multilayered, with the site coordinators having had the experience of working together on previous projects in face-to-face settings. Other participants meet and interact only through their work on ICLN. The personal contact and trust between the site coordinators helps to facilitate the functioning of other members of the group.

The locations represent a wide cultural and geographic diversity. Students enjoyed writing for and reading the work of other students even when they knew little about them. But with increasing knowledge about their partners came increased interest in the interactions. Exchange of other media—photos, audiotapes and videotapes—provided a common meeting ground for students who work together across distances. This exchange enabled students to create their own tasks on the network. In the absence of knowledge of participants, there seems to be a higher need for a well-specified task.

The size of the group varies with each project. The group of participants on a specific project would include the teachers and students from between three and eight classrooms as well as university students and researchers.

Organization of the Network Task

The activity approach to networking adopted by those who have organized ICLN ensures that participants are joined together to accomplish a specified goal. The task shared by all participants is to create functional learning environments in which students cooperate with peers and adults in other locations to share ideas, explore issues, and solve problems. The university researchers and students were interested in mapping out the properties of electronic message systems and their usefulness for instructional interaction. The pre-service and in-service teachers were interested in principles and design of cooperative learning on the network. The students were involved with the content of projects in science, social science, and language arts.

Examples of student projects include an analysis of international news coverage, a comparison of educational systems, a study of career choices and how these have changed across generations, a study of how the water cycle operates in different places and of techniques for dealing with water shortages, food prices and import and export policies, and comparisons of TV watching patterns.

Response Opportunity

The ease of access varied across the different locations. In sites with university support, the cost and technical support were supplied by the university. In cases of teachers working without this support, the cost in money and time was sometimes too great to assure regular interaction.

Response Obligation

Schools working closely with ICLN coordinators agreed to spend some part of the school week on the networking activities. Despite strong personal commitment to this project by most of the teachers, state- and district-mandated curriculum, differences in school holiday schedules, and testing periods sometimes resulted in response delays.

Coordination/Evaluation

To coordinate this network, a person in each location was designated as a "site coordinator." This person was responsible for locating and working with the teachers and students at each site. In addition there are "activity coordinators," who took the initiative in developing and running an activity on the network. These activity coordinators provided the group leadership that is so important to keeping a task functioning.

ICLN activities that lacked a coordinator were less likely to be successful, if success is equated with sustaining interaction. There were many messages with good ideas for projects that were exchanged. Those that had at least one person strongly committed to the project were likely to continue. Good ideas without the commitment of a coordinator rarely instigated much activity. A strong coordinator seemed to be a necessary but not a sufficient condition. It is the purpose or function of the activity from the perspective of the participants that seems to determine its likelihood of success.

Evaluation is a critical element of ICLN. The rest of the analysis presented in this chapter provides some of the strategies we are developing for examining the interaction on networks.

The design and development of the ICLN draw upon the framework of a participant structure analysis of networking. This framework gives us a way to see the dimensions of variant possibilities in this new institutional medium. However, the most important fact leading to successful educational networks is the presence of an important function that the network serves. The nature of this function determines the particular form that the network should have.

INTERMESSAGE REFERENCE ANALYSIS

In reading through a set of electronic messages, one gets a strong feeling that there are "multiple threads": multiple topics that are being pursued in parallel. Previous research has pointed to the "multiple thread" nature of electronic message interaction (Black et al. 1983; Quinn et al. 1983). These previous approaches relied on an analysis of the topic content of the discussion.

In order to trace these "multiple threads" more easily, we have developed an alternative approach, which we call Intermessage Reference Analysis. This is a more "syntactically" based analysis, performing the analogue of a repeated reference analysis for text. For each message, a coder determines whether reference is made to previous messages. Sometimes these references are clear: if the message sender used an "Answer" or "Reply" command in the message system, the program will automatically place in the "Subject" line of the header a reference to the previous message. Sometimes the message sender will include an explicit reference to a message in the text of the message: "...your message yesterday...." Other times, the reference is less explicit, as when a message supplies an answer to a question asked in a previous message: "...Yes, I agree."

Although this analysis leaves the analyst scratching his/her head about some borderline cases, the reliability between coders is fairly high. Two independent codings of a corpus of 104 messages agreed on the intermessage references in 99 of the messages, reaching 95 percent reliability. From this analysis, we can immediately address a number of questions. Which messages are referenced a lot? Does that depend on the sender of the message, or the topic of the message, or how the message is addressed? Who references whose messages? That is, is the referencing stratified according to the different roles of the participants, or does it cross role boundaries?

To address the questions raised above, we selected a corpus of messages in the ICLN: those messages sent during April 1986. There were 104 messages sent during this time period, and there were 76 intermessage references made in these 104 messages. Table 8.1 shows the number of times messages were referenced by other messages.

Table 8.1   How Often Were Messages Referenced by Other Messages?

# of References	# of Messages	% of Messages
5	1	1
4	3	3
3	6	6
2	13	13
1	25	24
0	56	54

As can be seen, a few messages were referenced multiple times (one message was referenced by five other messages; four messages were referenced by three others; etc.), while a majority of messages (54%) were never referenced. There is an interesting analogy between the results of this analysis and the results of citation analyses: most papers published in journals never are cited by other papers, while a few papers are cited again and again (Garfield 1972).

What determines whether a message is referenced or not? Are messages from adult participants referenced more than those from children? Let us start with the question of whose messages are referenced. Are the messages from the adults referenced and those by children ignored? Table 8.2 shows that this is not the case. In fact, it shows that messages from students are referenced slightly more often than those from adults. It also shows that a majority of messages from each group are not referenced.

This table shows us that messages from participants in the different roles in the network are referenced. But it doesn't tell us anything about who is referencing whose messages. Do adults in the network reference only other adults' messages? Do the stu-

Table 8.2 Whose Messages Are Referenced?

Author's Group	# of Messages	Percent Referenced
Site coordinators	35	42.9
University students	33	48.5
Precollege students	28	46.4
Unknown author	2	50.0
Joint authors across categories	6	66.7

Table 8.3 Who References Whom?

Author of Referenced Msg	Author of Referring Msg					Total	Percent
	AD	US	ST	AD&US	UK		
AD	11	3	1			15	17.4
US	14	11	8		2	35	40.7
ST	15	2	11	1		29	33.7
UK	2					2	2.3
AD&ST	2					2	2.3
AD&US	1					1	1.2
US&ST		2				2	2.3
Total	45	18	20	1	2	86	
Percent	52.3	20.9	23.3	1.2	2.3		100

Key: AD = Adults (site coordinators, graduate students, teachers)
US = Undergraduate student
ST = Precollege student
UK = Unknown author
XX&XX=Joint authorship

dents reference only other students? Table 8.3 shows who references whom.

These data shows that there is a weak tendency for people in a given role to reference messages of those in the same role. But there is also a lot of crossover. The correlation is 0.015, which is very low.

These are the kinds of global facts we can derive from the intermessage reference analysis. However, a much more powerful outcome is what we call a "message map." Each reference of one message to another can be thought of as a link in a graphical representation of the messages. So, if we lay the messages out in a space with time as the horizontal axis and different senders as the vertical axis, a particular set of messages can be displayed as a message map, with the intermessage references as directed links (arrows) between the messages. Figure 8.1 shows a simple message map.

Each rounded rectangle in this map is a message, and the arrows point from each message to a previous message that it references. Time is the horizontal axis, labeled in weeks at the top, and different senders are listed along the vertical axis. The naming convention for messages is that the first two letters indicate the sender; the next three or four the date sent; and the last, either the destination or the topic of the message. To simplify the diagram, several reference links to the same message are sometimes joined into a thicker line. The name of the cluster is the subject header of the "root" message, which is in quotes below the root message. This cluster is "Mexican Aliens Migration to America," shown near the bottom of Figure 8.1. This message was referenced by five other messages, which were in turn referenced by other messages. Even this simple message map shows that these electronic interactions deviate from the most common face-to-face "whole group" instructional pattern, which is a string of alternations in turns between teacher and different students (Mehan 1978). Figure 8.2 shows the message map for all the messages sent during the months of April and May 1986 on the ICLN.

This message map is quite complicated, and difficult to read. However, the nature of its complexity is informative. It certainly makes clear the "multiple thread" nature of electronic message interaction, previously documented by Black et al. (1983) and Quinn et al. (1983). Perhaps of greater utility is the possibility of using the intermessage reference analysis, which created this messy messages map, to pull out smaller and more manageable clusters of messages. A cluster consists of all messages that are interlinked with reference links. Figure 8.3 shows the map of the largest such cluster during this period. We will name these

Figure 8.1 A Simple Message Map

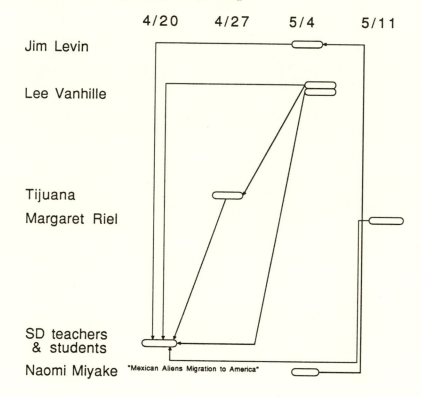

Figure 8.2 The Complete Message Map for April-May 1986

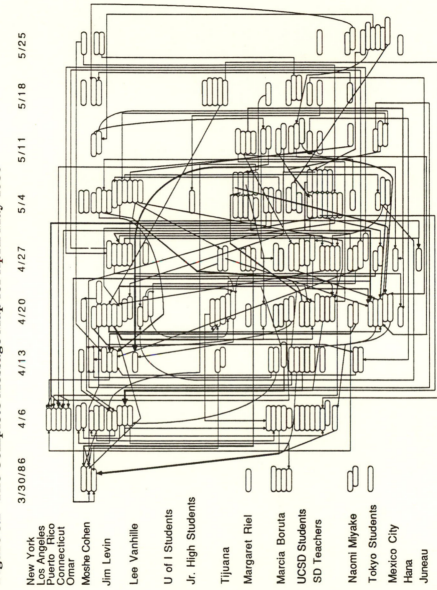

3/30/86   4/6   4/13   4/20   4/27   5/4   5/11   5/18   5/25

New York
Los Angeles
Puerto Rico
Connecticut
Omar

Moshe Cohen

Jim Levin

Lee Vanhille

U of I Students

Jr. High Students

Tijuana

Margaret Riel

Marcia Boruta

UCSD Students

SD Teachers

Naomi Miyake

Tokyo Students

Mexico City

Hana

Juneau

197

Figure 8.3 The Largest Cluster of Messages Among the April-May Messages

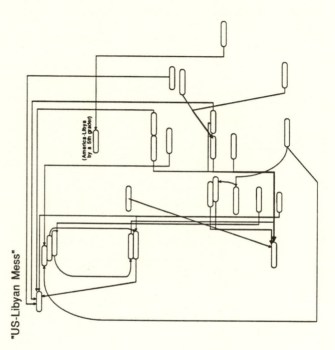

3/30/86 4/6 4/13 4/20 4/27 5/4 5/11 5/18 5/25

New York
Los Angeles
Puerto Rico
Connecticut
Omar

Moshe Cohen

Jim Levin

Lee Vanhille

U of I Students

Jr. High Students

Tijuana

Margaret Riel

Marcia Boruta

UCSD Students

SD Teachers

Naomi Miyake

Tokyo Students

Mexico City

Hana

Juneau

"US-Libyan Mess"

(America-Libya by a 5th grader)

largest such cluster during this period. We will name these clusters by the "Subject" header of the root message (the first message in the cluster to be sent). Figure 8.3 shows the "U.S.-Libya mess" cluster.

Using the intermessage reference analysis, we can identify 77 clusters in the 218 April-May messages, ranging from singleton clusters (those messages that aren't referenced by another message) to the 25-message cluster shown in Figure 8.3. Table 8.4 shows the distribution of sizes of clusters.

Table 8.4 Distribution of Message Cluster Sizes in April-May 1986 Messages

Size of Cluster	Number of Clusters This Size
1	57
2	6
3	3
4	1
5	2
6	1
7	2
10	1
14	1
16	1
17	1
24	1
25	1

Looking at a number of these message maps, it becomes apparent that some messages trigger off a large set of other messages (as at least partially measured by the intermessage reference analysis), while others have little or no impact. What determines whether a message is "influential" or not in an electronic mail interaction? Before we can address this question, we need some sort of measure of "influence." The simplest measure would be the number of direct references. This is the measure implicit in Table 8.2 —the most influential message with this metric would be the one that was referenced five times. However, a message often sets off a long sequence of other messages, not all of which directly reference the initial message. For example, in Figure 8.3, one "root" message of the "U.S.-Libya mess" cluster is directly referenced 5 times, and the other only 8 times, even though they are the root of a cluster of 25 messages. To better measure this cascade effect, we developed an "influence" measure that is the sum of all messages that reference a message, either directly or indirectly (by referencing a message that references the original message, etc.). An even more sophisticated measure would count these indirect measures but would dilute their impact in proportion to their indirectness. For our purposes, a simple sum has been sufficient.

The Intermessage Reference Analysis described here can be criticized for largely ignoring the content of the messages, focusing instead almost entirely on the relatively superficial repeated references. However, language typically has sufficient redundancy that one measure of connectivity is highly correlated to other measures. So, even though we admit that there is more to the structuring of message interactions than references between messages, we also claim that analyzing these references is a good initial approach to sketching out the interactional patterns.

As a start, the Intermessage Reference can serve as a way to identify clusters of messages that we can then analyze more deeply with other techniques. For example, Waugh, Miyake, Levin, and Cohen (1988) use it as an initial step for the Semantic Trace Analysis that Miyake developed. In this chapter, we will use it as a first step in an alternative semantic analysis, which we call a "message act analysis."

MESSAGE ACT ANALYSIS

Individual utterances have been analyzed by philosophers of language, linguists, psychologists, and others according to the "speech acts" that they perform (Austin 1962; Searle 1969; d'Andrade and Wish 1985). In oversimplified terms, a speech act is the function that an utterance is to accomplish. We have carried out an analogous analysis of messages, aimed at identifying the functions that each message is to accomplish. We call this analysis a "message act analysis." While we have not completed a general message act analysis, we can report here a more specific message act analysis, one focused on instructional functions.

Mehan (1978) developed a partial classification of instructional speech acts in documenting a common classroom interactional pattern that he calls "IRE sequences." These sequences consist of an initiation act by the teacher, a reply by a student, and then an evaluation by the teacher. Here is an example that Mehan (1978) gives of this pattern:

Initiation by teacher:	Uh, Prenda, ah, let's see if we can find, here's your name. Where were you born, Prenda?
Reply by student:	San Diego.
Evaluation by teacher:	You were born in San Diego, all right.
Initiation by teacher:	Um, can you come up and find San Diego on the map?
Reply by student:	(goes to board and points)
Evaluation by teacher:	Right there, okay.
Initiation by teacher:	Now, where, where did, where was your mother born, where did your mother come from?
Reply by student:	Oh, Arkansas.
Evaluation by teacher:	Okay.

This pattern is very common. In fact, Mehan (1978) found that "This sequence was the predominant form of teacher-student interaction, comprising 53 percent of the total in the nine lessons that Mehan and his associates analyzed," pp. 41-2.

We analyzed the messages in our corpus, classifying them according to whether they initiated a new topic, replied to a previous message, or evaluated a previous message. Figure 8.4 shows the IRE pattern for a cluster of messages.

Note that the conventional IRE sequence is largely missing. Instead, there are much more complex patterns of initiation, reply, and evaluation in this interaction. While the patterns are complex, there seem to be two common patterns among the messages we've analyzed. One is a "star" pattern, as shown in Figure 8.5 below.

In this pattern, the replies are largely to some one initiation. A second pattern is more linear in structure, with a chain of replies. This is much more similar to the kinds of discussion "threads" found in other electronic interactions (for example, Quinn et al. 1983). Figure 8.6 shows this "thread" pattern.

We did find a few instances of the IRE sequences that Mehan found to be so common in face-to-face instruction, but they were rare and usually embedded in a more complex pattern. For

Figure 8.4   An "IRE" Cluster of Messages

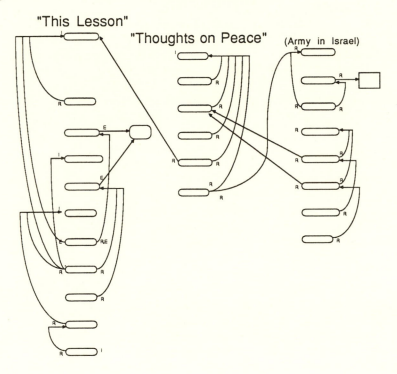

"This Lesson"

"Thoughts on Peace"

(Army in Israel)

Figure 8.5 A "Star" IRE Cluster

"US-Libyan Mess"

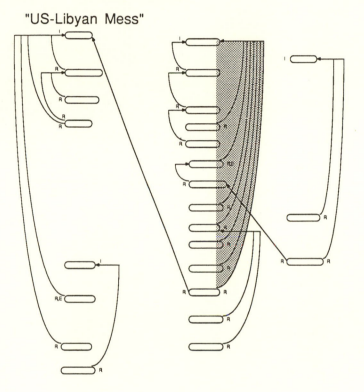

203

Figure 8.6 A "Thread" IRE Cluster

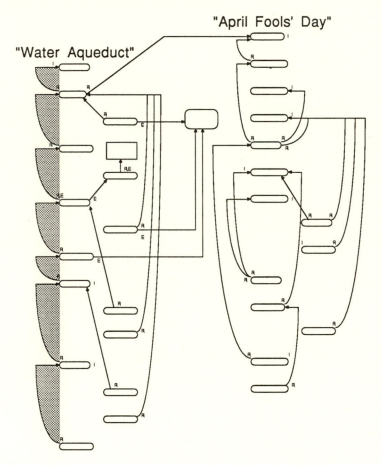

"April Fools' Day"

"Water Aqueduct"

204

Figure 8.7 A Cluster With a Simple IRE Sequence as Part

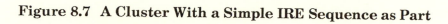

"Mexican Aliens Migration to America"   "InterCultural Crossword Puzzle"   "Communication Protocol"

example, Figure 8.7 shows one of these "pure" IRE sequences, as part of a larger, more complex cluster.

In the Mehan analysis, almost all initiations and evaluations were by the teacher, and almost all replies were by the students. Table 8.5 shows who made the initiations, replies, and evaluations in the network interactions analyzed here. While a majority of the evaluations (71%) were made by the adults, there were a substantial number by students. Less than half (39%) of the initiations were made by adults.

Table 8.5 The Distribution of Initiations, Replies and Evaluations Across Groups

Author	Initiation	Reply	Evaluation	R,E	R,I
AD	27	63	17	10	
US	14	20	1	3	
ST	20	20	1	5	2
AD & ST	6	6			
US & ST	1				
UK	2				
TOTAL	70	109	19	18	2

Key: AD = Adults (site coordinators, graduate students, teachers)
      US = Undergraduate student
      ST = Precollege student
      UK = Unknown author
      XX & XX = Joint authorship

One of the main conclusions that we can draw from this "message act analysis" is that there are substantial differences between face-to-face instruction and instruction conducted using electronic networks.   However, there are also important similarities. Our next analysis points out some of these.

MESSAGE FLOW ANALYSIS

One of the simpler kinds of analyses to perform on a set of messages is to plot the density of messages per unit time, and follow that across time. Anyone who has participated in electronic message interactions has certainly experienced the feeling that there is an ebb and flow in messages. We have plotted the flow of all the messages in the ICLN across a full year (March 31, 1986-March 31, 1987). Figure 8.8 shows the plot of the number of messages per week.

The top line shows the total number of messages, and the lower lines chart the flow of messages sent by several of the most active sites (San Diego, Illinois, Tokyo, Jerusalem). The most notable thing to learn from this view of message activity is how the ebb and flow of messages corresponds to the ebb and flow of school activity in general. That is, valleys occur during vacations, and peaks occur at midsemester. By itself this is not surprising at all. But an examination in the activity generated by the different sites shows peaks and valleys at different times from those of other sites. Spring vacation in one site does not correspond to spring vacation at another, especially those in very different places. If we had southern hemisphere locations involved, their summer vacation in December and January obviously would not correspond to the July and August lull shown on this chart.

So, the general level of activity of instructional networking is very similar to that of face-to-face instruction. This is not at all surprising, since both occur within the context of the same institutions, and are constrained by the schedules of those institutions. Yet it is important to keep this fact in mind when organizing network instructional activities. If you don't, you end up assuming that everyone else on the network has the same schedule that you do, and then fail to understand a lack of response.

Another important point to learn from this global message flow analysis is how long it takes for activity to start at the beginning of each semester. Partly because not all schools start at the same time in the fall and partly because some of the participants needed some training to be able to participate fully, the ramp up to fall activity took longer than the ramp up for the spring semester (14 weeks in the fall vs. 6 weeks in the spring).

Using the Intermessage Reference Analysis to identify clusters of messages, we can carry out the Message Flow Analysis on individual messages. Some activities arise and reach a peak of activity over a short period of time, while others start out more slowly. This is shown in Figure 8.9 below.

Figue 8.8 Flow of Messages Across a Year

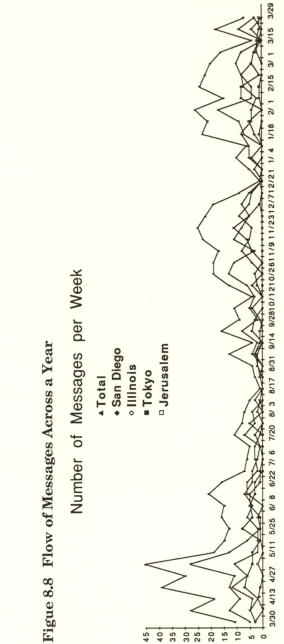

Number of Messages per Week

▲ Total
● San Diego
○ Illinois
■ Tokyo
□ Jerusalem

208

Figure 8.9 Message Flows for Two Clusters

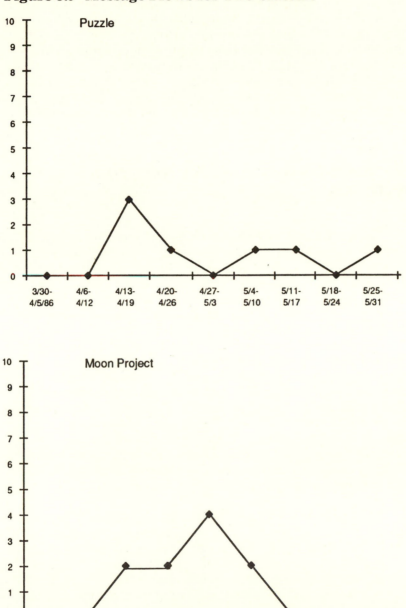

We are currently examining the shapes of these message flow diagrams for different clusters, trying to see whether there are systematic differences in message flow that are related to different kinds of network activities. But the simple analysis done here shows how even the most rapidly developing clusters take weeks to rise to a peak. The nature of this nonreal time medium is to stretch interaction out over time. This time stretching is at least somewhat compensated for by breadth at any moment created by the multiple threads that people can participate in.

IMPLICATIONS OF THESE ANALYSES FOR INSTRUCTION

Now that we've developed these different ways of analyzing message interactions, what have we learned about instruction? Although we have found some similarities to face-to-face instruction, we have also found some important differences. And we've learned that we can't blindly transfer existing instructional activities to this new interactive medium and expect them to work well, because of the important differences we have found.

What is the nature of educational activities that flourish in this new instructional medium? We know that they are different from conventional instruction. Are they more similar to other computer-based activities? Let us compare these network activities with other computer-based educational activities. One of the most common uses of computers is for drill-and-practice programs. Interestingly, the interactional pattern of these programs is very close to the strict IRE sequences that Mehan found in classroom instruction. The computer initiates, the student replies, the computer evaluates, the computer initiates again, and so on.

The next most common use of computer (according to Becker 1986) is for programming. Although this is sometimes viewed as the student teaching the computer (Papert 1980; Taylor 1980), in fact most programming is more like direction giving or order giving. The programmer issues a command, the computer follows that command, the programmer gives another command (or tries to figure out why the first command didn't work). It is different from the conventional instructional pattern in that the programmer seldom communicates an evaluation to the computer (although many programmers issue quite strong evaluations verbally, few computers hear them). The interactional pattern, however, is quite different from the kinds of patterns we've found through the analyses presented here. Similarly, attempts to develop intelligent tutor systems have produced systems that have more linear kinds of dialogue interactions. They are also quite different from the patterns seen here.

What are more appropriate models of the interaction? There are two functioning interactional patterns that we propose as more similar to the interactional patterns we found: teletask forces and teleapprenticeships. One aspect we can trace with the analyses described previously is the fluid nature of participation in electronic network activities. Participants drop out; others join in later; others participate for the duration of the activity. Activities end; new ones form, either proposed de novo or emerging out of other activities. A model of interaction we can draw upon is that of a task force, a group of people drawn together to accomplish some task, usually for a limited time. Task forces often draw in additional people, either those solicited by the existing members or those attracted to the activity. So, the patterns we have seen here may point to a new pattern of educational interaction, "teletask forces," groups of people of diverse abilities drawn together for a short-term interaction.

Instruction also depends on longer-term arrangements. Apprenticeship is a long-term instructional pattern that predates schooling. In this kind of learning environment, instruction occurs within the context of the target domain. From the start, novices learn the overall structure of the task to be mastered, and then acquire expertise in the subparts within this context. Even in our highly schooled society, apprenticeships are the pattern used at the most advanced levels of education: law internships, advanced study, medical residencies and internships. The reason apprenticeships aren't used more widely is their high cost.

Patterns that we've observed in instructional electronic network interaction resemble those described in face-to-face apprenticeships (Lave 1977). Thus we may see emerging a new pattern, "teleapprenticeships," with some of the properties of face-to-face apprenticeships (Levin, Riel, Miyake, and Cohen 1987).

These two models, teletask forces and teleapprenticeships, are presented here to illustrate that new ways of thinking about instruction will be required to use the new interactive media effectively. And as these new instructional models emerge, they will allow us to see more clearly aspects of face-to-face instruction by their contrasts.

REFERENCES

Au, K. H. (1980). On participation structures in reading lessons. *Anthropology and Education Quarterly, 2*: 91-115.

Austin, J. (1962). *How to do things with words*. Cambridge, MA: Harvard University Press.

Becker, H. (1986). *Instructional uses of school computers*. Reports from the 1985 National Survey, no. 1. Baltimore: Johns Hopkins University, Center for Social Organization of Schools.

Black, S. D., Levin, J. A., Mehan, H. & Quinn, C. N. (1983). Real and nonreal time interaction: Unraveling multiple threads of discourse. *Discourse Processes, 6* (1): 59-75.

Cohen, M., Levin, J. A., & Riel, M. M. (1986). *An intercultural electronic network for social science learning*. Technical report. Champaign: University of Illinois, Department of Educational Psychology.

d'Andrade, R. G., & Wish, M. (1985). Speech act theory in quantitative research on interpersonal behavior. *Discourse Processes, 8*: 229-59.

Florio, S. (1978). *Learning how to go to school*. Unpublished doctoral dissertation, Harvard University.

Garfield, E. (1972). Citation analysis as a tool in journal evaluation. *Science, 178*: 471-79.

Hiltz, S. R., & Turoff, M. (1978). *The network nation: Human communications via computer*. Reading, MA: Addison-Wesley.

Katz, M. M., McSwiney, E., & Stroud, K. (1987). *Facilitating collegial exchange among science teachers: An experiment in computer-based conferencing*. Technical report. Cambridge, MA: Harvard Graduate School of Education, Educational Technology Center.

Lave, J. (1977). Tailor-made experiments and evaluating the intellectual consequences of apprenticeship training. *Quarterly Newsletter of the Laboratory of Comparative Human Cognition, 1*: 1-3.

Levin, J. A. & Cohen, M. (1985). The world as an international science laboratory: Electronic networks for science instruction and problem solving. *Journal of Computers in Mathematics and Science Teaching 4* (4): 33-5.

Levin, J. A., Riel, M., Miyake, M., & Cohen, M. (1987). Education on the electronic frontier: Teleapprentices in globally distributed educational contexts. *Contemporary Educational Psychology, 12*: 254-60.

Levin, J. A., Waugh, M., & Kolopanis, G. (1988). Science instruction on global electronic networks. *Spectrum: The Journal of the Illinois Science Teachers Association, 13*: 19-23.

Mehan, H. (1978). Structuring school structure. *Harvard Educational Review, 48*: 32-64.

———— (1979). *Learning lessons.* Cambridge, MA: Harvard University Press.

Mehan, H., Moll, L., & Riel, M. M. (1985). *Computers in classrooms: A quasi-experiment in guided change.* La Jolla, CA: University of California, San Diego.

Newman, D. (1986). Local and long distance computer networking for science classrooms. Paper presented at the American Educational Research Association Meetings, San Francisco, April.

Papert, S. (1980). *Mindstorms. Children, computers, and powerful ideas.* New York: Basic Books.

Philips, S. (1972). Participant structures and communicative competence. In C. Cazden et al. (eds.), *Functions of language in the classroom.* New York: Teachers College Press.

———— (1982). *The invisible culture: Communication in classroom and community on the Warm Springs Indian Reservation.* New York: Longmans.

Quinn, C. N., Mehan, H., Levin, J. A., & Black, S. D. (1983). Real education in nonreal time: The use of electronic message systems for instruction. *Instructional Science, 11* (4): 313-27.

Riel, M. M. (1985). The Computer Chronicles Newswire: A functional learning environment for acquiring literacy skills. *Journal of Educational Computing Research, 1* (3): 317-37.

Riel, M. M., & Levin, J. A. (1985). Educational electronic networks: How they work (and don't work). Paper presented at the American Educational Research Association Meetings, Chicago, April.

Searle, J. R. (1969). *Speech acts: An essay in the philosophy of language.* Cambridge: Cambridge University Press.

Taylor, R. P. (1980). *The computer in the school: Tutor, tool, tutee.* New York: Teachers College Press.

Waugh, M., Miyake, N., Levin, J. A., & Cohen, M. (1988). Problem solving interactions on electronic networks. Paper presented at the American Educational Research Association Meetings, New Orleans, April.

Chapter 9
Hypertextual Perspectives on Educational Computer Conferencing

Richard Wolfe

Computer conferencing is an important kind of computer-mediated communication system; it is the computerized analogue of a meeting, allowing a group of participants to exchange and share messages and generate a common record of the discussion. Computer conferencing has been used for scientific and professional knowledge networking, for discussion and coordination of business work, and for general-purpose communication in environments such as university computing communities.

A recent and promising application of computer conferencing is delivery of formal education courses at the postsecondary level and in professional development. In many cases, computer conferencing implements distance education. In these contexts, the structure of a computer conference is parallel to that in a conventional course: There are students and there is a teacher; there is a specific time line and there are specific educational goals and objectives; there is a need for individual accomplishments and individual evaluation; a course is generally a recurring process, with the same teacher and new students. In some recent work, there has been experimentation with special computer conferencing techniques involving whole group and subgroup seminars, paired learner activities, and other tasks that structure the learner population, the content, and the time line of a course (Harasim 1987).

Computer conferencing can be conceptualized as a form of hypertext, which we may begin to define as a nonlinear networking of textual information (see Conklin 1987). The theoretical origins of hypertext go back several decades to efforts to control scientific information databases, and further theory and practice have been connected to the development of advanced computer systems. Until a few years ago, computerized hypertext systems were available only on advanced computing equipment, especially artificial intelligence work stations. One of the more advanced implementation is Notecards (Halasz, Moran, and Trigg 1987), which runs on Xerox LISP work stations. Starting in about 1985, various commercial programs for idea processing became available and popular for personal computers. These programs provide some level of hypertext ability. Then in the summer of 1987, the Hypercard system for the Apple Macintosh computer was released; it has generated a flurry of interest in hypertext and commercial development of hypertext databases and interfaces.

A computer conference is an instance of hypertext. It consists of text items with complex linkages and identification. The participants can view the conference at different levels of detail or abstraction, through application of branching and browsing mechanisms. But the existing computer conferencing systems are rather limited and awkward instances of hypertext. Furthermore, the participants and organizers of computer conferences have very weak hypertext tools for organizing and viewing the conference. Consequently, we find conference users inventing their own hypertext adjuncts. One evidence for the problem is that the participants in a computer conference—especially an extensive one, such as for a graduate-level course—need to adopt elaborate manual systems to keep track of the conference and their reading of it. For example, we have a number of cases of students printing the conference as it occurs, cutting the transcript into individual notes or items, and reorganizing these by theme—either categorizing and linking the themes by posting the notes on a wall or storing notes in manila folders categorized by topic (Harasim 1988): manual hypertext. More sophisticated users employ their computer disk storage and word processor for similar purpose (Harasim 1988).

My interest in connecting computer conferencing and hypertext is twofold: first, as we shall see below, recasting computer conferences in more powerful hypertext systems facilitates content analysis—a qualitative determination of who said what, when in the chronological sequence or logical sequence things were said, and how things were said. With a hypertext system, we can split a conference into its items, label and categorize the items, make explicit our interpretations of the linkages, and read back and tabulate what we find. The second reason to relate hypertext and computer conferencing is to lead to improvements in the interface design model for computer conferencing. We would like to provide the moderator and the participants in a computer conference with a better grasp of overall content and structure of the conference in progress, better navigation tools, and a more efficient process of contribution and interpretation.

HYPERTEXTUAL ANALYSIS OF COMPUTER CONFERENCES

As noted in the preface, there were a number of preliminary computer conferences that led to the chapters in the present book, and I was a participant in the conferences. For purposes of illustrating hypertextual analysis of computer conferences, one of these conferences, a discussion of the Feenberg chapter on social factors, was captured to disk, reformatted, carved up into individual items, and copied into one kind of hypertext system, the IZE program (Kleinberger and Blanks 1988).

As readers familiar with the literature on hypertext will realize, I am using the term "hypertext" in a somewhat idiosyncratic fashion. The manufacturers of the IZE software do not market their product as hypertext, and hypertext research specialists usually restrict their attention to more elaborate, graphically oriented systems. But for me the term "hypertext" should be applied when both of the following conditions are met:

1. There is a textual database that has a complex organization
2. The operator of the software can view the database through multiple paths and perspectives.

Both these conditions apply to the IZE program in its application to the computer conference on social factors.

The 37 notes in the social factors conference were lightly edited, reformatted, and separated into 37 files. The files were pulled into IZE and given keywords. The assignment of keywords initially was done manually. With IZE, the operator (me) moves the cursor to a word in a text and hits a special key (F4). That causes the word to be highlighted on the screen, and treated for analysis and retrieval purposes as a keyword. When the text did not contain a word considered to be an appropriate keyword, it was added not to the text; rather, a different special key (ALT-F4) was hit, entering it in a box that would pop up. The text and nontext keywords function identically for analysis and retrieval. The initial assignment of keywords was done thoughtfully. Then some more automatic tools were employed. The IZE program can be made to look through the bodies of all texts and flag keywords from a provided list or from the set of all keywords currently in use; it also can flag words that are specially marked or set off in the texts. In this way, keywords were added for themes that had been identified in the manual operation (themes such as Searching, Branching, CoSy, etc.). The name of the conference item writer was added to the keyword list.

The IZE program has the usual hypertext facilities for building arbitrary links from one item to another, so that when a person browsing through the database sees a special "button" in the text, he or she can press the button and jump to read another item. The unique capability of IZE, however, is its method of employing the keywords to prepare and display an outline structure of the database. An overall structure for the 37 social factor conference items is given in Figure 9.1(a). This is a table of contents restricted to "", that is, not restricted at all. The program has analyzed the frequency of the keywords and determined a major division into branching, features, options, Feenberg, etc. How this is done is never explained; it has something to do with maximizing the information in the outline, and it is artificially intelligent. Within the outline, the major and minor keywords combine to give either an exact description of an item, marked in the outline with the symbol ">," or a count of items that have some further keyword articulation, indicated with the count enclosed in "{ }". For example, there is one item, in outline position I-E, with keywords "branching," "Henri," "reordering," "searching," and "Features." There are three items, in outline position II, with the keyword "features" and some combination of other keywords.

Once IZE has an outline on the screen, the operator has three ways to look further. First, he or she can select and display any of the fully described items, marked with ">," by moving the cursor on the outline and hitting the "enter" key. Second, any of the incompletely articulated items, or any branch containing incompletely articulated items, can be selected and expanded, which yields a new outline. Third, the sequence of items in a branch can be examined one after another—this is called browsing.

The outline is displayed by IZE in response to a search request, which is phrased in a conventional Boolean notation. Figure 9.1(b) is the outline for a selection with one specified term, "branch,*" which means any keyword, such as "branch," "branching," "branches." The outline is specialized to the 18 items that had such a keyword. Figures 9.1(c) and 9.1(d) give the outlines of further searches made on the social factors conference items. The IZE program has mechanisms, not illustrated here, for guiding the construction of outlines according to a specified divi-

sion of contents, for filtering out keywords, for affecting the outlines, and for selecting texts using full-text scans.

The essence of the IZE outline is that it gives a comprehen-
sible perspective on the contents of the database or a section of the
database. At the highest level, it may show a simple marginal
tabulation of keywords. As a search focuses on a smaller area of
the database, the outline becomes more articulated and complete,
until all the available keywords are in the outline (there are no
unexpanded branches) or the operator is looking at a single item.
This allows an unprecedented grasp of the multivariate nature of
the keyword assignments. For example, in Figure 9.1(d), we see
that Branching was a major topic of discussion with respect to
specific conferencing software systems, we see some evident comparison of CoSy, Forum, and Parti in terms of their provision of
filtering; and we see some isolated discussion of other points.

Before leaving this example, it should be noted that some
kinds of hypertextual analysis are not present in the IZE application. First of all, the structure is determined by keywords and is
always fluctuating, according to the set of items selected. This
contrasts with a hierarchical hypertext, like that provided by an
outline processor such as MORE (Winer, Baron, and Winer 1986),
in which the structure is actually fixed and then expanded or contracted during viewing. Second, in IZE, the categories of the organization, the nodes of the outline, are not explicitly labeled; they
are identified with the keywords or items as selected and displayed. In other hypertext systems, the superstructure is explicitly graphed and its elements are named. With full-blown systems such as Notecards (Halasz, Moran, and Trigg 1987), the
paths connecting items or objects that are named or have data in
them.

DESIGNING A HYPERTEXTUAL INTERFACE FOR
EDUCATIONAL COMPUTER CONFERENCING

From the point of view of computer programming, a conferencing system is a database of text messages with some degree
of organization and control and an interface through which the
conference participants gain access, input and output, to the
database. The interface comprises the central conferencing
software and the software in the participant's terminal or
microcomputer. I want to concentrate on the design of the interface in terms of the information it contains and the logical power it
provides, leaving aside technical and practical matters such as

menus, pointing devices, automated dialing, uploading and downloading, etc.

I shall also concentrate here on a passive hypertextual interface for the student in an educational conference. For the instructor, there are additional information and processing requirements involved in starting and repeating a course and in monitoring and evaluating participation roles. And as I shall mention later, there are interesting possibilities for creating a more active computer conferencing interface—that is, one with explicit logic and processes to motivate the participant's behavior and to shape the course of the conference.

Choice of a Metaphor

The experienced user of a computer conferencing system might be unaware that he or she is operating in a metaphor, as Monsieur Jordan was unaware that he was speaking in prose. That is to say, we conventionally use a concrete terminology for the conferencing material and processing that is only metaphorically related to the detailed electro-mechanical computer operation or the mathematical data structure of the conferencing database. For many systems and many users, the metaphor is one of the "message central," where you receive notes as on a teleprinter, and tear them off to read and act on them, or replay them from a backup store, and type in new messages to be sent off. This metaphor is suggested by the system documentation and training materials and by the textual trim that is put around conference text.

Some kind of metaphor is required: we cannot think constantly in bits and bytes. The goals of a metaphor must be to give the user a grasp of the communication medium, a terminology for thinking and talking about the elements and procedures of the computer conference. What does the conference "look like" at a particular point in time, and "where" is the user relative to the progress or content of the conference? The metaphor provides the participant with a medium for gaining a sense of size, depth, and organization of the current content of a conference and for understanding the magnitude and direction of his/her task.

The metaphor of a message central could be reprogrammed in a hypertextual redesign of computer conferencing and replaced with one of the following metaphors:

1. The conference is taking place in a meeting room, with the participants sitting around a table. Each person has a pile of notes which can be passed around, copied,

read out. There is a chalkboard for everyone to look at.

2. The conference is a tree with a trunk, a pattern of branches, and leaves with notes. It can be traversed, looked at from afar, augmented with new leaves or branches; limbs can be removed or grafted.

3. The conference is the annotated transcript of the conference, with line numbers, interlinear commentary, cross-references, attributions, and emendations. Participants have different levels of editorial power and responsibility.

4. The conference participants are adventurers travelling through physical space, encountering materials to be studied and discussed, keeping logs of their travels, and annotating a map of where they have been.

The Apple Macintosh computer interface, based on earlier work by Xerox, provides the metaphor of a office desktop and office files. The objects such as texts and programs are represented as icons on the screen (the desktop), specifically located, able to be opened, moved around, labeled, color-coded (on a color Macintosh), thrown away, filed in folders, copied, stored on disk machines, etc. This kind of metaphor could be adapted for a computer conferencing interface with the addition of some essential features. It is especially important to be able to judge the size of an element or branch of the conference.

Organizational Abilities

In current practice with computer conferencing, there is an emphasis and concern about navigating about a conference and searching for material, so that a participant can locate items related to one being read or follow a thread of discussion. There is a logical duality between searching and organizing, and my hypertextual interface would emphasize the latter. There should be extensive mechanisms in the interface to facilitate indexing, categorizing, labeling, and "placing" the components of a conference. Good conference organization will facilitate searching in a conference, because items will be grouped and quick approximate selection can be made. It should also motivate searching, by providing the participant with a sense of what kinds of content are available. As is well known from psychology, the activity of sorting and categorizing items is an extremely efficient way of learning and remembering them.

The organizational ability should be exercised when items are entered by their authors as indications of the intention of their contributions. The authors can incorporate content keys, make cross-references, and place their notes in specific locations or branches. Then further organization should be made when an item is read by each participant as the interpretation of the item. These interpretations are necessarily personal and idiosyncratic; that is, there will be as many interpretive organizations as there are participants. In the course of a conference, the moderator or the original author or perhaps the group in some way can provide a public reorganization, by rekeying or relocating items.

A conventional way to classify text items is to assign keywords. As in the IZE example given earlier, this might be done by attaching a list of keywords or by marking words in text—highlighting them with special visual marks or modes. Keywords implicitly define multidimensional classifications of items. Using a system like IZE, keywords can provide multiple organizational perspectives, allowing an on-going content analysis of the conference. A simpler procedure is to place items in categories. In a desktop metaphor, this could correspond to locating items in specific "places"—in-box, action-box, content folder, on the desk—or in particular physical spaces—such as the lower right quadrant of the computer screen.

From either verbal, keyword systems or nonverbal, categorical or spatial systems, the hypertextual interface should allow easy switching between specific notes in the conference and organizational perspectives, and the participant should be able to traverse the conference at the organizational level, and choose when to focus in on particular notes of interest.

Annotational Abilities

In current conferencing systems, there is always a mechanism for keeping track for each participant of which items have been read and which are new. This information is sometimes available to the moderator or to all participants. A hypertextual interface should extend this ability, which conceptually is an annotation imposed on the conference database. Partly the extension can be imbedded in the metaphor: items are in in-boxes or pending files or located on distribution lists. Also the categorization system can be used to provide finer levels of operation: tickler files, chronologies, statistics about online time and contributions, and graphics about the size of different parts of the conference.

The hypertextual environment should further allow a new layer of textual accumulation in the conference—what in hypertext systems are called metanotes.

An important purpose is to provide an analogue of the handwritten, interlinear annotation of a transcript. That is, the initial record is supplemented with an annotation. In the computer implementation, this might be accomplished by having specially bracketed material inserted into notes or by having flags inserted that invoke metanotes, say as pop-up windows. For the personal hypertext of an individual, these would work like underlining or highlighting or adding marginal notes when reading print material. On the other hand, the annotations might be written by an individual but made available to the group, or they might be commentary by the instructor or designated participant editors.

Annotation can also consist of cross-reference and linkage. A special key is inserted in a note to mark someone's notion of an appropriate reference to another note. This could be a simple citation or it could be, in a more elaborate hypertext system, an active button to invoke a move to that other note. This provides another way of navigating through a conference, an alternative to traversing the conference at a higher organizational level. Somewhat intermediate between these methods is the production and continuing maintenance of an index where participants can browse for or look up items.

HYPERTEXTUAL ISSUES FOR COMPUTER CONFERENCING ANALYSIS AND DESIGN

The design issues for hypertext interfaces for computer conferences are parallel to the research issues in analyzing what went on in a computer conference. Except, of course, that the participant in ongoing computer conference has a growing and evolving hypertext to deal with. The use of hypertextual interfaces for educational computer conferencing would seem to have some special design requirements that relate to the learning objectives of an educational course of study.

Labels Versus Categories

Categories are classes of items. Keywords define classes. But keyword systems and category systems are not the same thing conceptually or practically. It is a qualitatively different task to organize items into groups than to label the groups. Some hypertext systems allow one to make organizations that are unlabeled and based on seeing one, several, or all items of a category rather than a label for the category. In an education course, learning about the keywords, or terminology and categorical structure of the content domain, may be an important part of the objectives. This suggests that the categorical structure needs to be flexible and subject to periodic reappraisal. A methodology for studying categorization behavior is given in Miller, Wiley, and Wolfe (1986).

Categorization Versus Network

Category systems are the simplest way to organize items. In many cases, they may be sufficient. Keyword systems lead to multiple categorizations. More generally, networks allow complex linkage. But is such complexity really useful? The computer conference, as organized in a hypertext system, becomes a statement of the content of a course of study. Categorical structures and hierarchies may be more appropriate summarizations of the knowledge imparted and attained than the maze of paths and connections, which can be considered the object and not the result of study, the trees and not the forest. Many hypertext systems, however, such as Apple's Hypercard, concentrate on linkage rather than perspective.

Item Organization Versus Pointer Systems

Long conference items often consist of the concatenation of several distinct contributions. How could this be prevented or treated? Should they be split apart? An alternative is to make the hypertext system point to places in an item rather than to an item. Short items are easy to categorize and organize, but then the organizational structure becomes an important part of the knowledge structure that the hypertext represents. Eventually, the production of linear text may be an objective of an educational program. With the IZE program (Kleinberger and Blanks 1988), the keywording and indexing can be done outside the body of text and the final items being analyzed can be effective links to word-processing documents.

Process Control Versus Information Control

The hypertext system in which a computer conference is embedded can potentially be used for passive organization and access to the information or for active control of the process and sequence of interaction, collaboration, and contribution by participants. How much structure is useful? Teachers and learners either have to direct their activities or have their activities directed for them. To some extent, beginners in a field need to learn the sequence of information that requires consideration, and so some automation and mechanization of process may be useful. Extensive work in hypermedia that guides learning is being carried out in the CSILE project (Scardamalia et al. 1989), for *Computer Supported Intentional Learning Environments*.

Personal Versus Group Perspectives

Computer conferencing is a hypertext application with many participants. Should each have a personal hypertextual perspective on the conference, should there be a union hypertext, or should both kinds of organizations coexist? How do central and distributed hypertext copies diverge and become synchronized? To what extent is the hypertext or the computer conference an individual or isolated endeavor, and to what extent does it approach the global and seamless web of an electronic information community envisioned by Vannevar Bush in 1945?

CONCLUSIONS

In this chapter, I have considered conceptual and practical connections between computer conferencing and hypertext. Hypertext involves nonlinear networking of textual (or other) information and an ability to access information with multiple paths and perspectives. A computer conference—and I have concentrated on educational settings—consists of a network of text (or other) items contributed and read by conference participants, the learners and teachers in a course. That is, computer conferencing is conceptually an instance or application of hypertext. I illustrated this by recasting transcripts from educational computer conferences into hypertext databases. Practically, current computer conferencing systems are awkward implementations of hypertext, where the participants and organizers have only weak hypertext tools for organizing and viewing the content of the conference. I proposed that hypertext theory and practice can contribute to the understanding and analysis of educational computer conferencing and, further, can lead to redesign of capabilities and interfaces of computer conference systems. I concluded by raising issues that are especially pertinent for educational applications in such a redesign, because they affect the learning processes: methods of categorization and labeling, organizational methods, definition of the unit of analysis, control of process, and individual versus group hypertext perspectives.

This last issue is, I think, the key one for future merging of computer conferencing and hypertext systems. There is implicit in the individual-group arrangements an important and difficult educational design problem concerning the distribution, processing, control, and ownership of information and knowledge; and there is a technologically complex problem of building local and central hypertexts with efficient means for communication.

Figure 9.1 Keyword-based Outlines Produced by IZE

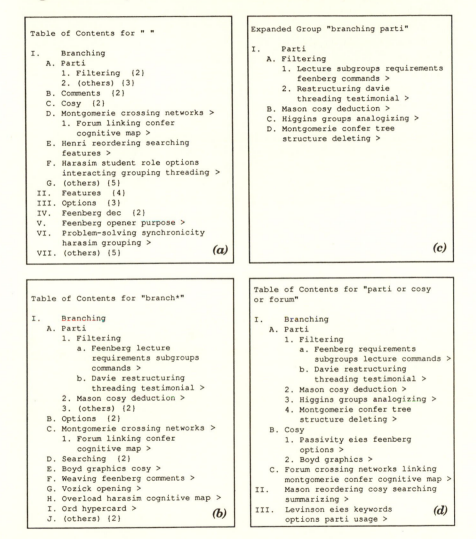

```
Table of Contents for " "

I.      Branching
   A. Parti
      1. Filtering  {2}
      2. (others)  {3}
   B. Comments  {2}
   C. Cosy  {2}
   D. Montgomerie crossing networks >
      1. Forum linking confer
         cognitive map >
   E. Henri reordering searching
      features >
   F. Harasim student role options
      interacting grouping threading >
   G. (others)  {5}
II.     Features  {4}
III.    Options  {3}
IV.     Feenberg dec  {2}
V.      Feenberg opener purpose >
VI.     Problem-solving synchronicity
        harasim grouping >
VII.    (others)  {5}
```
(a)

```
Expanded Group "branching parti"

I.      Parti
   A. Filtering
      1. Lecture subgroups requirements
         feenberg commands >
      2. Restructuring davie
         threading testimonial >
   B. Mason cosy deduction >
   C. Higgins groups analogizing >
   D. Montgomerie confer tree
      structure deleting >
```
(c)

```
Table of Contents for "branch*"

I.      Branching
   A. Parti
      1. Filtering
         a. Feenberg lecture
            requirements subgroups
            commands >
         b. Davie restructuring
            threading testimonial >
      2. Mason cosy deduction >
      3. (others)  {2}
   B. Options  {2}
   C. Montgomerie crossing networks >
      1. Forum linking confer
         cognitive map >
   D. Searching  {2}
   E. Boyd graphics cosy >
   F. Weaving feenberg comments >
   G. Vozick opening >
   H. Overload harasim cognitive map >
   I. Ord hypercard >
   J. (others)  {2}
```
(b)

```
Table of Contents for "parti or cosy
or forum"

I.      Branching
   A. Parti
      1. Filtering
         a. Feenberg requirements
            subgroups lecture commands >
         b. Davie restructuring
            threading testimonial >
      2. Mason cosy deduction >
      3. Higgins groups analogizing >
      4. Montgomerie confer tree
         structure deleting >
   B. Cosy
      1. Passivity eies feenberg
         options >
      2. Boyd graphics >
   C. Forum crossing networks linking
      montgomerie confer cognitive map >
II.     Mason reordering cosy searching
        summarizing >
III.    Levinson eies keywords
        options parti usage >
```
(d)

REFERENCES

Conklin, J. (1987). Hypertext: An introduction and survey. *IEEE Computer, 20* (9): 17-41.

Halasz, F. G., Moran, T. P. & Trigg, R. H. (1987). Notecards in a nutshell. In *Proceedings of CHI+GI (Toronto, April 5-9, 1987)*. New York: ACM, pp. 44-52.

Harasim, L. (1987). Teaching and learning online: Issues in computer-mediated graduate courses. *Canadian Journal of Educational Communication, 16* (2): 117-35.

———— (1988). *Issues in online learning*. Computer Conferencing Technical Report no.9. Toronto: Educational Evaluation Center, Ontario Institute for Studies in Education.

Kleinberger, P. & Blanks, N. (1988). IZE Version 1.0 [microcomputer software]. Madison, WI: Persoft, Inc.

Miller, D. M., Wiley, D. E., & Wolfe, R. G. (1986). Categorization methodology: an approach to the collection and analysis of certain classes of qualitative information. *Multivariate Behavioral Research, 21* : 135-67.

Scardamalia, M., Bereiter, C., McLean, R. S., Swallow, J., & Woodruff, E. (1989). Computer-supported intentional learning environments. *Journal of Educational Computing Research, 5* (1): 51-68.

Winer, P., Baron, D. & Winer, D. (1986). MORE [microcomputer software]. Mountain View, CA: Living Videotext, Inc.

Chapter 10
Bibliography on Educational CMC

Linda M. Harasim

The final chapter of this book presents a comprehensive bibliography on educational CMC. This bibliography will, it is hoped, contribute to disseminating research on educational CMC, valuable to researchers, designers, and implementors; it also offers a starting point for those new to the field.

In developing this bibliography, I have included publications about educational CMC from all educational levels and countries, written in English. Under the rubric of "CMC" I have included articles on applications of electronic mail, bulletin boards, and computer conferencing; while this collection emphasizes asynchronous communication, articles on synchronous-mode educational CMC have been included to reflect an important new line of research and development. This bibliography considers only systems that involve computer-mediated communication systems: literature on video and audio conferencing systems is not represented here. This collection also concentrates on publications dealing explicitly and primarily with educational CMC; however, selected key texts on general CMC, viewed as classics or as seminal to the field of CMC, have also been included as background for educators and researchers using these new environments. Another selection "criterion" was accessibility; hence I have included only material published as articles, books, reports, or papers in proceedings.

This bibliography draws together a "state of the art" of online education: accomplishments in educational CMC in the first decade. The pages that follow testify to a remarkable interest in spreading the word, as well as in deepening our understanding of the online educational experience. Much new ground has been covered: this work represents, however, only the first steps of activity and explorations. Subsequent developments have a history to build upon and a future to build.

Adams, D.M., & Bott, D.A. (1984). Tapping into the world: Computer telecommunications networks and schools. *Computers in the Schools, 1*(3), 3-17.

Alexander, G., & Lincoln, C. (1989). The thoughtbox: A computer based communication system for distance learning. In R. Mason & A.R. Kaye (Eds.), *Mindweave: Communication, computers and distance education* (pp. 86-100). Oxford: Pergamon Press.

Amara, R., & Vallee, J. (1974). Forum: A computer-based system to support interaction among people. In *Proceedings of the 1974 IFIP Congress*. Vol. 5 Systems for management and administration.

Andrews, J., & Strain J. (1985). Computer-assisted distance education: Off-line and on-line American experiences. *Distance Education, 6*(2), 143-157.

Arias, A., & Bellman, B. (1987). BESTNET: International cooperation through interactive Spanish/English transition telecourses. *Technology and Learning, 1*(3).

Atack, L. (1988). Learning by computer: Putting continuing education within reach of busy nurses. *The Canadian Nurse*, (March), pp. 24-26.

Bacsich, P.D. (1985). *Teleconferencing for distance education and training: Is the Open University experience typical?*. Optel Report No. 16) (ERIC Document Reproduction Service ED 273 258. Milton Keynes: The Open University.

Bacsich, P. (1989). Computer conferencing and electronic publishing: Cooperation or competition. In R. Mason & A.R. Kaye (Eds.), *Mindweave: Communication, computers and distance education* (pp. 247-251). London: Pergamon Press.

Baird, P., & Forer, B. (1987). An experiment in computer conferencing using a local area network. *Electronic Library, 5*(3), 162-69.

Baron, N.S. (1984). Computer mediated communication as a force in language change. *Visible Language, 18*(2), 118-140.

Bates, A.W. (1986). Computer assisted learning or communications: Which way for information technology in distance education? *Journal of Distance Education, 1*(1), 41-57.

Batson, T. (1988). The ENFI Project: A networked classroom approach to writing instruction. *Academic Computing, 2*(5), 32-33, 55-56.

Batson, T., & Peyton, J.K. (1986). The computer as fifth sense: Networking with deaf students to simulate natural language acquisition. *Teaching English to Deaf and Second Language Students, 4*(2), 12-18.

Bechtold, B., et al. (1972). EMISARI: Management information system designed to aid and involve people. In *Proceedings of the 4th International Symposium on Computer and Information Science*.

Beckwith, D. (1987). Group problem-solving via computer conferencing: The realizable potential. *Canadian Journal of Educational Communication, 16*(2), 89-106.

Berry, S. (1982). Educational resources — We deliver a computerized delivery system for Alaska's schools. *Educational Libraries, 7*(1-2), 12-14.

Bischoff, D. (1986). On-line learning. *The Village Voice (Guide to Summer Studies Supplement), April 29,* 11.

Bissell, S.A., Coombs, N.R., Medvedeff, D.J., & Rogers, S.M. (1987). Distance teaching techniques using electronic conferencing. In *Proceedings of the Second Guelph Symposium on Computer Conferencing* (pp. 3-9). Guelph, Ontario: University of Guelph.

Black, S.D., Levin, J.A., Mehan, H., & Quinn, C.N. (1983). Real and non-real time interaction: Unraveling multiple threads of discourse. *Discourse Processes, 6*(1), 59-75.

Bowen, D., & Kenealy, P. (1986). Isolated physics teachers: One solution. *The Physics Teacher,* (February), pp. 77-79.

Boyd, G.M. (1987). Emancipative educational technology. *Canadian Journal of Educational Communication, 16*(2), 167-172.

Boyd, G.M. (1989). The life-worlds of computer-mediated distance education. In R. Mason & A.R. Kaye (Eds.), *Mindweave: Communication, computers and distance education* (pp. 225-227). London: Pergamon.

Brienne, D., & Goldman, S.V. (1989). Networking: How it has enhanced science classes in New York schools...and how it can enhance classes in your school, too. *Classroom Computer Learning, 9*(7), 45-53.

Brochet, M.G. (1985a). Computer conferencing: A tool to enhance graduate student learning. In *Proceedings of the Guelph Symposium on Computer Conferencing and Electronic Messaging, January, 1985* . Guelph, Ontario: University of Guelph, Institute of Computer Science.

Brochet, M.G. (Ed.). (1985b). *Effective moderation of computer conferences.* Guelph, Ontario: University of Guelph, Computer Support Services.

Brochet, M.G. (1987). Computer conferencing as a seminar tool: A case study. In C. Crosby (Ed.), *Compendium of University of Guelph papers on computer conferencing: 1985-1987.* Guelph, Ontario: University of Guelph.

Brown, J.S. (1985a). Process versus product: A perspective on tools for communal and informal electronic learning. *Journal of Educational Computing Research, 1*(2), 179-201.

Brown, J.S. (1985b). Idea amplifiers — New kinds of electronic learning environments. *Educational Horizons, 63*(3), 108-122.

Brown, F.D. (1986). Telecommunications in higher education: Creating new information sources. *THE Journal: Technical Horizons in Education, 13,* 68-70.

Brown, E., & Sullivan, J. (1985). Electronic conferencing for faculty/student contact time. In Duncan K., & Harris, D. (Eds.), *Computers in education* (pp. 503-507). Amsterdam: Elsevier Science Publishing B.V.

Bugliarello, G. (1988). Toward hyperintelligence. *Knowledge: Creation, Diffusion, Utilization, 10*(1), 67-89.

Bull, G., Harris, J., Lloyd, J., & Short, J. (1989). The electronic academical village. *Journal of Teacher Education, 40*(4), 27-31.

Butler, G., & Jobe, H. (1987). The Australian-American connection. *The Computing Teacher, 14*(7), 25-26.

Cadsby, C.B. (1987). Computer conferencing and the teaching of economics: Application to a small advanced class. In C. Crosby (Ed.), *Compendium of University of Guelph papers on computer conferencing 1985-1987.* Guelph, Ontario: University of Guelph.

Caldwell, R.L., Van Nest, W.D., Tynan, A.A., & Leach, R.A. (1987). Conferencing selection and implementation: University of Arizona case history. In *Proceedings of the Second Guelph Symposium on Computer Conferencing* (pp. 209-222). Guelph, Ontario: University of Guelph.

C.A.L.L. Digest, Special Issue on Telecommunications for Language Teachers and Learners. Vol. 3, No. 5, 1987.

Carr, R. (1988). Computer conferencing and the university community. *Open Learning*, 3(2), 37-40.

Cartwright, G.F. (1977). Computer conferencing as an educational tool. *Learning and development*, 8(5).

Case, D. (1985). The personal computer: Missing link to the electronic journal? *Journal of the American Society for Information Science*, 36(5), 309-313.

Castro, A.S. (1988). Teaching and learning as communication: The potentials and current applications of computer-mediated communication systems for higher level education. In *Higher level distance education. Perspectives for international cooperation and new developments in technology*. Paris: UNESCO.

Castro, A., Stirzaker, L., Northcott, P., & Bacsich, P. (1986). Applications of computer communications technology to distance education. *Media in Education and Development*, 19(2), 92-96.

Chapman, D.T. (1986). Campus-wide networks: Three state-of-the-art demonstration projects. *THE Journal: Technical Horizons in Education*, 13, 66-70.

Chesebro, J.W. (1985). Computer-mediated interpersonal communication. In B.D. Ruben (Ed.), *Information and behavior* (pp. 202-222). New Brunswick, NJ: Transaction Books.

Clark, G.C. (1988). What goes up, must come down—Learning by Satellite. *The Computing Teacher*, 16(2), 13-15.

Clark, G.C. (1989). Distance education in United States schools. *The Computing Teacher*, 16(6), 7-10.

Cohen, M. & Riel, M.M. (1988). The effect of distant audiences on students' writing. *American Educational Research Journal*, (In press).

Cohen, M., Levin, J.A., & Riel, M.M. (1985). *The world as functional learning environment: An intercultural learning network* (Tech.Rep. No. 5). San Diego: University of California, Interactive Technology Laboratory.

Cohen, M., Levin, J.A., & Riel, M.M. (1986). *An intercultural electronic network for social science learning* (Technical Report). Champaign: University of Illinois, Department of Educational Psychology.

Cohen, M., & Miyake, N. (1986). A world wide intercultural network: Exploring electronic messaging for instruction. *Instructional Science, 15*(3), 257-273.

Cohen, M., & Riel, M. (1986). *Computer networks: Creating real audiences for students' writing.* Technical Report 15. San Diego: University of California, Interactive Technology Laboratory.

The Computing Teacher, Special Telecommunication Issue, May, 1988.

Coombs, N. (1987). Computer conferencing at RIT. *EDU, 44*(Spring), 17-18.

Coombs, N. (1989). Using CMC to overcome physical disabilities. In R. Mason, & A.R. Kaye (Eds.), *Mindweave: Communication, computers and distance education* (pp. 180-184). London: Pergamon.

Cox, W.F. (1985). *Observations on some tele-education trends and developments.* (Internal Report). Melbourne: Telecom Australia.

Crosby, C., & Hunter, C.S. (1987). A partial bibliography of references related to computer conferencing. In *Proceedings of the Second Guelph Symposium on Computer Conferencing* Guelph, Ontario: University of Guelph.

Cross, T.B. (1983a). Computer tele-conferencing and education. *Educational Technology, 23*(4), 29-31.

Cross, T.B. (1983b). Learning without going there: Education via computer tele/conferencing. In *Proceedings of the 4th Canadian Symposium on Instructional Technology, Winnipeg, Manitoba, October 19-21* (pp. 165-172). National Research Council of Canada.

Crowley, M.L. (1987). Curricular implications for teleconferencing in the classroom: Observations from two Canadian studies. *Education & Computing, 3*, 201-206.

Crowley, M.L. (1989). Organizing for electronic messaging in the schools. *The Computing Teacher, 16*(7), 23-26.

Crowston, K., Malone, T.W., & Lin, F. (1987-88). Cognitive science and design: A case study of computer conferencing. *Human Computer Interaction, 3*, 59-85.

Danowski, J.A. (1982). Computer-mediated communication: A network-based content analysis using a CBBS conference. In M. Burgoon (Ed.), *Communication Yearbook 6* (pp. 905-924). Beverly Hills: Sage Publications.

Davie, L.E. (1987a). Facilitation of adult learning through computer conferencing. In *Proceedings of the Second Guelph Symposium on Computer Conferencing* (pp. 11-21). Guelph, Canada: University of Guelph.

Davie, L.E. (1987b). Learning through networks: A graduate course using computer conferencing. *Canadian Journal of University Continuing Education, 13*(2), 11-26.

Davie, L.E. (1988). The facilitation of adult learning through computer mediated distance education. *Journal of Distance Education, III*(2), 55-69.

Davie, L.E. (1989). Facilitation techniques for the on-line tutor. In R. Mason & A.R. Kaye (Eds.), *Mindweave: Communication, computers and distance education* (pp. 74-85). London: Pergamon Press.

Davie, L.E., & Palmer, P. (1985). Computer-teleconferencing for advanced distance education. *Canadian Journal of University Continuing Education, 10*(2), 56-66.

Davies, D. (1989). Computer-supported cooperative learning: Interactive group technologies and distance learning systems. In R. Mason & A. Kaye (Eds.), *Mindweave: Communication, computers and distance education* (pp. 228). Oxford: Pergamon.

Davis, B., & Marlowe, C. (1984). The computer as a networking and information resource for adult learners. *New Directions for Continuing Education, 29*, 89-95.

Dede, C., Bowman, J., & Kierstead, F. (1982). Communications technologies and education: The coming transformation. In Didsbury, H.F., Jr. (Ed.), *Communications and the future* (pp. 174-182). Bethesda, MD: World Future Society.

DeLoughry, T.J. (1988). Remote instruction using computers found as effective as classroom sessions. *The Chronicle of Higher Education*, (April 20).

Derycke, A.C., & Nora, C. (1985). Data communication and computer networks: A proposal for a curriculum and a survey of different pedagogical aids. In Duncan, K., & Harris, D. (Eds.), *Computers in education* (pp. 245-249). Amsterdam: Elsevier Science Publishing B.V.

Dickson, M., Franklin, J., & Hill, A. (1987). Attitudinal changes through computer conferencing. In *Proceedings of the Second Guelph Symposium on Computer Conferencing* (pp. 63-68). Guelph, Canada: University of Guelph.

Dodd, W.P. (1987). Information exchange in the research community. In *Proceedings of the Second Guelph Symposium on Computer Conferencing* (pp. 307-322). Guelph, Canada: University of Guelph.

Dodge, B. & Dodge, J. (1987). Selecting telecommunication software for educational settings. *The Computing Teacher*, (April), pp. 10-12.

Dodge, B. & Dodge, J. (1989). *Modems, methods, and magic: A guide to telecommunications for educators*. Franklin, Beedle & Associates.

Dodge, J. & Dodge, B. (1987). Readiness activities for telecommunications. *The Computing Teacher*, *14*(7), 7-9.

Duranti, A. (1986). Framing discourse in a new medium: Openings in electronic mail. *The Quarterly Newsletter of the Laboratory of Comparative Human Cognition*, *8*(2), 64-71.

Ehrmann, S. (1988). Assessing the open end of learning: Roles for new technologies. *Liberal Education*, *74*(3), 5-11.

Ehrmann, S. (1989). Improving a distributed learning environment with computers and telecommunications. In R. Mason & A.R. Kaye (Eds.), *Mindweave: Communication, computers and distance education* (pp. 255-258). Oxford: Pergamon Press.

Eldridge, J.R. (1982). New dimensions in distance learning. *Training and Development Journal, 36*(10), 42-44, 46-47.

Ellenwood, W.C. (1987). Commodore users: On line. *The Computing Teacher, 14*(7), 13-14.

Ellis, M.L., & McCreary, E.K. (1985). The structure of message sequences in computer conferences: A comparative case study. In the *Proceedings of the Guelph Symposium on Computer Conferencing and Electronic Messaging, January, 1985*. Guelph, Ontario: University of Guelph.

Emms, J., & McConnell, D. (1988). An evaluation of tutorial support provided by electronic mail and computer conferencing. In *Aspects of educational technology XXI: Designing new systems and technologies for learning*. London: Kogan Page.

Engelbart, D.C., & Hooper, K. (1988). The augmentation system framework. In S. Ambron, & K. Hooper (Eds.), *Interactive media*. Washington: Microsoft Press, Apple Computer, Inc.

Ergener, D. & Wellens, A.R. (1985). A split-screen electronic messaging system for Apple II computers. *Behavior Research Methods, Instruments and Computers, 17*, 556-64.

Erickson, A. (1987). An ACOT experiment in learning. *The Computing Teacher, 14*(7), 31-32.

Fanning, T., & Raphael, B. (1986). Computer teleconferencing experience at Hewlett-Packard. In *Proceedings of the CSCW' 86 Conference on Computer-Supported Cooperative Work, December* (pp. 291-306). New York, NY: ACM.

Fano, R.M. (1985). Computer-mediated communication. *IEEE Technology and Society Magazine, 4*(1), 3-6.

Feenberg, A. (1986). Network design: An operating manual for computer conferencing. *IEEE Transactions on Professional Communication, 29*(1), 2-7.

Feenberg, A. (1987). Computer conferencing and the humanities. *Instructional Science, 16*, 169-186.

Feenberg, A. (1989a). The planetary classroom. *Proceedings of the IFIP Conference on Message Handling, 6.5*. Amsterdam: North Holland.

Feenberg, A. (1989b). The written world. In R. Mason, & A.R. Kaye (Eds.), *Mindweave: Communication, computers and distance education* (pp. 22-39). Oxford: Pergamon Press.

Feldman, M. (1986). Constraints on communication and electronic messaging. Proceedings of the CSCW '86 Conference on Computer-Supported Cooperative Work, pp. 73-90, Austin, Texas.

Ferguson, J.A. (1977). PLANET: A computer conferencing system and its evaluation through a case study. *Behavior Research Methods, Instruments and Computers, 9*, 92-95.

Field, A. (1985). Turning computers into college classrooms. *Business Week*, (October 14).

Finn, T.A. (1983). *Process and structure in computer-mediated group communication (conferencing)*. Unpublished doctoral dissertation, *Dissertation Abstracts International*, 45, 4502B. (University Microfilms No. AAC8410614).

Fischer, M. (1987). Selecting software: A survey of telecommunications software for the Apple II family. A+ *Magazine*, (April).

Flavin, R.A., Williford, J.D., & Barzali, H. (1986). Computer conferencing data structures in the GRANDiose system. *IEEE Transactions on Professional Communication, 29*(1), 34-44.

Florini, B. (1989). *Computer conferencing: A technology for adult education* (Technical Report No. 1). Syracuse, NY: Syracuse University Kellog Project.

Florini, B., & Vertrees, D. (1989). The institutional context for computer conferencing. In R. Mason & A.R. Kaye (Eds.), *Mindweave: Communication, computers and distance education* (pp. 232-235). Oxford: Pergamon.

Foster, D.L. (1985). *Educator's guide to conferencing using computers*. Washington, DC: National Institute of Education.

Freeman, L., & Freeman, S. (1980). A semi-visible college: Structural effects on a social networks group. In *Proceedings of Electronic Communication: Technology and Impacts. AAAS Selected Symposium 52* . Boulder, CO: Westview Press.

Gilcher, K., & Johnstone, S. (1988). *A critical review of the use of audiographic conferencing systems, by educational institutions for instructional delivery*. College Park, MD: University of Maryland, University College.

Gleason, B.J. (1987). Giving quizzes online on EIES and other VC tools. Technical Report, New Jersey Institute of Technology.

Glossbrenner, A. (1984). On-line college. *PC Magazine*, *3*(21), 297-298.

Goldberg, F. (1988). Telecommunications and the classroom: Where we've been and where we should be going. *Computer Teacher*, *15*(8), 26-30.

Goyens, C. (1985). The electronic university. *InfoAge*, *4*(8), 29-31.

Gray, R. (1989). CMC for in-service training. In R. Mason & A.R. Kaye (Eds.), *Mindweave: Communication, computers and distance education* (pp. 185-188). London: Pergamon Press.

Grint, K. (1989). Accounting for failure: Participation and non-participation in CMC. In R. Mason & A.R. Kaye (Eds.), *Mindweave: Communication, computers and distance education* (pp. 189-191). Oxford: Pergamon Press.

Guihot, P. (1989). Using Teletel for learning. In R. Mason & A.R. Kaye (Eds.), *Mindweave: Communication, computers and distance education* (pp. 192-195). London: Pergamon Press.

Guillaume, J. (1980a). Computer conferencing and our relationship to work. *ACM SIGSOC Bulletin 7*.

Guillaume, J. (1980b). Computer conferencing and the development of an electronic journal. *The Canadian Journal of Information Science*, *5*, 21-29.

Gurd, G., & Picot, J. (1987). A study of Atlantic Canadian user reactions to two inter-university electronic networks. In *Proceedings of the Second Guelph Symposium on Computer Conferencing* (pp. 245-261). Guelph, Canda: University of Guelph.

Gwen, R. & Longworth, N. (1988). Pluto—A European network for teacher education. *Proceedings of the Fifth International Conference on Technology and Education*. Edinburgh, Scotland: CEP Consultants, Ltd.

Halasz, I.M. (1984). *Feasibility study of telecommunications and electronic technologies useful to the National Academy for Vocational Education*. Final Administrative Report: Year One, Vol. II, . Columbus, OH: National Center for Research in Vocational Education, Ohio State University.

Handler, M. (1988). A second grade class lets their fingers do the talking. *The Computing Teacher*, *16*(2), 17-19.

Harasim, L.M. (1986a). Computer learning networks: Educational applications of computer conferencing. *Journal of Distance Education*, *1*(1), 59-70.

Harasim, L.M. (1986b). *Implementing the women educators' computer conferencing research project.* Toronto, Canada: Federation of Women Teachers' Associations of Ontario.

Harasim, L.M. (1987a). Computer-mediated cooperation in education: Group learning networks. In *Proceedings of the Second Guelph Symposium on Computer Conferencing, June 1-4* (pp. 171-186). Guelph, Canada: University of Guelph.

Harasim, L.M. (1987b). Teaching and learning on-line: Issues in computer-mediated graduate courses. *Canadian Journal for Educational Communication*, *16*(2), 117-135.

Harasim, L.M. (1989). Online Education: A new domain. In R. Mason & T. Kaye (Eds.), *Mindweave: Communication, computers and distance education* (pp. 50-62). Oxford: Pergamon Press.

Harasim, L.M., & Johnson, E.M. (1985). Educational applications of computer conferencing for teachers in Ontario. In *Proceedings of the Workshop of Computer Conferencing and Electronic Mail, January 22-23* . Guelph, Canada: Institute of Computer Science.

Harasim, L.M., & Johnson, E.M. (1986a). Computer conferencing and online education: Designing for the medium. *Canadian Journal for Information Science*.

Harasim, L.M., & Johnson, E.M. (1986b). *Educational applications of computer networks for teachers/trainers in Ontario.* Toronto, Ontario: Ministry of Education/Ontario Institute for Studies in Education.

Harasim, L.M., & Smith, D. (1988). *The women educators' computer conferencing research project.* Toronto, Ontario: Federation of Women Teachers' Associations of Ontario. The Ontario Institute for Studies in Education.

Harasim, L. & Winkelmans, T. (1988). *Computer-mediated scholarly collaboration: A case study of an online workshop.* Research Report. Toronto: Ontario Institute for Studies in Education.

Harasim, L.M., & Wolfe, R.G.   (1988). *Research analysis and evaluation of computer conferencing and networking in education* (Final Report). Toronto, Canada: Ontario Institute for Studies in Education.

Harasim, L.M. & Chandler-Crichlow, C. (1989). *Hypertextual transcript analyses of educational computer conferences.* Research Report # 15. Toronto, ON: Ontario Institute for Studies in Education.

Hargreaves, A., & Harasim, L. (1986). Net results in education: The electronic classroom. *EDU Magazine*, (41, Spring), pp. 27-29.

Harris, J.B. (In press). Tailoring telecommunications innovations to fit educational environments: The mode makes all the difference. *Educational Technology*.

Harris, M., Hannah, L., Matus, C., Watson, W.Jr., Kline, J., Zellers, S., & Erwin, J. (1987). Four on-line networking projects. *The Computing Teacher*, *14*(7), 33-34.

Hart, J., MacDonald, P.M., & MacDonald, I.C. (1987). A low cost system for interactive transmission of text and voice in distance education. In *Proceedings of the Second Guelph Symposium on Computer Conferencing* (pp. 263-269). Guelph, Canada: University of Guelph.

Hart, R. (1987). Towards a third generation distributed conferencing system.   *Canadian Journal for Educational Communication*, *16*(2), 137-152.

Hauptman, O., & Allen, T.J. (1987). *The influence of communication technologies on organizational structure: A conceptual model for future research* (Sloan School of Management Working Paper No. 90s: 87-038). Cambridge, MA: Massachusetts Institute of Technology.

Heidelback, R. (1984). Maryland education microcomputer network and Marynet. In *Proceedings, National Educational Computing Conference (June, 1984)*.

Heimstra, R., & Vertrees, D. (1987). ADNET - A single discipline network. In University of Guelph (Ed.), *Proceedings of the Second Guelph Symposium on Computer Conferencing* (pp. 323). Guelph, Ontario: University of Guelph.

Henri, F. (1988). Distance education and computer-assisted communication. *Prospects, 18*(1), 85-90.

Hiemstra, G. (1982). Teleconferencing: Concern for face and organizational culture. In M. Burgoon (Ed.), *Communication Yearbook* (pp. 874-904). Beverly Hills: Sage Publications.

Hiltz, S.R. (1984). *Online communities: A case study of the office of the future.* New Jersey: Ablex Publishing Corporation.

Hiltz, S.R. (1986). The "virtual classroom": Using computer-mediated communication for university teaching. *Journal of Communication, 36*(2), 95-104.

Hiltz, S.R. (1988). Collaborative learning in a virtual classroom. In *Proceedings of the Conference on Computer-Supported Cooperative Work,* (pp. 282-290). Portland, Oregon.

Hiltz, S.R., Johnson, K., & Agle, G.M. (1978). *Replicating Bales problem solving experiments on a computerized conference: A pilot study.* Newark, NJ: Computerized Conferencing and Communications Center, New Jersey Institute of Technology.

Hiltz, S.R., Johnson, K., Aronovitch, C., & Turoff, M. (1980). *Face-to-face vs. computerized conferences: A controlled experiment. Vol. 1: Findings* (Research Report No. 12). Newark, NJ: Computerized Conferencing and Communications Center, New Jersey Institute of Technology.

Hiltz, S.R., Johnson, K., & Turoff, M. (1986). Experiments in group decision making, 1: Communications process and outcome in face-to-face vs. computerized conferences. *Human Communications Research, 13*(2), 225-252.

Hiltz, S.R., & Kerr, E.B. (1986). Learning modes and subsequent use of computer-mediated communication systems. In *Proceedings of the CHI'86* (April): 149-155.

Hiltz, S.R., Kerr, E.B., & Johnson, K. (1985). *Determinants of acceptance of computer-mediated communication systems: A longitudinal study of four systems* (Research Report No. 22). Newark, NJ: Computerized Conferencing and Communications Center, New Jersey Institute of Technology.

Hiltz, S.R., & Turoff, M. (1978). *The network nation: Human communication via computer.* Reading, Mass.: Addison-Wesley Publishing Company, Inc.

Hiltz, S.R., & Turoff, M. (1981). The evolution of user behaviour in a computerized conferencing system. *Communications of the ACM, 24*(11), 739.

Hiltz, S.R., & Turoff, M. (1985). Structuring computer-mediated communications systems to avoid information overload. *Communications of the ACM, 28*(7), 680-689.

Hiltz, S.R., Turoff, M., & Johnson, K. (1981). The effect of structure, task, and individual attributes on consensus in computerized conferences. In Uhlig, R.P. (Ed.), *Computer message system*. Amsterdam: North Holland.

Hiltz, S.R., Turoff, M., & Johnson, K. (1985). *Mode of communication and the "risky shift": A controlled experiment with computerized conferencing and anonymity in a large corporation* (Computerized Conferencing and Communications Center Research Report No. 21). Newark, NJ: New Jersey Institute of Technology.

Hsu, E.Y.P., & Geithman, D.T. (1987). "Virtual Lab" and management education: An experiment in the use of a computer mediated conferencing system. In *Proceedings of the Sixteenth Annual Regional Conference, April 2-3* . Atlantic City, NJ: Decision Sciences Institute .

Hsu, E.Y.P., & Geithman, D.T. (1988). "Virtual management practices lab": Revisted research up-date. In *Proceedings of the Seventeenth Annual Regional Conference, March 23-25* . Newport, Rhode Island: Decision Sciences Institute.

Humphrey, C. (1985). Getting a turnout: The plight of the organizer. *Iassist Quarterly, 9*(2), 14-27.

Janda, K. (1987, October). Computer augmented teaching in large lecture courses: The case of the American government. *American Computing, 2*(2), 34-35, 42-43.

Johansen, R. (1984). *Teleconferencing and beyond: Communications in the office of the future.* New York, NY: McGraw-Hill.

Johansen, R., & Bullen, C. (1988). Thinking ahead: What to expect from teleconferencing. In I. Greif (Ed.), *Computer-supported cooperative work: A book of readings* (pp. 185-198). San Mateo, CA: Morgan Kaufmann Publishers.

Johansen, R., & DeGrasse, R. (1979). Computer-based teleconferencing: Effects on working patterns. *Journal of Communication, 29*(3), 30-41.

Johansen, R., DeGrasse, R., & Wilson, T. (1978). Group communication through computers. Volume 5: Effects on working patterns. (Report R-41). Washington, D.C.: National Institute of Education (Eric Reports).

Johansen, R., McNeal, B., & Nyhan, M. (1981). Telecommunications and developmentally disabled people: Evaluations of audio conferencing, personal computers, computer conferencing, electronic mail. (Report R-50) Menlo Park, CA: Institute for the Future.

Johansen, R., McNulty, M., & McNeal, B. (1978). *Electronic education: Using teleconferencing in post-secondary organizations.* Report R-2. Menlo Park, CA: Institute for the Future.

Johansen, R., Miller, R.H., & Vallee, J. (1974). Group communication through electronic media: Fundamental choices and social effects. *Educational Technology*, (August), pp. 7-20.

Johansen, R., Miller, R.H., & Vallee, J. (1975). Group communication through electronic media: Fundamental choices and social effects.. In H.A. Linstone & M. Turoff (Eds.), *The Delphi method: Techniques and applications* (pp. 517-534). Reading: Addison-Wesley Publishing Company.

Johansen, R., & Schuyler, J.A. (1975). Computerized conferencing in an educational system: A short-range scenario. In H.S. Linstone & M. Turoff (Eds.), *The Delphi method: Techniques and applications*. Reading, Mass.: Addison-Wesley.

Johansen, R., Schuyler J.A., & Vallee, J. (1975). Computerized conferencing in an educational system: A short range scenario. In H.A. Linstone & M. Turoff (Eds.), *The Delphi method: Techniques and applications* (pp. 517-534). Reading, MA: Addison-Wesley.

Johansen, R., Vallee, J., & Collins, K. (1978). Learning the limits of teleconferencing: Design of a teleconference tutorial. In *Evaluating new telecommunications services: Proceedings of the NATO Symposium on Telecommunications, Bergamo, Italy* . New York: Plenum.

Johansen, R., Vallee, J., & Spangler, K. (1979). *Electronic meetings: Technical alternatives and social choices*. Reading, MA: Addison-Wesley.

Kaplan, N. (1987). Writing courses in the electronic age. *EDUCOM Bulletin*, (Fall), pp. 10-12.

Karabenick, S.A. (1987). Computer conferencing: Its impact on academic help-seeking. In *Proceedings of the Second Guelph Symposium on Computer Conferencing* (pp. 69-76). Guelph, Canada: University of Guelph.

Katz, M.M., McSwiney, E., & Stroud, K. (1987). Supporting secondary science teachers: The role of common interests. In *Proceedings of the Second Guelph Symposium on Computer Conferencing* (pp. 147-150). Guelph, Canada: University of Guelph.

Kaye, A.R. (1987a). Computer conferencing and electronic mail. In M. Thorpe & D. Grugeon (Eds.), *Open learning for adults*. Harlow, Longman.

Kaye, A.R. (1987b). Integrating computer conferencing into distance education courses: A discussion paper. In *the Second Guelph Symposium on Computer Conferencing* (pp. 23-32). Guelph, Canada: University of Guelph.

Kaye, A.R. (1987c). Introducing computer-mediated communication into a distance education system. *Canadian Journal of Educational Communication, 16*(2), 153-166.

Kaye, A.R. (1989). Computer-mediated communication and distance education. In R. Mason, & A.R. Kaye (Eds.), *Mindweave: Communications, computers and distance education* (pp. 3-21). Oxford: Pergamon Press.

Kelleher, K. & Cross, T.B. (1985). *Teleconferencing: Linking people together electronically*. Englewood Cliffs, NJ: Prentice-Hall.

Kerr, E.B. (1984). *Moderating online conferences*. Computerized Conferencing and Communications Center, Research Report 20, NJIT, Newark, NJ.

Kerr, E.B. (1986). Electronic leadership: A guide to moderating on-line conferences. *IEEE Transactions on Professional Communication, 29*(1), 12-18.

Kerr, E.B., & Hiltz, S.R. (1982). *Computer-mediated communications systems: Status and evaluation.* New York: Academic Press.

Kiesler, S., Siegel, J., & McGuire, T. (1984). Social psychological aspects of computer-mediated communication. *American Psychologist, 39*(10), 1123-34.

Kiesler, S., Zubrow, D. & Moses, A.M. (1985). Affect in computer-mediated communication: An experiment in synchronous terminal to terminal discussion. *Human-Computer Interaction, 1,* 77-104.

Kiesler, S., Zubrow, D., Moses, A.M., & Geller, V. (1984). Affect in computer mediated communication: An experiment in synchronous terminal-to-terminal discussion. *Human Computer Interaction, 1*(1), 77-104.

Kimmel, H., Kerr, E.B., & O'Shea, M. (1987a). Computerized collaboration. *The Computing Teacher, 15*(3), 36-38.

Kimmel, H., Kerr, E.B., & O'Shea, M. (1987b). Computer conferencing for delivering educational services. In University of Guelph (Ed.), *The second Guelph symposium on computer conferencing, June 1-4, 1987* (pp. 187-191). Guelph, Ontario: University of Guelph.

Kimmel, H., Phipps, D., Heimerdinger, M., & Schulman, E. (1984). Enhancing educational effectiveness: The Electronic Information Exchange System. In *Proceedings, National Conference Association Educational Data Systems, May,* pp. 235-239.

Knapp, L.R. (1986). The computer chronicles. A Newswire network for kids. *Classroom Computer Learning, 10*(7), 38-41.

Knapp, L.R. (1987). Teleconferencing: A new way of communications for teachers and kids. *Classroom Computer Learning, 7*(6), 37-41.

Knowledge Engineering (1985). AI course on-line for graduate credit. *Knowledge Engineering,* (November), pp. 6-7.

Kremers, M. (1988). Adams Sherman Hill meets ENFI: An inquiry and a retrospective. *Computers and Composition, 5*(3), 69-77.

Kremers, M., & Haile, P. (1986/87). Teaching writing by interdisciplinary computer conference. *Educational Technology Systems, 15*(2), 213-219.

Kurland, N. (1983). Have computer, will not travel: Meeting electronically. *Phi Delta Kappan, 65*(2), 124-126.

Lake, D. (1988). Two projects that worked: Using telecommunications as a resource in the classroom. *The Computing Teacher, 16*(4), 17-19.

Laliberte, S.M. (1988). MIX-The McGraw-Hill information exchange. In S. Ambron & R. Pennington (Eds.), *Toward a seamless society: Networking in education* (pp. 75-92). Learning Tomorrow Series. Cupertino, CA: Apple Education Advisory Council.

Lederberg, J. (1978). Digital communications and the conduct of science: The new literacy. *Proceedings of the IEEE, 66*(11), 1314-19.

Lerch, I. (1983). The movable conference. *BYTE, 8*(5), 104-120.

Levin, J.A., & Cohen, M.S. (1985). The world as an international science laboratory: Electronic networks for science instruction and problem solving. *Journal of Computers in Mathematics and Science Teaching, 4*(4), 33-35.

Levin, J.A., Riel, M., Miyake, N., & Cohen, M. (1987). Education on the electronic frontier: Teleapprentices in globally distributed educational contexts. *Contemporary Educational Psychology, 12*, 254-260.

Levin, J.A., Riel, M., Rowe, R.D., & Boruta, M.J. (1984). Muktuk meets jacuzzi: Computer networks and elementary school writers. In S.W. Freedman (Ed.), *The acquisition of written language: Revision and response* (pp. 160-171). Norwood, NJ: Ablex.

Levin, J.A., Waugh, M., & Kolopanis, G. (1988). Science instruction on global electronic networks. *Spectrum: The Journal of the Illinois Science Teachers Association, 13*, 19-23.

Levinson, P. (1986a). Connected Education and the international community. *International Informatics Access, 1*(3), 1-2.

Levinson, P. (1986b). Marshall McLuhan and computer conferencing. *IEEE Transactions on Professional Communications PC, 29*(1), 9-11.

Levinson, P. (1988a). Impact of personal information technologies on American education, interpersonal relations, and business, 1985 - 2010. In P. Durbin (Ed.), *Technology and contemporary life* (pp. 177-191). Boston, MA: Reidel Press.

Levinson, P. (1988b). *Mind at large: Knowing in the technological age*. Greenwich, CT: JAI Press.

Levinson, P. (1989). Media relations: Intergrating computer telecommunications with educational media. In R. Mason & A.R. Kaye (Eds.), *Mindweave: Communication, computers and distance education* (pp. 40-49). London: Pergamon.

Licklider, J.C.R. (1968). The computer as a communication device. *Science and Technology, 76*, 21.

Lorentsen, A. (1989). Evaluation of Computer Conferencing in Open Learning. In R. Mason & A.R. Kaye (Eds.), *Mindweave: Communication, computers and distance education* (pp. 196-197). Oxford: Pergamon Press.

Malone, T.W. (1985a). *Computer support for organizations: Towards an organizational science* (Sloan School of Management Working Paper No. 85-012). Cambridge, MA: Massachusetts Institute of Technology.

Malone, T.W. (1985b). *Organizational structure and information technology: Elements of a formal theory* (Sloan School of Management Working Paper No. 130). Cambridge, MA: Massachusetts Institute of Technology.

Marlett, N. (1988). Empowerment through computer telecommunications. In B. Glastonbury, W. LaMendola, & S. Toole (Eds.), *Information technology and the human services* (pp. 244-264). Chichester: John Wiley & Sons.

Marshall, J.G. (1987). The use of data-conferencing as an instructional technique. In *Proceedings of the Second Guelph Symposium on Computer Conferencing* (pp. 151-154). Guelph, Canada: University of Guelph.

Mason, R. (1988a). Computer conferencing: A contribution to self-directed learning. *British Journal of Educational Technology, 19*(1), 28-42.

Mason, R. (1988b). Computer conferencing and the university community. *Open Learning, 3*(2), 37-40.

Mason, R. (1989). An evaluation of CoSy on an Open University course. In Robin Mason & Anthony Kaye (Eds.), *Mindweave: Communication, computers, and distance education* (pp. 115-145). Oxford: Pergamon Press.

Maxcy, D.O. & Maxcy, S.J. (1986/87). Computer/telephone pairing for long distance learning. *Educational Technology Systems*, *15*(2), 201.

McConnell, D. (1987). Computer conferencing in the development of teacher inservice education. In *Proceedings of the Second Guelph Symposium on Computer Conferencing* . Guelph, Canada: University of Guelph.

McCord, S.A. (1985). Measures of participation, leadership, and decision quality by participants in computer conferencing and nominal group technique decision-making exercises. *Dissertation Abstracts International*, *46*, 4605A. University Microfilms No. AAC8514143.

McCreary, E. (1989). Computer-mediated communication and organisational culture. In Robin Mason & Anthony Kaye (Eds.), *Mindweave: Communication, computers and distance education* (pp. 101-114). Oxford: Pergamon Press.

McCreary, E., & van Duren, J. (1987). Educational applications of computer conferencing. *Canadian Journal of Educational Communication*, *16*(2), 107-115.

McDonnell, D. & Raymond, J. (1987). Integration of the electronic blackboard and the electronic overhead projector. In *Proceedings of the Second Guelph Symposium on Computer Conferencing* (pp. 193-197). Guelph, Canada: University of Guelph.

McGuire, T.W., Kiesler, S., & Siegel, J. (1986). *Group and communication effects in risk choice.* (Committe on Social Science Research in Computing Research Paper). Pittsburg, PA: Carnegie-Mellon University.

McQueen, R. (1987). Distributed conferencing systems: A practical, easily implementated architecture. In *Proceedings of the Second Guelph Symposium on Computer Conferencing* (pp. 227-237). Guelph, Canada: University of Guelph.

Meeks, B.N. (1985a). An overview of conferencing systems. *Byte*, *10*(13), 169-184.

Meeks, B.N. (1985b). Life at 300 baud: The electric schoolhouse. *Profiles*, *3*(2), 16-18, 78-79.

Meeks, B.N. (1987). The quiet revolution: On-line education becomes a real alternative. *BYTE Magazine*, *12*(2), 183-190.

Mills, M.K. (1987). Computer alliances for international faculty development. In *Proceedings of the Second Guelph Symposium on Computer Conferencing* (pp. 41-50). Guelph, Canada: University of Guelph.

Mills, M.K. (1986/87). Ombudsmen, expediters, and hosts: Teaching management through telecommunications. *Educational Technology Systems, 15*(1), 81.

Mojkowski, C., & Pietro, D. (1982). The school practices information network and file: A nationwide network for sharing educational practice information. *Education Libraries, 7*(1-2), 15-17, 24.

Molnar, A.R. (1982). The search for new intelligent technology. *THE Journal: Technological Horizons in Education, 9*(September).

Montgomerie, T.C. (1987). Facilitating 'extended campus' graduate education through electronic communication. *Canadian Journal of Educational Communication, 16*(3), 239-256.

Moore, G.A.B. (1987). The introduction of asynchronous electronic communication for distance education in developing countries: A case study in Thailand. In *Proceedings of the Second Guelph Symposium on Computer Conferencing* (pp. 51-58). Guelph, Canada: University of Guelph.

Moore, J.W. (1985). CHYMNET. *Chemical Engineering News,* (Feb. 18), pp. 9.

Morabito, M. (1986). Teaching telecomputing in schools. *Link-Up,* (September).

Morin, A.J. (1988). SpecialNet — A national computer-based communications network. In S. Ambron & R. Pennington (Eds.), *Towards a seamless society: Networking in education* (pp. 13-34). Learning Tomorrow Series. Cupertino, CA: Apple Education Advisory Council.

Murray, D.E. (1986). *Conversation for action: The computer terminal as medium of communication.* Unpublished doctoral dissertation, Doctoral dissertation, Stanford University. *Dissertation Abstracts International,* 47, 4702A.

Murrel, S.L. (1983). The impact of communicating through computers (electronic mail, conference). *Dissertation Abstracts*

International, *44*, 4412A. University Microfilms No. AAC8405370.

Muzio, J. (1989). Email and electronic transfer of data files for a distance education course. In R. Mason & A.R. Kaye (Eds.), *Mindweave: Communication, computers and distance education* (pp. 198-200). London: Pergamon.

Newman, J.A. (1985). *The KNOW-NET dissemination project (Knowledge network of Washington). Final Report.* Washington, D.C.: National Institute of Education.

Newman, D. (1987). Local and long distance computer networking for science classrooms. *Educational Technology, 27*(6), 20-23.

Newman, D. & Goldman, S.V. (1986/87). Earth Lab: A local network for collaborative classroom science. *Educational Technology Systems, 15*(3), 237.

Newman, D., Goldman, S.V., Brienne, D., & Jackson, I. (1986). *Earth lab: Progress report.* New York: Bank Street College of Education, Center for Children and Technology.

Newman, D., Goldman, S.V., Brienne, D., Jackson, I., & Magzamen, S. (1989). Peer collaboration in computer-mediated science investigations. *Journal of Educational Computing Research, 5*(2), 151-66.

Newsted, P.R., Sheehan, B.S., & Licker, P.S. (1987). A value-added model of computer-aided instruction. In *Proceedings of the Second Guelph Symposium on Computer Conferencing* (pp. 155-164). Guelph, Canada: University of Guelph.

Nipper, S. (1989). Third generation distance learning and computer conferencing. In R. Mason & A.R. Kaye (Eds.), *Mindweave: Communication, computers and distance education* (pp. 63-73). Oxford: Pergamon Press.

Novemsky, L., Dios, R., Gautreau, R., Hsu, E., Kimmel, H., O'Connor, J., O'Shea, M., & Reynolds, W. (1987). Humanizing the new education technologies. *Bull. Sci. Tech. Soc.*, 7(STS Press), 995-1000.

O'Shea, M.R. (1987). Computer conferencing for delivering educational services. In *Proceedings of the Second Guelph Symposium on Computer Conferencing* . Guelph, Ontario: University of Guelph.

O'Shea, M.R., Kimmel, H., & Kerr, E.B. (1986). Accessing science information. *Science Scope*, (April), pp. 9.

Ohler, J. (1989). What's on line for educators. *Electronic Learning Magazine*, 8(6), 34-35.

Oldsen, C.F. (1982). *Communication linkage implementation study. Final Report.* Washington, D.C.: Office of Vocational and Adult Education.

Opper, S. (1983). Meetings of the minds: A step beyond electronic mail. *Data Training*.

Osgood, D. (1986). The electronic university network. *BYTE*, 11(3), 171-176.

Owen, T. (1989a). Computer-mediated writing and the Writer in Electronic Residence. *The Association of Educators of Gifted, Talented and Creative Children in BC*, 10(3).

Owen, T. (1989b). Computer-mediated writing: The writer in electronic residence. In R. Mason & A.R. Kaye (Eds.), *Mindweave: Communication, computers and distance education* (pp. 208-210). Oxford: Pergamon Press.

Paulsen, M.F. (1987/88). In search of a virtual school. *THE Journal: Technological Horizons in Education*, 14(December/January), 71-76.

Paulsen, M.F. (1989). EKKO: A virtual school. In R. Mason & A.R. Kaye (Eds.), *Mindweave: Communication, computers and distance education* (pp. 201-207). London: Pergamon.

Peyton, J.K. (1988). Cross-age tutoring on a local area computer network: Moving from informal to formal academic writing. *The Writing Instructor*, 8(2), 53-60.

Peyton, J.K., & Batson, T. (1986). Computer networking: Making connections between speech and writing. *ERIC/CLL News Bulletin*, 10(1), 1-7.

Peyton, J.K., & Mackinson, J. (1987). Computer networks: A collaborative approach to literacy development. *Dialogue*, 4(3), 6-7.

Peyton, J.K., & Mackinson, J. (1989). Writing and talking about writing: Computer networks with elementary students. In D. Roen & D.M. Johnson (Eds.), *Richness in writing: Empowering minority students* (pp. 100-119). New York: Longman.

Pfaffenberger, B. (1986). Research networks, scientific communication, and the personal computer. *IEEE Transactions on Professional Communication*, 29(1), 23-29.

Phillips, A.F. (1983). Computer conferences: Success or failure?. In R.N. Bostrm (Ed.), *Communication yearbook 7* (pp. 837-856). Beverly Hills: Sage Publications.

Phillips, A.F., & Pease, P.S. (1985). Computer conferencing and education: Complementary or contradictory concepts? Paper presented at the 35th Annual meeting of the International Communication Association, Human Communication Technology Special Interest Group, Honolulu. Washington, D.C.: National Institute of Education. (Eric Reports.)

Phillips, G.M., Santoro, G.M., & Kuehn, S.A. (1988). The use of computer-mediated communication in training students in group problem-solving and decision-making techniques. *The American Journal of Distance Education*, 2(1), 38-51.

Por, G. (1985). Have micro, get tel-education. *Link-Up*, (September), pp. 26-27.

Pournelle, J. (1985). Grasping the power of CMC. *Popular Computing*, 5(2), 39-42.

Price, C. (1975). Conferencing via computer: Cost effective communication for the era of forced choice. In H.A. Linstone & M. Turoff (Eds.), *The Delphi Method: Techniques and Applications*. Reading, MA: Addison-Wesley.

Pullinger, D.J. (1986). Chit-chat to electronic journals: Computer conferencing supports scientific communication. *IEEE Transactions on Professional Communications PC*, 29(1), 23-29.

Quarterman, J.S., & Hoskins, J.C. (1986). Notable computer networks. *Communications of the ACM*, 29(10), 932-971.

Quinn, C.N., Mehan, H., Levin, J.A., & Black, S.D. (1983). Real education in non-real time: The use of electronic message systems for instruction. *Instructional Science*, 11(4), 313-327.

Resta, P. (1988). Europe on line. *The Computing Teacher*, 16(1), 54-56.

Reynolds, K.E. (1984). Reynolds' rap. *Science Scope*, (Sept), pp. 16.

Rhodes, L.A. (1984). Reaching out by electronic communication. *Educational Leadership, 42*(3), 80-81.

Rice, R.E. (1980a). Computer conferencing. In B. Dervin & M.J. Voigt (Eds.), *Progress in communication sciences, Vol. 1* (pp. 215-40). Norwood, NJ: Ablex.

Rice, R.E. (1980b). The impacts of computer-mediated organizational and interpersonnel communication. In M.E. Williams (Ed.), *Annual review of information science and technology* (pp. 221-249). White Plains, NY: American Society for Information Science.

Rice, R.E. (1982a). *Human communication networking in a teleconferencing environment.* Unpublished doctoral dissertation, Department of Communication, Stanford University. Stanford.

Rice, R.E. (1982b). Communication networking in computer-conferencing systems: A longitudinal study of group roles and system structure. In M. Burgoon (Ed.), *Communication yearbook* (pp. 925-944). Beverly Hills, CA: Sage Publications.

Rice, R.E. (1984). Evaluating new media systems. In J. Johnston (Ed.), *Evaluating the New Information Technologies* (pp. 53-71). San Francisco: Jossey-Bass.

Rice, R.E. (1986). Applying the human relations perspective to the study of new media. *Computers and Society, 15*(4), 32-37.

Rice, R.E. (1987). Computer-mediated communication and organizational innovation. *Journal of Communication, 37*(4).

Rice, R.E. and Associates. (1984). *The new media: Communication, research, and technology.* Beverly Hills: Sage.

Rice, R.E. & Case, D. (1983). Electronic message systems in the university: A description of use and utility. *Journal of Communication, 33*(1), 131-152.

Rice, R.E. & Love, G. (1987). Electronic emotion: Socio-emotional content in a computer-mediated communication network. *Communication Research, 14*(1), 85-108.

Riedl, R. (1986). CompuServe in the classroom. *Computing Teacher*, *13*(6), 62-64.

Riedl, R. (1989). Patterns in computer-mediated discussions. In R. Mason & A.R. Kaye (Eds.), *Mindweave: Communication, computers and distance education* (pp. 215-219). London: Pergamon.

Riel, M. (1983). Education and ecstasy: Computer chronicles of students writing together. *The Quarterly Newsletter of the Laboratory of Comparative Human Cognition*, *5*(3), 59-67.

Riel, M. (1985). The Computer Chronicles Newswire: A functional learning environment for acquiring literacy skills. *Journal of Educational Computing Research*, *1*(3), 317-37.

Riel, M. (1986). *The educational potential of computer networks*. Technical Report No. 16. San Diego: University of California, Interactive Technology Laboratory.

Riel, M. (1987). The InterCultural Learning Network. *The Computing Teacher*, *14*(7), 27-30.

Roberts, L. (1988). Computer conferencing: A classroom for distance learning. *ICDE Bulletin, 18*.

Rogers, A. (1988). CMS School-net. A practical approach to effective school networking. In S. Ambron & R. Pennington (Eds.), *Toward a seamless society: Networking in education* (pp. 187-202). Learning Tomorrow Series. Cupertino, CA: Apple Education Advisory Council.

Rogers, E. & Kincaid, L. (1981). *Communication networks: Toward a new paradigm for research*. New York: Free Press.

Rogers, E.M., & Rafaeli, S. (1985). Computers and communication. In B. Ruben (Ed.), *Information and Behavior (pp. 95-112)*.

Rousseau, R., & Moreau, L. (1987). A model of individual adjustment process to computers. In *Proceedings of the Second Guelph Symposium on Computer Conferencing* (pp. 77-89). Guelph, Canada: University of Guelph.

Rumble, G. (1989). On-line costs: Interactivity at a price. In R. Mason & A.R. Kaye (Eds.), *Mindweave: Communication, computers and distance education* (pp. 146-165). London: Pergamon Press.

Ryan, M.G. (1981). Telematics, teleconferencing and education. *Telecommunications Policy*, *5*(4), 315-322.

Saba, F. & Twitchell, D. (1988/89). Integrated Services Digital Network: How it can be used for distance education. *Educational Technology Systems*, *17*(1), 15.

Saunders, C., & Heyl J. (1988). Evaluating educational computer conferencing. *Journal of Systems Management*, (April), pp. 33-7.

Sayers, D. (1989). Bilingual sister classes in computer writing networks. In Duane Roen & Donna M. Johnson (Eds.), *Richness in writing: Empowering minority students* (pp. 120-133). New York: Longman.

Sayers, D., & Brown, K. (1987). Bilingual education and telecommunications: A perfect fit. *The Computing Teacher*, *14*(7), 23-24.

Schack, M. (1987). The electronic link: Computer bulletin boards. *Media and Methods*, (January/February).

Schroeder, R.E. (1981). Computer conferencing: Exploding the classroom walls. *THE Journal: Technological Horizons in Education*, *8*(2), 46.

Schroff, R., & Gabrovsky, P. (1987). Representing educational materials in Prolog. In *Proceedings of the Second Guelph Symposium on Computer Conferencing* (pp. 199-206). Guelph, Canada: University of Guelph.

Scrogan, L. (1987a). Telecomputing: How to overcome the roadblocks. *Classroom Computer Learning*, *7*(5), 40-45.

Scrogan, L. (1987b). What's new in online information services. *Classroom Computer Learning*, *7*(7), 48-51.

Scrogan, L. (1988). The online underworld. *Classroom Computer Learning*, (February).

Sevel, F. (1984). What if we gave a teleconference and nobody said anything? *Online Today*, *3*(3), 33-36.

Sewell, D.F., & Rotheray, D.M. (1985). Instructional influences on the design and implication of computer-mediated learning. In Duncan, K. & Harris, D. (Eds.), *Computers in education* (pp. 1019-1023). Amsterdam: Elsevier Science Publishing B.V.

Shatzer, L.   (1987).   Cost-effective analysis of tele-training. *Performance and Instruction*, *26*(9/10), 48-51.

Shea, G.   (1984).   Information services: The new frontier of communication. *Electronic Learning*, (Nov/Dec), pp. 33-34.

Sheppard, M.   (1986).   Communications technologies: Challenges and solutions for isolated school learners. *Media in Education and Development*, *19*(3), 130-133.

Sheridan, T.J., Moray, N., Stoklosa, J., Guillaume, J., & Makepeace, D.   (1981).   *Experimentation with a multi-disciplinary teleconference and electronic journal on mental workload*. Cambridge, MA: Massachusetts Institute of Technology.

Siegel, J., Dubrovsky, V., Kiesler, S., & McGuire, T. (1986). Group processes in computer-mediated communication. *Organizational Behaviour and Human Decision Processes*, *37*, 157-187.

Sinclair, G.   (1988a).   EUREKA! (from An Electronic Net-Rider's Journal). In S. Ambron & R. Pennington (Eds.), *Towards a seamless society: Networking in education* (pp. 333-346). Cupertino, CA: Apple Education Advisory Council.

Sinclair, G.   (1988b).   The EXCITE Center. *Minds in Motion*, *1*(Winter), 55-56.

Sirc, G.   (1988).   Learning to write on a LAN. *THE Journal: Technological Horizons in Education*, *15*(8), 100-104.

Slatta, R.   (1985).   Setting up your own bulletin board. *Link-Up*, (December).

Smith, D.J.   (1985).   *Information technology and education: Signposts and research directions*. London, Eng.: Economic and Social Research Council.

Smith, J.Y.   (1986).   Communication quality in information systems development: The effect of computer-mediated communication on task-oriented problem solving (teleconferencing). *Dissertation Abstracts International*, *47*, 4704A. University Microfilms No. AAC8616055.

Smith, R.C.   (1988).   Teaching special relativity through a computer conference. *American Journal of Physics*, *56*(2), 142-47.

Southworth, J.H. (1988). The Hawaii global TELEclass project and multimedia computer-based educational telecommunication (CBET). In Sueann Ambron & Randy Pennington (Eds.), *Toward a seamless society: Networking in education* (pp. 273-294). Learning Tomorrow Series. Cupertino, CA: Apple Education Advisory Council.

Spielvogel, R.A. (1988). Learning link - A model for low-cost educational networks. In Sueann Ambron & Randy Pennington (Eds.), *Toward a seamless society: Networking in education* (pp. 165-184). Learning Tomorrow Series. Cupertino, CA: Apple Education Advisory Council.

Spitzer, M. (1986). Writing style in computer conferences. *IEEE Transactions on Professional Communication*, *29*(1), 19-22.

Spragge, J.G. (1987). If computer users are a community, the conference must be the town meeting. In *Proceedings of the Second Guelph Symposium on Computer Conferencing* (pp. 91-104). Guelph, Canada: University of Guelph.

Sproull, L. (1986). Using electronic mail for data collection in organizational research. *Academy of Management Journal*, *29*(1), 159-169.

Sproull, L., & Kiesler, S. (1986). *Reducing social context cues: The case of electronic mail* (Committee on Social Science Research in Computing Research Paper). Pittsburgh, PA: Carnegie-Mellon University.

Stahr, L. (1985). Tactics for teleconferencing. *PC World*, *3*(5), 218-225.

Stefik, M., Foster, G., Bobrow, D.G., Kahn, K., Lannry, S., & Suchman, L. (1987). Beyond the chalkboard: Computer support for collaboration and problem-solving in meetings. *Communications of the ACM*, *30*(1), 32-47.

Steinfield, C.W. (1986). Computer mediated communication systems. In M.E. Williams (Ed.), *Annual review of information science and technology, Vol. 21* (pp. 167-202). Washington, DC: American Society for Information Science.

Stevens, C.H. (1980). Many-to-many communication through inquiry networking. *World Future Society Bulletin*.

Stevens, C.H. (1986). *Electronic organization and expert networks: Beyond electronic mail and computer conferencing*

(Sloan School of Management Working Paper No. 90s: 86-021). Cambridge, MA: Massachusetts Institute of Technology.

Stix, A.H. (1987). Computer conferences: What makes them difficult, and for what types of conferencing situations are they most suited. In *Proceedings of the Second Guelph Symposium on Computer Conferencing* (pp. 105-121). Guelph, Canada: University of Guelph.

Stoll, P.F. (1988). Telecommunications and distance learning systems in New York State. In S. Ambron & R. Pennington (Eds.), *Toward a seamless society: Networking in education* (pp. 259-271). Learning Tomorrow Series. Cupertino, CA: Apple Education Advisory Council.

Sullivan, M.F. (1988). METN-Networking in Maryland. In S. Ambron & R. Pennington (Eds.), *Toward a seamless society: Networking in education* (pp. 153-159). Learning Tomorrow Series. Cupertino, CA: Apple Education Advisory Council.

Tamshiro, R. & Hoagland, C. (1987). Telecomputing a chain story. *The Computing Teacher, 14*(7), 37-39.

Tennis, J. (1985/86). Telecomputing Diary. *Electronic Learning,* (September-May).

Thomas, R. (1989). The implications of electronic communication for the OU. In R. Mason & A. Kaye (Eds.), *Mindweave: Communication, computers and distance education* (pp. 166-177). Oxford: Pergamon Press.

Thompson, D. (1987). Teaching writing on a local area network. *THE Journal: Technological Horizons in Education, 14*(2), 92-97.

Thompson, D. (1988a). Conversational networking: Why the teacher gets most of the lines. *Collegiate Microcomputers, 6*(3), 193-201.

Thompson, D. (1988b). Interactive networking: Creating bridges between speech, writing, and composition. *Computers and Composition, 5*(3), 2-27.

Thompson, D., & Simpson, C. (1988). The computer connection: Team teaching a joint course at two sites. *The Northern Virginia Review,* (Spring), pp. 28-30.

Thompson, G. (1989). *Learner participation in online graduate courses*. Unpublished M.Ed. Thesis, Ontario Institute for Studies in Education, Toronto, Ontario.

Thompson, G.B. (1972). Three characterizations of communications revolutions. In *Computer communication: Impacts and implications. Proceedings of the First International Conference on Computer Communication*. Washington, DC: .

Thorson, E. & Buss, T.F. (1977). Using computer conferencing to formulate a computer simulation of transitive behavior. *Behavior Research Methods, Instruments and Computers*, *9*, 81-86.

Toles, M.T. (1983). Creating electronic communities: Mass and vernacular technologies for interpersonal communication via computer. *Dissertation Abstracts International*, *44*, 4406A. University Microfilms No. AAC8321908.

Toner, P.D. (1983). Computer conferencing in formative evaluation: The development and evaluation of a new model of tryout-revision. *Dissertation Abstracts International*, *44*, 4403A. Doctoral dissertation, Michigan State University.

Tracz, G. (1980). Computerized conferencing: An eye-opening experience with EIES. *Canadian Journal of Information Science*, *5*, 11-20.

Tucker, M.S. (1983). The turning point: Telecommunications and higher education. *Journal of Communication*, *33*(1), 118-130.

Turoff, M. (1987). Computer mediated communication: Possibilities and potential. In *Proceedings of the Second Guelph Symposium on Computer Conferencing*. Guelph, Ontario: University of Guelph.

Turoff, M., Foster, G., Hiltz, S.R., Ng. (1989). The TEIES design and objectives: Computer-mediated communications and tailorability. In *Proceedings of the Hawaii International Conference on System Sciences, January, Hawaii*.

Turoff, M., & Gage, H. (1976). *Computerized conferencing and the homebound handicapped* (Computerized Conferencing and Communications Center Research Report No. 6). Newark, NJ: New Jersey Institute of Technology.

Turoff, M., & Hiltz, S.R. (1977). *EIES Development and evaluation project final report.* Newark, NJ: Computerized Conferencing and Communications Center, New Jersey Institute of Technology.

Turoff, M., & Hiltz, S.R. (1980). *International potentials of computer conferencing.* Computerized Conferencing and Communications Center: New Jersey Institute of Technology.

Turoff, M., & Hiltz, S.R. (1981). Exploring the future of human communication via computer. *Technology and Society, 1*(1), 1-6.

Turoff, M., & Hiltz, S.R. (1982). The electronic journal: A progress report. *Journal of the American Society for Information Science, 33*(4), 195-202.

Uhlig, R.P., Farber, D.J., & Bair, J.H. (1979). *The office of the future: Communication and computers.* Amsterdam: North-Holland Publishing Co.

Ujimoto, V. & James, D.A. (1987). The adoption of information technology in academic setings. In *Proceedings of the Second Guelph Symposium on Computer Conferencing* (pp. 123-144). Guelph, Canada: University of Guelph.

Umpleby, S. (1986). Online educational techniques. *ENA Netweaver, 2*(1), article 6.

Upton, E.M. (1987). Computer conferencing: A tool for hospitality professionals. In *Proceedings of the Second Guelph Symposium on Computer Conferencing* (pp. 165-166). Guelph, Canada: University of Guelph.

Utsumi, T., Rossman, P., & Rosen, S. (1988). The global electronic university. *The American Journal of Distance Education, 2*(2).

Vallee, J. (1982). *The network revolution: Confessions of a computer scientist.* Berkeley, CA: And/Or Press Inc.

Vallee, J. (1984). *Computer message systems.* New York: McGraw Hill.

Vallee, J., Johansen, R., Randolph, R., & Hastings, A. (1974). *Group communication through computers: A study of social effects. Vol. 2.* Menlo Park: Institute for the Future.

Vallee, J., Lipinski, H.M., & Miller, R.H. (1974). *Group com-munication through computers: Design and use of the FORUM system, Vol. 1.* Menlo Park: Institute for the Future.

Vallee, J., Johansen, R., & Spangler, K. (1975). The computer conference: An altered state of communication? *The Futurist*, (June), pp. 116-121.

Vallee, J., Johansen, R., Lipinski, H.M., Spangler, K., Wilson, T., & Hardy, A. (1975). *Group communication through computers: Pragmatics and dynamics. Vol. 3.* Menlo Park, CA: Institute of the Future.

Van Duren, J. (1989). CMC at Athabasca University. In R. Mason & A.R. Kaye (Eds.), *Mindweave: Communication, computers and distance education* (pp. 211-214). Oxford: Pergamon.

Vaughan, L. (1988a). Superintendents at the workstation?. In S. Ambron & R. Pennington (Eds.), *Toward a seamless society: Networking in education* (pp. 143-151). Learning Tomorrow Series. Cupertino, CA: Apple Education Advisory Council.

Vaughan, L. (1988b). Visions of the Future-Considerations for shaping educational networking. In S. Ambron & R. Pennington (Eds.), *Toward a seamless society: Networking in education* (pp. 299-308). Learning Tomorrow Series. Cupertino, CA: Apple Education Advisory Council.

Vivian, V. (1986). Electronic mail in a children's distance education course: Trial and evaluation. *Distance Education*, 7(2), 237-260.

Vlahakis, R. (1987). The other side: Snapshot of a social studies simulation in action. *Classroom Computer Learning*, (May), pp. 42-45.

Waggoner, M.D. (1987). Explicating expert opinion through a computer conferencing delphi. *Dissertation Abstracts International*, *48*, 4802A. University Microfilms No. AAC8712234.

Waggoner, M.D. & Goldberg, A.L. (1986). A forecast for technology and education: The report of a computer conferencing Delphi. *Educational Technology*, *26*(6), 7-14.

Watson, F.C. (1988). Florida information resource network. In S. Ambron & R. Pennington (Eds.), *Toward a seamless society: Networking in education* (pp. 99-110). Learning Tomorrow Series. Cupertino, CA: Apple Education Advisory Council.

Watson, J.A., Eichhorn, M.I., & Scanzoni, J. (1988/89). A home/university computer network: Test of a system to study families. *Educational Technology Systems, 17*(4), 319.

Watt, M., & Watt, D. (1988). New Hampshire-A case study: Getting started in educational telecommunications. In S. Ambron & R. Pennington (Eds.), *Toward a seamless society: Networking in education* (pp. 113-122). Learning Tomorrow Series. Cupertino, CA: Apple Education Advisory Council.

Welsch, L.A. (1982). Using electronic mail as a teaching tool. *Communications of the ACM* [Association for Computing Machinery], *25*(2), 105-108.

Wenger, M. (1987). The role of interactive technology in education. *Educational Media International, 24*(1).

Williams, F., & Rice, R.E. (1983). Communication research and the new media technologies. In R.N. Bostrom (Ed.), *Communication Yearbook 7* (pp. 200-224). Beverly Hills: Sage Publications.

Wilson, J.A. (1985). Structuring learning networks: The possibilities for networked software. In Duncan, K., Harris, D. (Eds.), *Computers in education* (pp. 491-496). Amsterdam: Elsevier Science Publishing B.V.

Wingfield-Stratford, P. (1989). Applications of CMC within community organizations. In R. Mason & A. Kaye (Eds.), *Mindweave: Communication, computers and distance education* (pp. 220). Oxford: Pergamon.

Winkelmans, T. (1988). *Educational computer conferencing: An application of analysis methodologies to a structured small group activity*. Unpublished master's thesis, University of Toronto. Toronto, Ontario.

Wu, C. (1987/88). New age of satellite education. *Educational Technology Systems, 16*(3), 231.

Zimmerman, D.P. (1987). Effects of computer conferencing on the language use of emotionally disturbed adolescents. *Behavior Research Methods, Instruments, & Computers, 19*(2), 224-230.

Zinn, K.L. (1977). Computer facilitation of communication within professional communities. *Behavior Research Methods, Instruments and Computers, 9*(2), 96-107.

Zuboff, S. (1982, September-October). New worlds of computer mediated work. *Harvard Business Review*, pp. 142-152.

Zuboff, S. (1988). *In the age of the smart machine: The future of work and power*. New York, NY: Basic Books.

Contributors

Editor's Biography

LINDA HARASIM:
   Associate Professor, Department of Communication, Simon
   Fraser University

   Linda Harasim began researching into educational applications of CMC in the early 1980s, and has been teaching
   university courses online, via computer conferencing, since
   1985. The focus of her teaching and research is educational
   and organizational applications of computer-mediated communication and groupware. She is interested in the design
   of online collaborative environments to enhance knowledge
   networking and is currently examining the use of hypertextual interfaces for computer conferencing, both as a user interface and as a tool to conduct content and process analyses
   of online transcripts. She has designed and evaluated computer conferencing networks in Canada, the USA, and Latin
   America and was the organizer of the online educational
   research workshop that led to this book. During the period in
   which this book was written, Dr. Harasim was Senior
   Research Associate and Computer Communications Coordinator with the Ontario Institute for Studies in Education
   (the Graduate School of Education for the University of
   Toronto). She has published widely on educational CMC and
   has presented her research findings at national and international conferences.

Contributors' Bios

BERYL BELLMAN: Professor, Department of Communication
   Studies, California State University at Los Angeles, and
   Research Associate, Western Behavioral Sciences Institute

   Beryl Bellman has served on the faculties of California Institute of the Arts, State University of New York at
   Stonybrook, University of California at San Diego, and is
   currently at California State University in Los Angeles as
   well as serving as a Research Associate with WBSI. He has
   published three books, *Village of Curers and Assassins*
   (1975), *A Paradigm for Looking: Cross-Cultural Research
   with Visual Media* (1977) and *The Language of Secrecy*
   (1984) and over twenty essays in journals and edited
   volumes.   He has conducted extensive research in both
   Africa and Latin America, and is currently the Director of
   the Binational English and Spanish Telecommunications
   Network (BESTNET), a network for online education and
   faculty research seminars among eighteen academic institutions in the US and Mexico.

ANDREW FEENBERG: Professor of Philosophy at San Diego
   State University; Research Associate at the Western Behavioral Sciences Institute

   Andrew Feenberg began working with computer conferencing in 1982, teaching the first course of the Western Behavioral Sciences Institute School of Management and
   Strategic Studies, a continuing education program for high
   level executives which was the second course ever taught by
   computer conferencing. He has written several articles on
   computer conferencing and has served as a consultant to the
   Digital Equipment Corporation, leading a research project at
   WBSI on the adaptation of communications programs to the
   needs of users working together in groups on networks. In
   the framework of this project, he developed the "social factors model" for research into the social bases of user acceptance. This model is under continuing development at the
   WBSI with support from DEC.

ROXANNE HILTZ: Professor, New Jersey Institute of Technology and Associate Director, Computerized Conferencing and Communications Center, New Jersey Institute of Technology.

Roxanne Hiltz has been active in researching and developing computer conferencing since the 1970s, and has published four books and over one hundred articles and professional papers on the subject. *The Network Nation: Human Communication via Computer*, co-authored with Murray Turoff, won the 1978 award of the Association of American Publishers for the outstanding technical publication of the year. This book, together with *Computer-Mediated Communication* (co-authored with Elaine Kerr) and more recently *Online Communities: A Case Study of the Office of the Future*, are considered classics in the field. In recent years Dr. Hiltz has focussed her research interests on educational computer-mediated communications, in particular with a major study on the Virtual Classroom. The Virtual Classroom project centered upon the development and application of social science methodologies to the study of the educational impacts of computer conferencing.

TONY KAYE: Senior Lecturer, Institute of Educational Technology, The Open University, U.K.

Tony Kaye was instrumental in introducing the use of electronic mail and computer conferencing into a number of courses at the Open University. He works on a range of projects including a multi-media course on the Social and Technological Aspects of Information Technology, with 1,500 students and over 60 tutors, all of whom used the OU's CoSy conferencing system. He has published several articles and reports on the educational applications of computer-mediated communication, co-authored a number of books on distance education and recently co-edited *Mindweave: Communication, Computers and Distance Education*, with Robin Mason.

HAESUN KIM: Doctoral Candidate, Department of Educational Psychology, University of Illinois.

Haesun Kim is conducting her doctoral research on instructional electronic networks. She is also the "sysop" of the University of Illinois node of the FrEdMail Network. She plans to continue her work with long-distance educational networks in Korea when she returns after completing her studies.

JAMES A. LEVIN: Associate Professor, Department of Educational Psychology, University of Illinois.

Jim Levin has been exploring the implications of long-distance electronic networks for education, especially focusing on novel instructional activities made possible by the new interactive media. His paper on research methodologies describes work he has been doing with researchers in San Diego, Tokyo, and Jerusalem, analyzing educational network activities that he and colleagues have been organizing among children around the world since 1983. Dr. Levin has published many articles on educational computer networks, and presented his research at scholarly conferences.

PAUL LEVINSON: President, Connected Education, Inc., and Professor at the New School of Social Research.

Paul Levinson is founder and president of Connected Education, Inc., a not-for-profit corporation that since 1985 has been offering courses entirely via computer conferencing, for graduate and undergraduate credit in conjunction with The New School for Social Research. He is a philosopher of technology, with a special interest in the history and future of communications media. He is author of *Mind at Large: Knowing in the Technological Age*, 1988, as well as numerous other books and articles on the subject of computer-mediated communication.

ROBIN MASON: Research Assistant, and Doctoral Candidate, Open University, U.K.

Robin Mason is completing her doctoral research on the educational applications of computer conferencing. She has worked at the British Open University for many years in the Student Research Programme and since 1987 has been involved in preparing materials for and evaluating the introduction of computer conferencing into the OU's multi-media distance education course on Information Technology, which is the largest scale educational application of conferencing to date. She has published articles on applications of computer networking for adult education, and co-edited *Mindweave: Communication, Computers and Distance Education* with Tony Kaye. She is also concerned with evaluation methods and the development of a research field in computer conferencing.

ELAINE McCREARY: Assistant Professor, Department of Rural Extension Studies, University of Guelph.

Elaine McCreary's main area of interest over the last 20 years has been epistemology and explorations in the philosophy of knowledge. Her interest in educational CMC includes application of conferencing for distance delivery of graduate credit program and transcript analysis of the educational interactions. Dr. McCreary has published several articles on educational CMC, has presented at conferences, and supervises a number of graduate theses on CMC.

DENIS NEWMAN: Senior Scientist, BBN Labs Inc., Cambridge, MA.

Denis Newman's academic background is Developmental Psychology, with a particular interest in children's communication. In the mid-1980s he was Project Director, Center for Children and Technology, Bank Street College of Education, working on a variety of projects, including working with science teachers who were using Bulletin Boards and The Source to help them work with each other and with their pupils. While at Bank Street College, Dr. Newman directed the Earth Lab project which developed local area network software applications and curriculum units for elementary science classrooms. He also established computer-mediated communication systems for teacher training and staff development projects. Currently, at BBN, Dr. Newman is conducting formative research and instructional design for two projects developing intelligent training systems. He is continuing his research on situated cognition and social processes in cognitive change and maintains research interest in the role of the local environment in distance communication.

MARGARET RIEL: Educational Consultant, AT&T Long Distance Learning Network

Margaret Riel works with AT&T to develop the Long Distance Learning Network (LDLN) which extends the Inter-Cultural Network approach to a large scale project, involving 200 classrooms in the U.S., Canada, France, Germany, the Netherlands, and Australia. She developed the Curriculum Guide for the LDLN and has authored many articles on educational CMC. Her goal is to document the learning that takes place when students have access to social resources outside of the classroom.

RICHARD WOLFE: Head, Computing Services Group, Ontario Institute for Studies in Education (OISE)

Richard Wolfe is on the faculty of the Department of Measurement, Evaluation, and Computer Applications, at OISE as well as heading OISE's Computing Services. Over the last several years he has used computer networking to coordinate the analysis and publications from a large international study of mathematics education, has developed a laboratory for advanced computing applications, and has carried out research analysis of computer conferencing, focusing on statistical and hypertextual analysis of transcripts. He has a continuing interest in the theory and application of complex data structures and the educational uses of computer communications and hypertext technology.

Index